Garfield PIGS OUT

BY JIM DAVIS

Ballantine Books • New York

A Ballantine Books Trade Paperback Original

Copyright © 2006 by PAWS, Inc. All rights reserved.
"GARFIELD" and the GARFIELD characters are trademarks of PAWS, Inc.

Published in the United States by Ballantine Books, an imprint of The Random House Publishing Group,
a division of Random House, Inc., New York.

BALLANTINE and colophon are registered trademarks of Random House, Inc.

Library of Congress Control Number: 2005906938

ISBN 0-345-46466-4

Printed in the United States of America

www.ballantinebooks.com

9 8 7 6 5 4 3 2 1

FOR the BIRDS

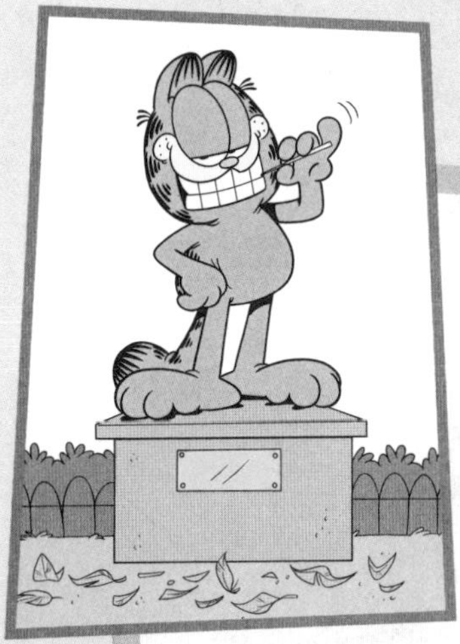

Save a statue.
Eat a pigeon.

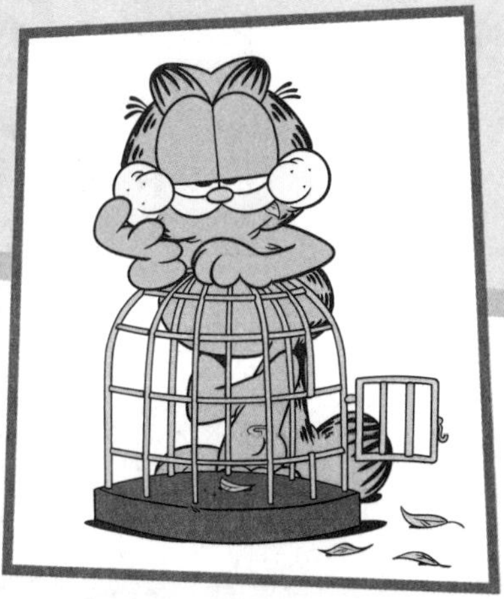

Tastes like
chicken.

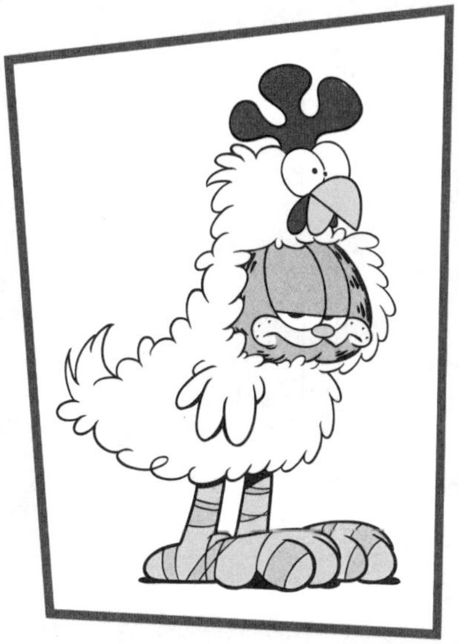

How do I get
out of this
chicken outfit?

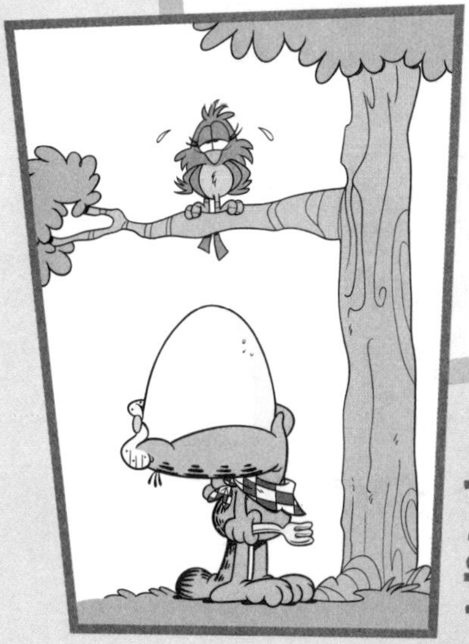

Breakfast
is served!

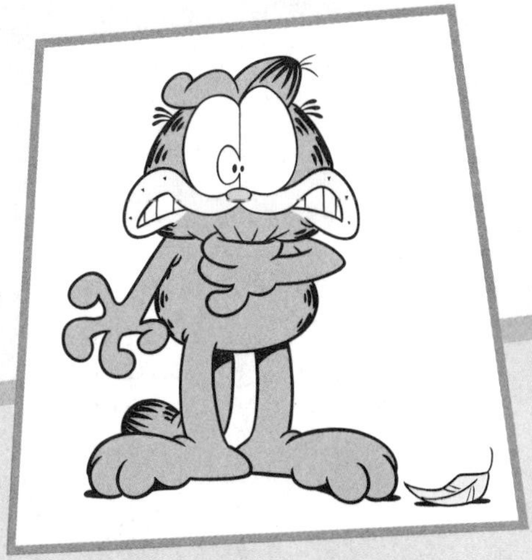

Ever have a
canary go down
the wrong pipe?

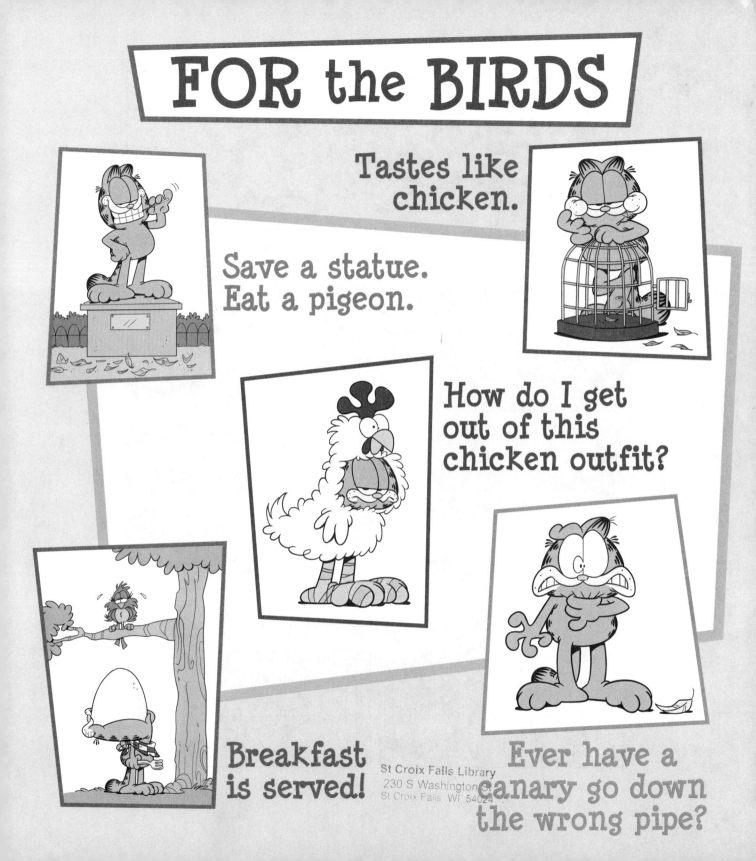

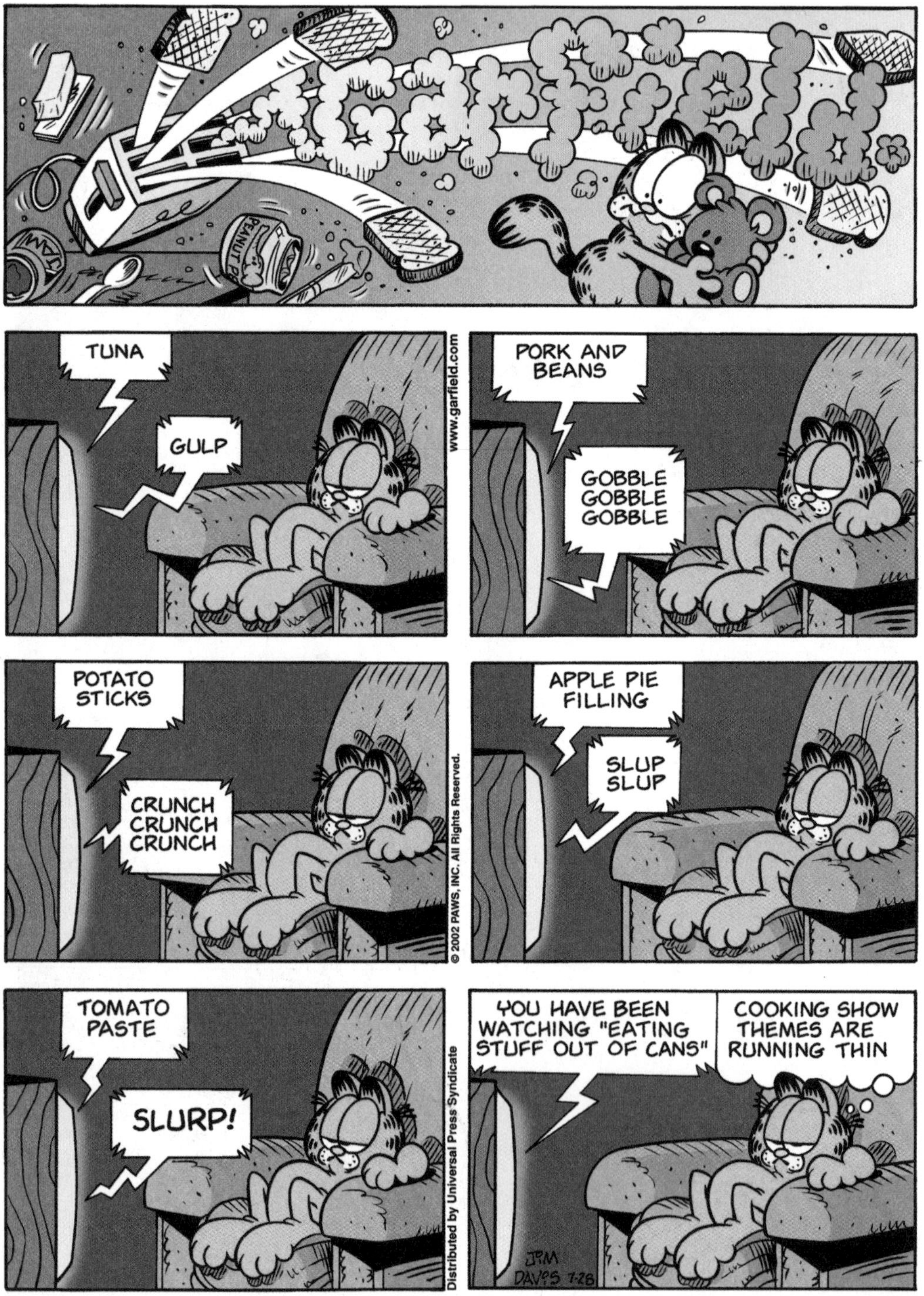
GARFIELD
JAM
PEANUT
TUNA
GULP
www.garfield.com
PORK AND BEANS
GOBBLE GOBBLE GOBBLE
POTATO STICKS
CRUNCH CRUNCH CRUNCH
© 2002 PAWS, INC. All Rights Reserved.
APPLE PIE FILLING
SLUP SLUP
TOMATO PASTE
SLURP!
Distributed by Universal Press Syndicate
YOU HAVE BEEN WATCHING "EATING STUFF OUT OF CANS"
COOKING SHOW THEMES ARE RUNNING THIN
JPM DAVIS 7-28

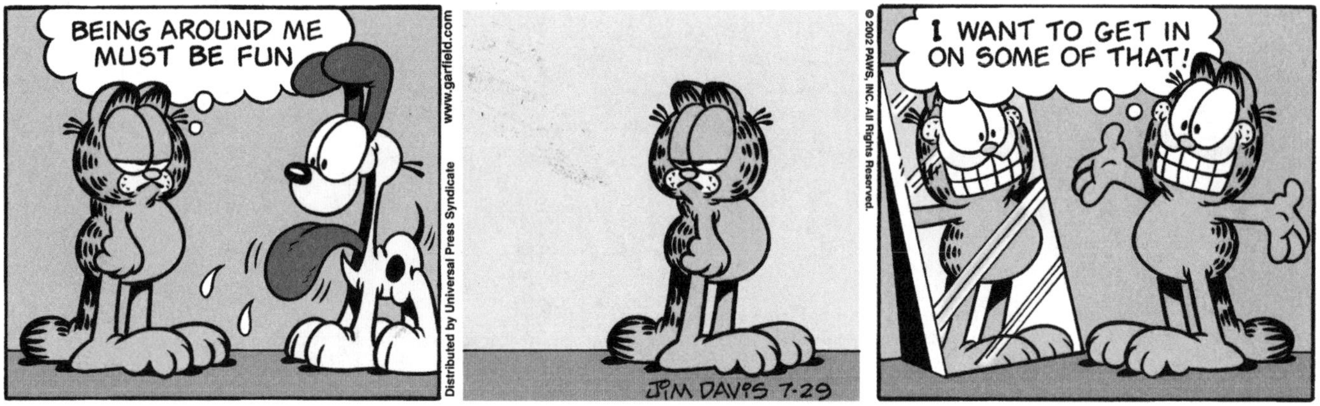
BEING AROUND ME MUST BE FUN
Distributed by Universal Press Syndicate www.garfield.com
JIM DAVIS 7-29
© 2002 PAWS, INC. All Rights Reserved.
I WANT TO GET IN ON SOME OF THAT!

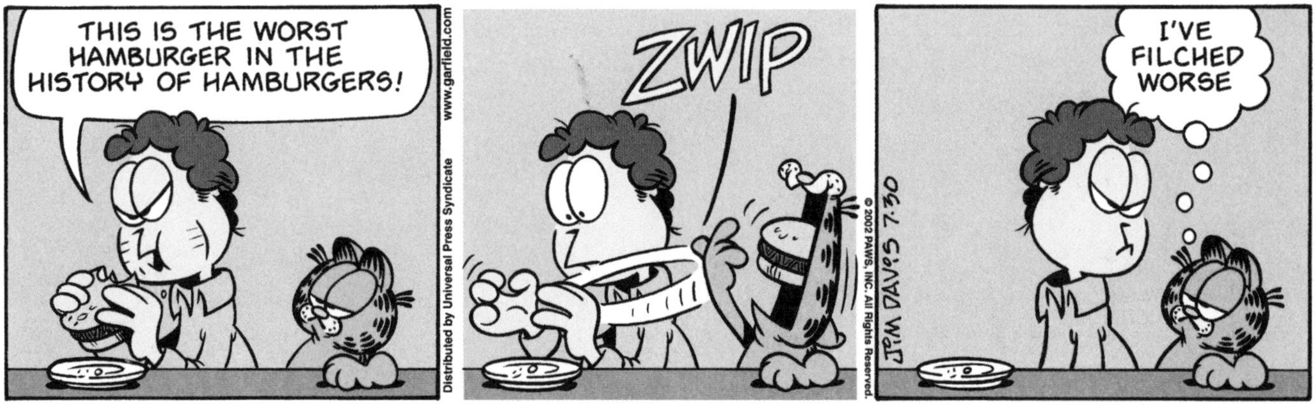
THIS IS THE WORST HAMBURGER IN THE HISTORY OF HAMBURGERS!
Distributed by Universal Press Syndicate www.garfield.com
ZWIP
© 2002 PAWS, INC. All Rights Reserved.
JIM DAVIS 7-30
I'VE FILCHED WORSE

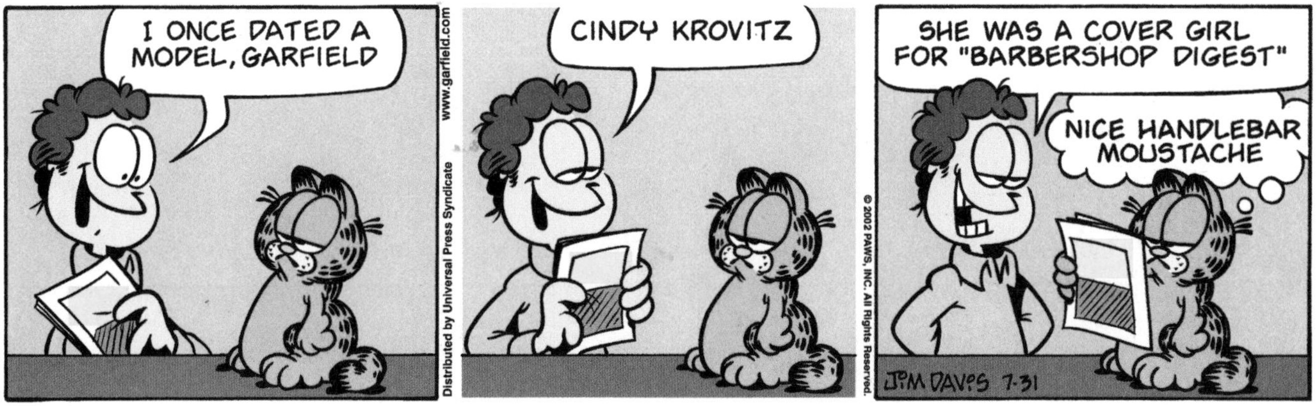
I ONCE DATED A MODEL, GARFIELD
Distributed by Universal Press Syndicate www.garfield.com
CINDY KROVITZ
© 2002 PAWS, INC. All Rights Reserved.
SHE WAS A COVER GIRL FOR "BARBERSHOP DIGEST"
NICE HANDLEBAR MOUSTACHE
JIM DAVIS 7-31

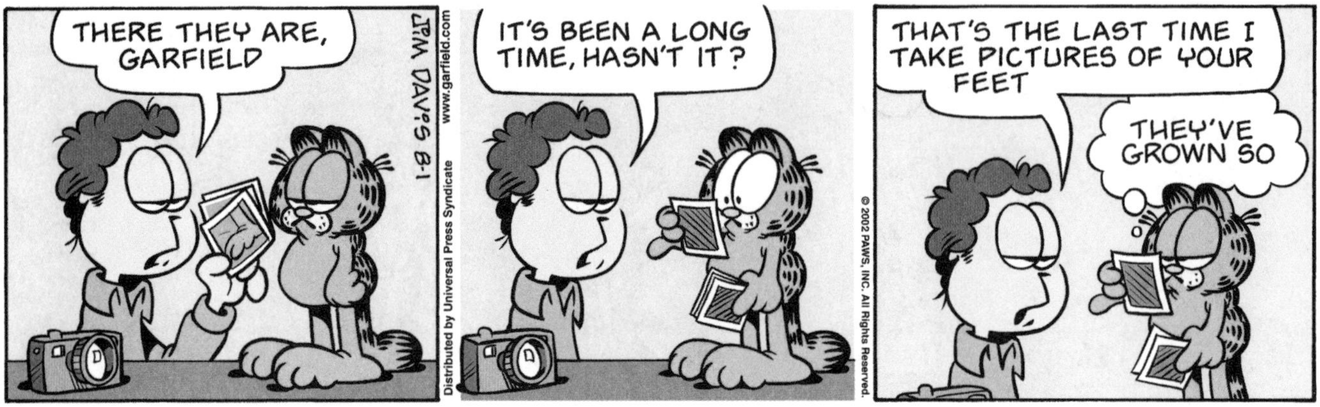
THERE THEY ARE, GARFIELD
JIM DAVIS 8-1
www.garfield.com
Distributed by Universal Press Syndicate
IT'S BEEN A LONG TIME, HASN'T IT?
© 2002 PAWS, INC. All Rights Reserved.
THAT'S THE LAST TIME I TAKE PICTURES OF YOUR FEET
THEY'VE GROWN SO

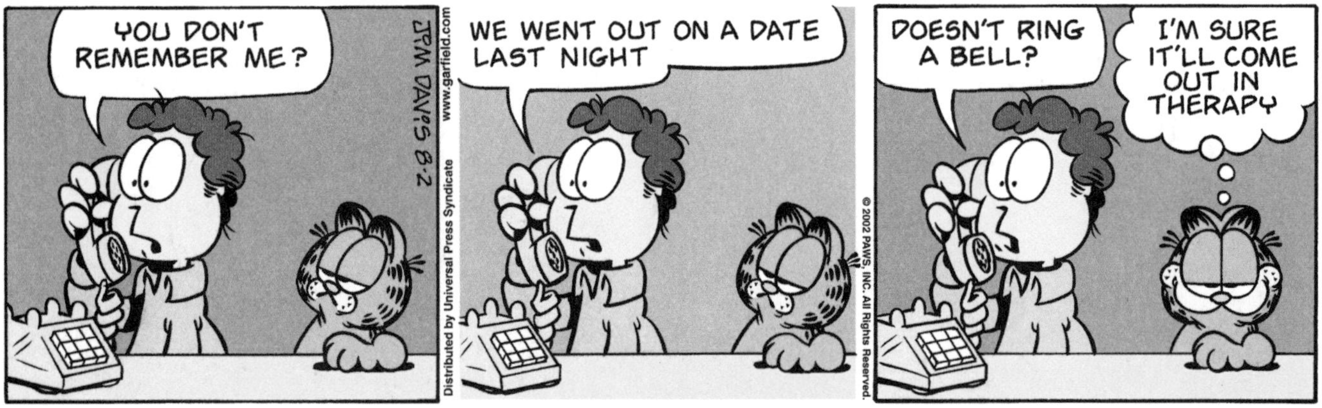
YOU DON'T REMEMBER ME?
JIM DAVIS 8-2
www.garfield.com
Distributed by Universal Press Syndicate
WE WENT OUT ON A DATE LAST NIGHT
© 2002 PAWS, INC. All Rights Reserved.
DOESN'T RING A BELL?
I'M SURE IT'LL COME OUT IN THERAPY

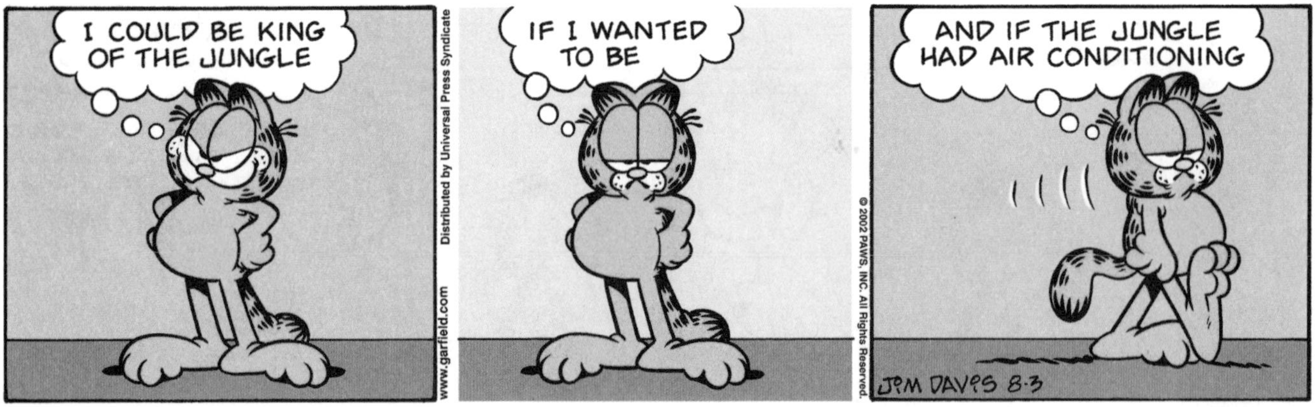
I COULD BE KING OF THE JUNGLE
Distributed by Universal Press Syndicate
www.garfield.com
IF I WANTED TO BE
© 2002 PAWS, INC. All Rights Reserved.
AND IF THE JUNGLE HAD AIR CONDITIONING
JIM DAVIS 8-3

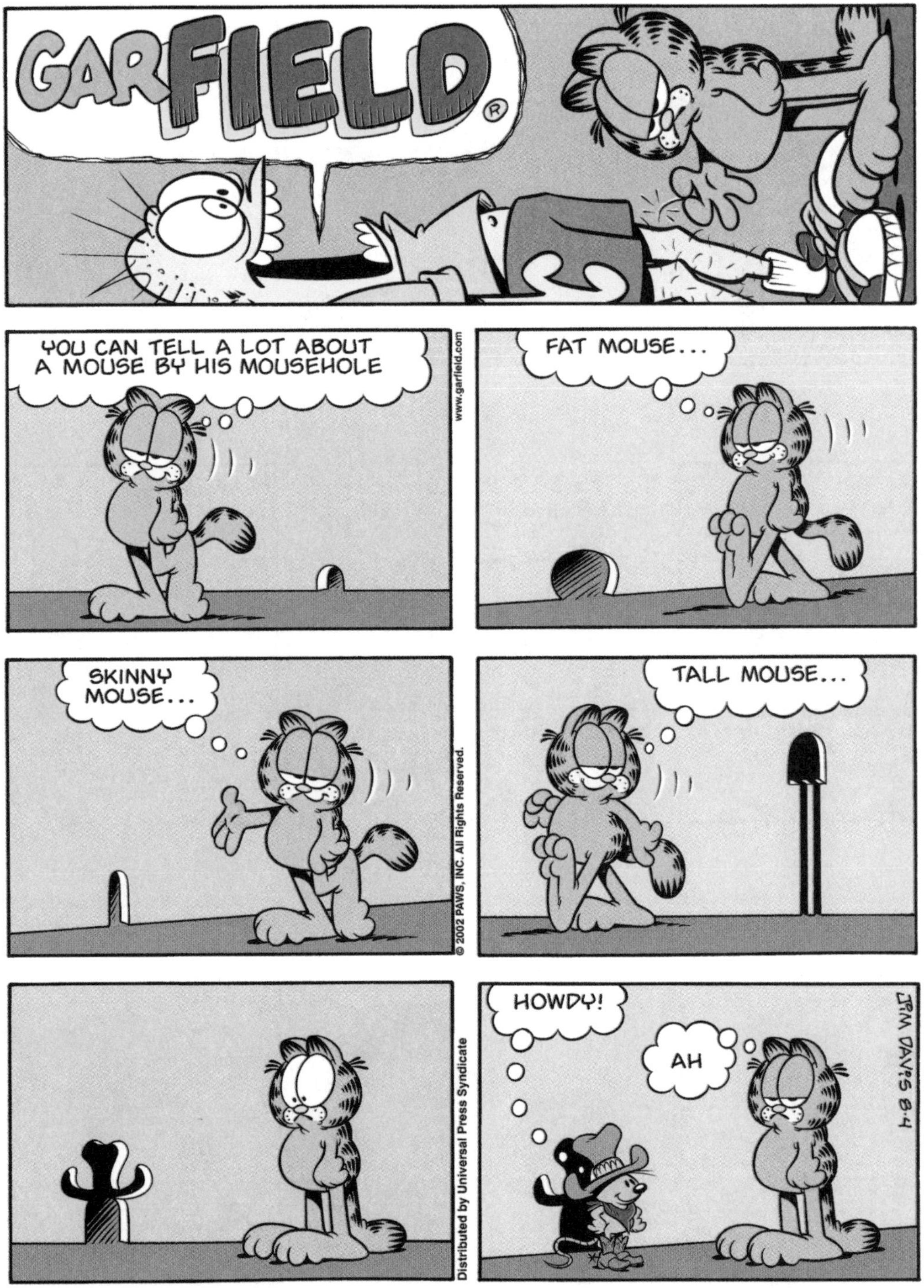

GARFIELD®
YOU CAN TELL A LOT ABOUT A MOUSE BY HIS MOUSEHOLE
FAT MOUSE...
SKINNY MOUSE...
TALL MOUSE...
HOWDY!
AH
JIM DAVIS 8-4
www.garfield.com
© 2002 PAWS, INC. All Rights Reserved.
Distributed by Universal Press Syndicate

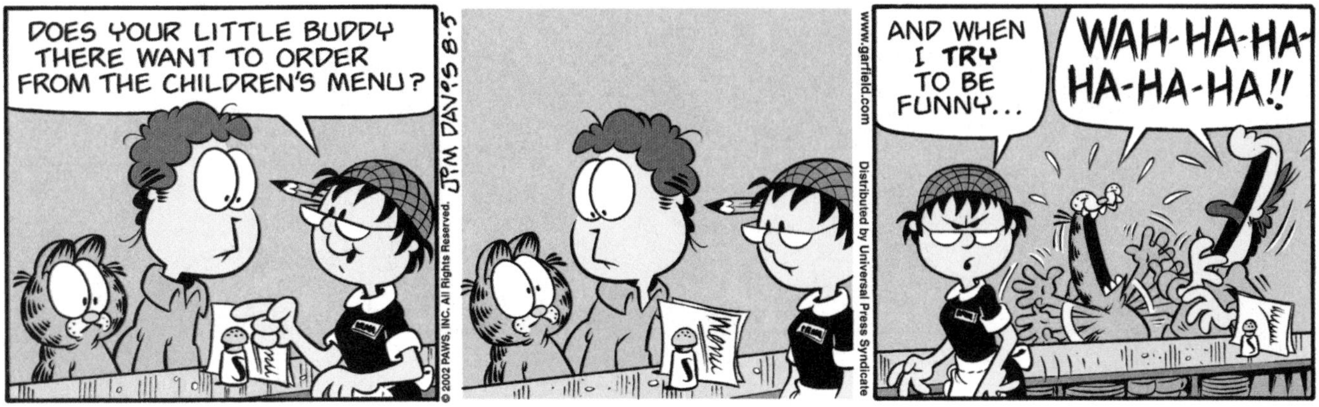
DOES YOUR LITTLE BUDDY THERE WANT TO ORDER FROM THE CHILDREN'S MENU?
AND WHEN I TRY TO BE FUNNY...
WAH-HA-HA-HA-HA-HA!!

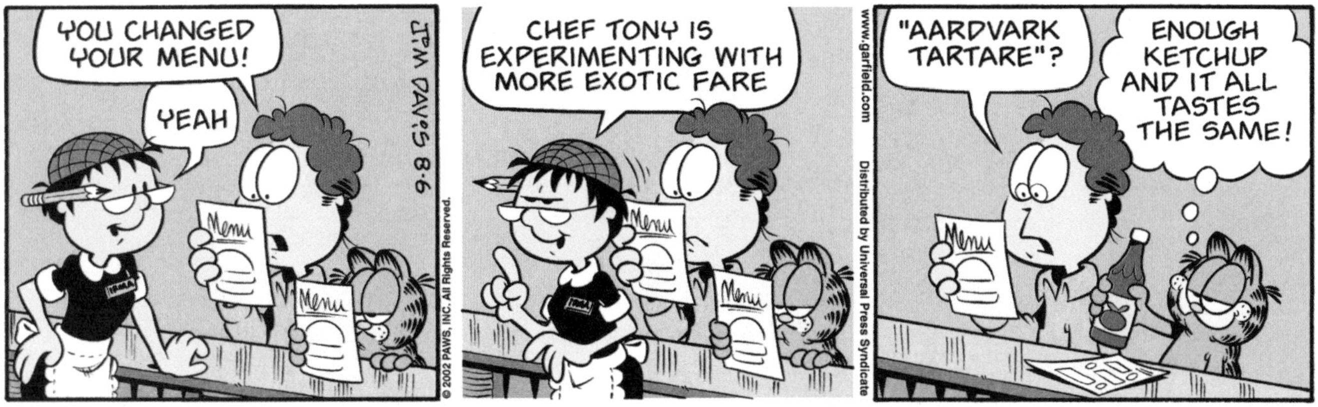
YOU CHANGED YOUR MENU!
YEAH
CHEF TONY IS EXPERIMENTING WITH MORE EXOTIC FARE
"AARDVARK TARTARE"?
ENOUGH KETCHUP AND IT ALL TASTES THE SAME!

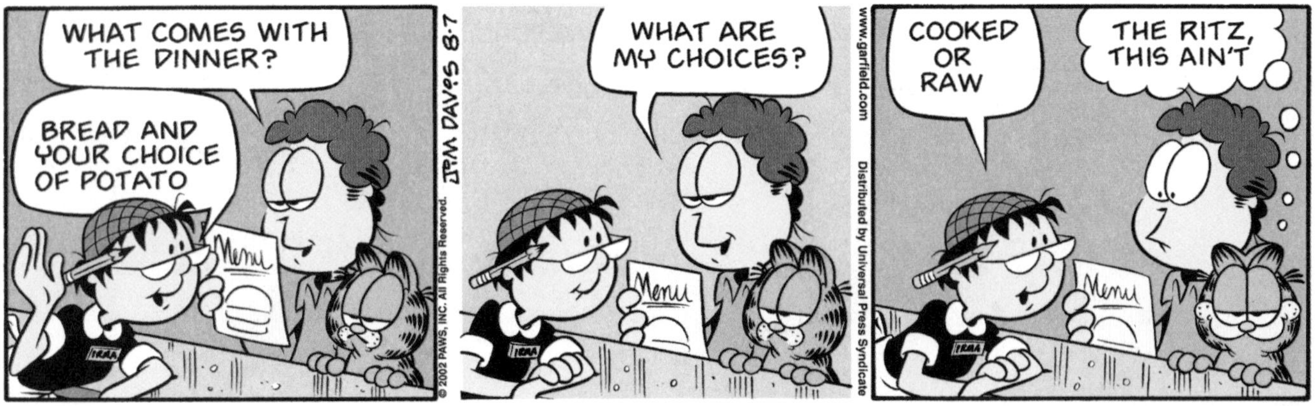
WHAT COMES WITH THE DINNER?
BREAD AND YOUR CHOICE OF POTATO
WHAT ARE MY CHOICES?
COOKED OR RAW
THE RITZ, THIS AIN'T

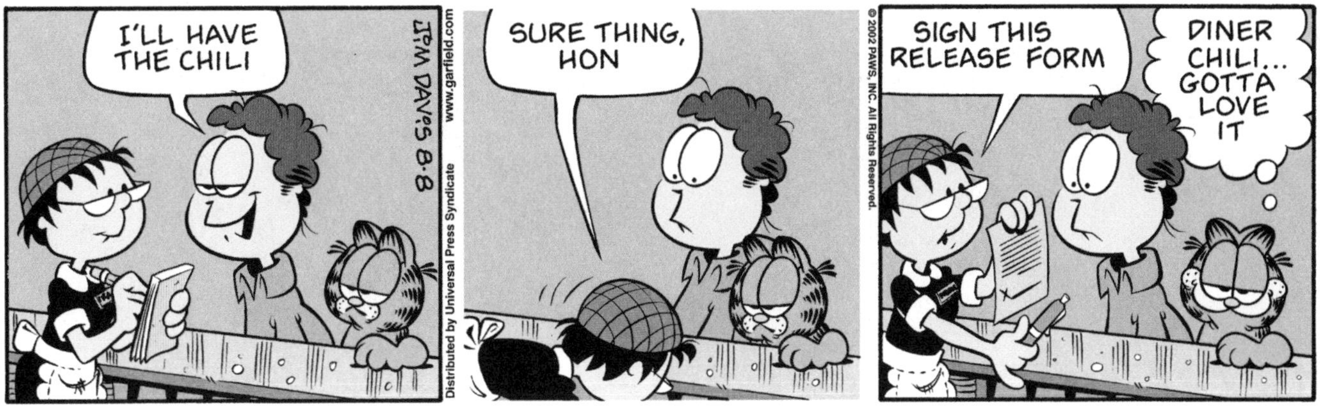
I'LL HAVE THE CHILI
JIM DAVIS 8-8
www.garfield.com
Distributed by Universal Press Syndicate
SURE THING, HON
© 2002 PAWS, INC. All Rights Reserved.
SIGN THIS RELEASE FORM
DINER CHILI... GOTTA LOVE IT

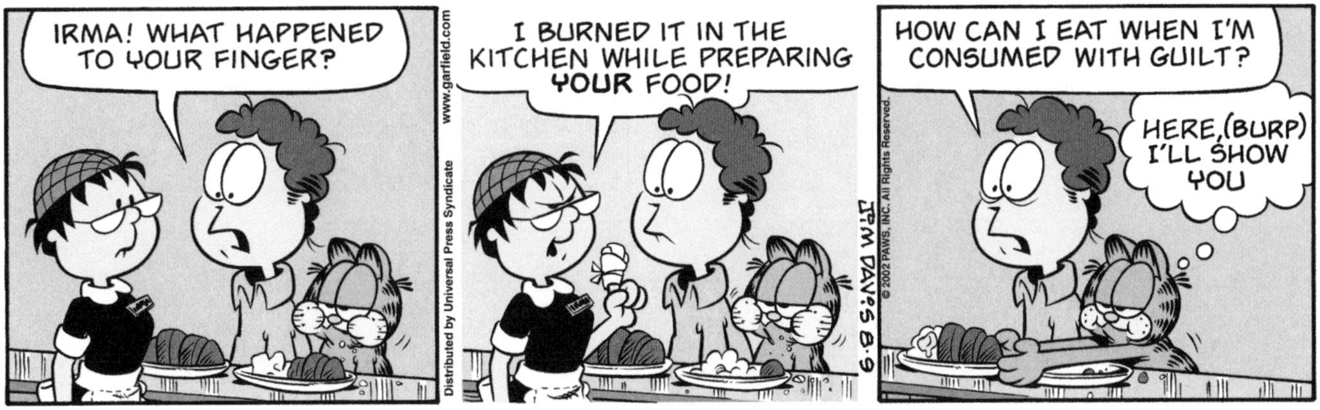
IRMA! WHAT HAPPENED TO YOUR FINGER?
www.garfield.com
Distributed by Universal Press Syndicate
I BURNED IT IN THE KITCHEN WHILE PREPARING **YOUR** FOOD!
JIM DAVIS 8-9
© 2002 PAWS, INC. All Rights Reserved.
HOW CAN I EAT WHEN I'M CONSUMED WITH GUILT?
HERE, (BURP) I'LL SHOW YOU

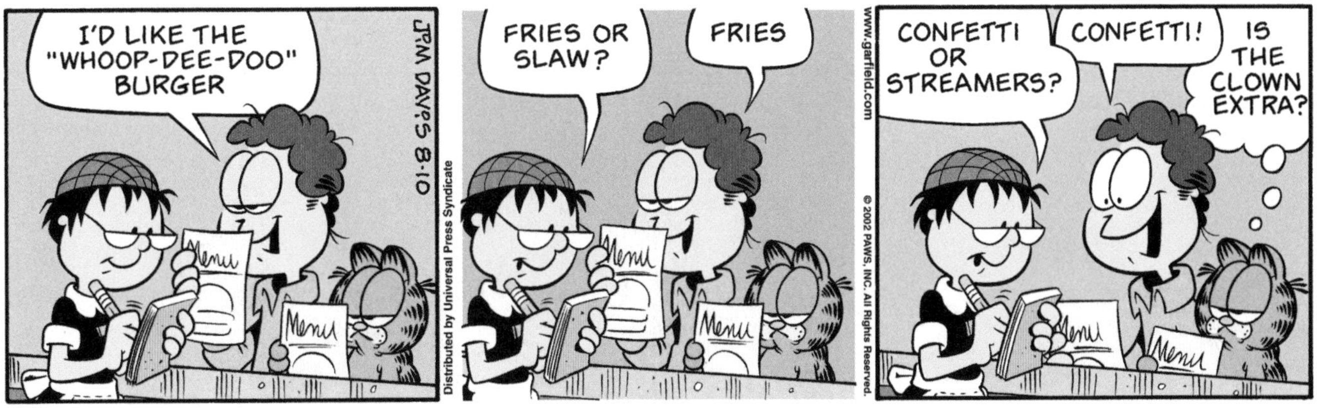
I'D LIKE THE "WHOOP-DEE-DOO" BURGER
JIM DAVIS 8-10
Distributed by Universal Press Syndicate
FRIES OR SLAW?
FRIES
www.garfield.com
© 2002 PAWS, INC. All Rights Reserved.
CONFETTI OR STREAMERS?
CONFETTI!
IS THE CLOWN EXTRA?

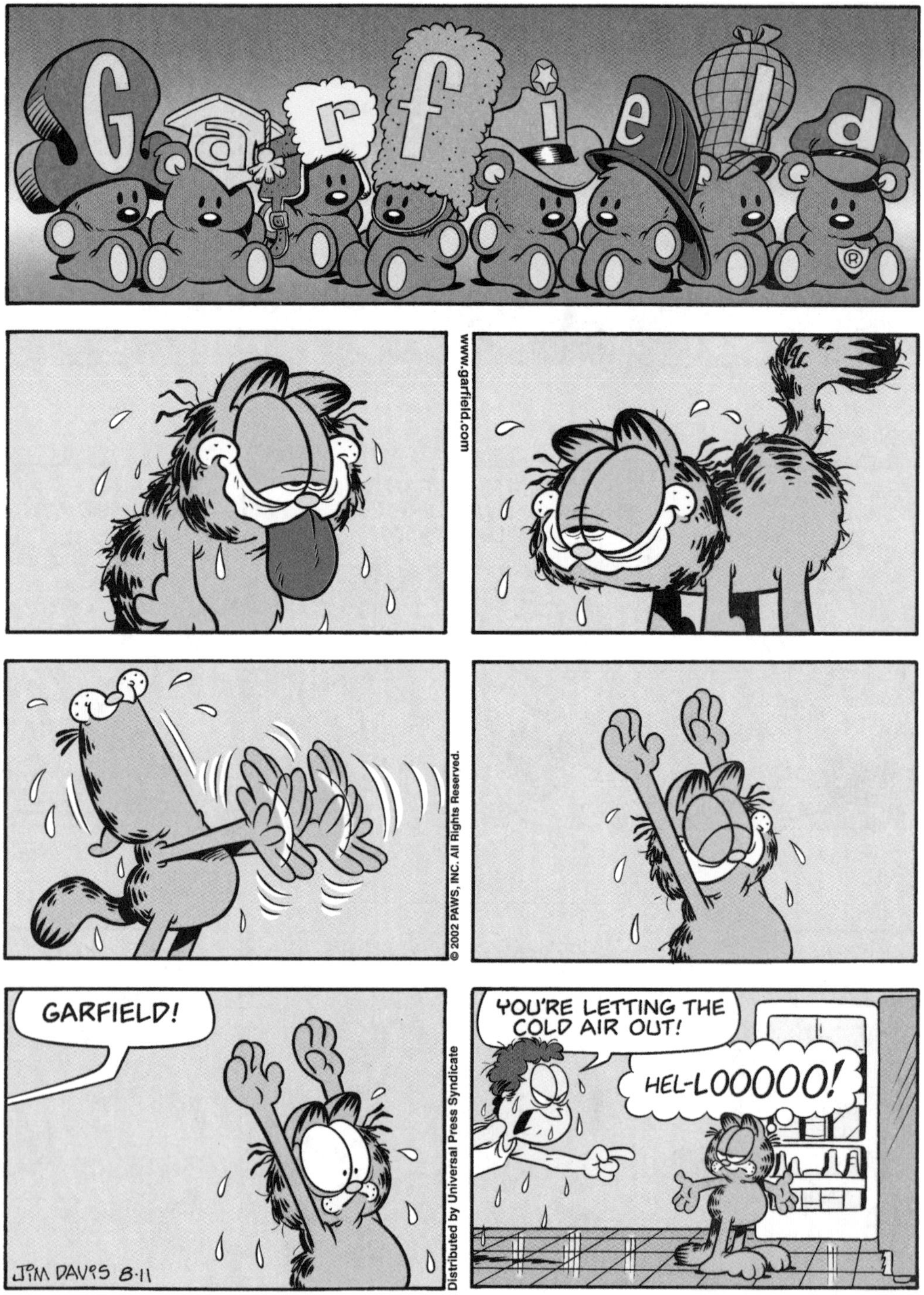
Garfield
www.garfield.com
© 2002 PAWS, INC. All Rights Reserved.
Distributed by Universal Press Syndicate
GARFIELD!
JIM DAVIS 8·11
YOU'RE LETTING THE COLD AIR OUT!
HEL-LOOOOO!

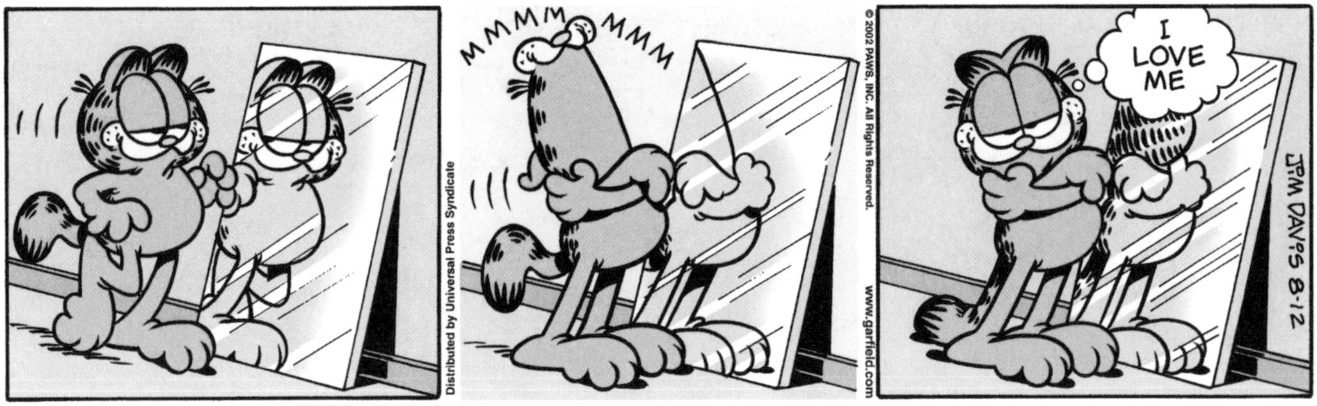
MMMM MMM
I LOVE ME
JIM DAVIS 8-12
Distributed by Universal Press Syndicate
© 2002 PAWS, INC. All Rights Reserved.
www.garfield.com

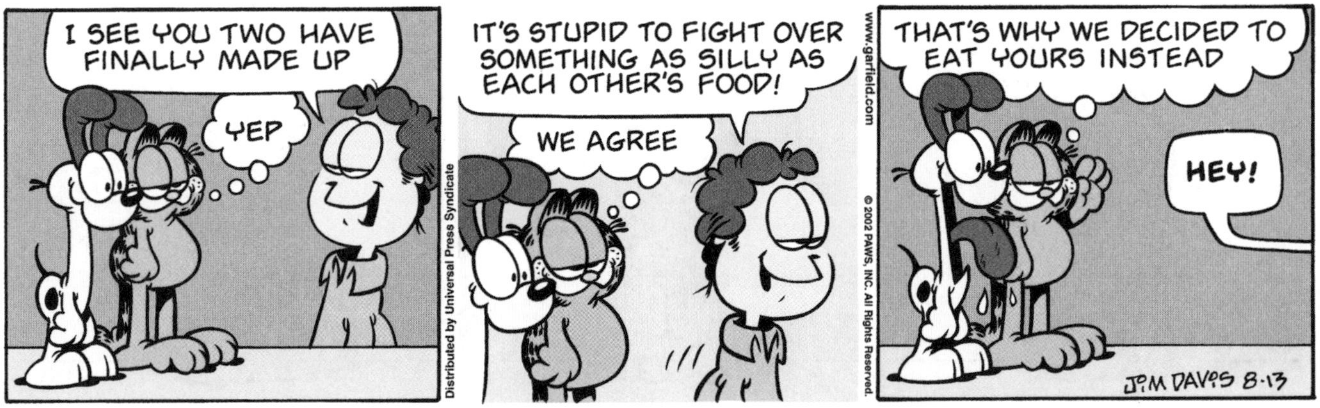
I SEE YOU TWO HAVE FINALLY MADE UP
YEP
IT'S STUPID TO FIGHT OVER SOMETHING AS SILLY AS EACH OTHER'S FOOD!
WE AGREE
THAT'S WHY WE DECIDED TO EAT YOURS INSTEAD
HEY!
JIM DAVIS 8-13
Distributed by Universal Press Syndicate
www.garfield.com
© 2002 PAWS, INC. All Rights Reserved.

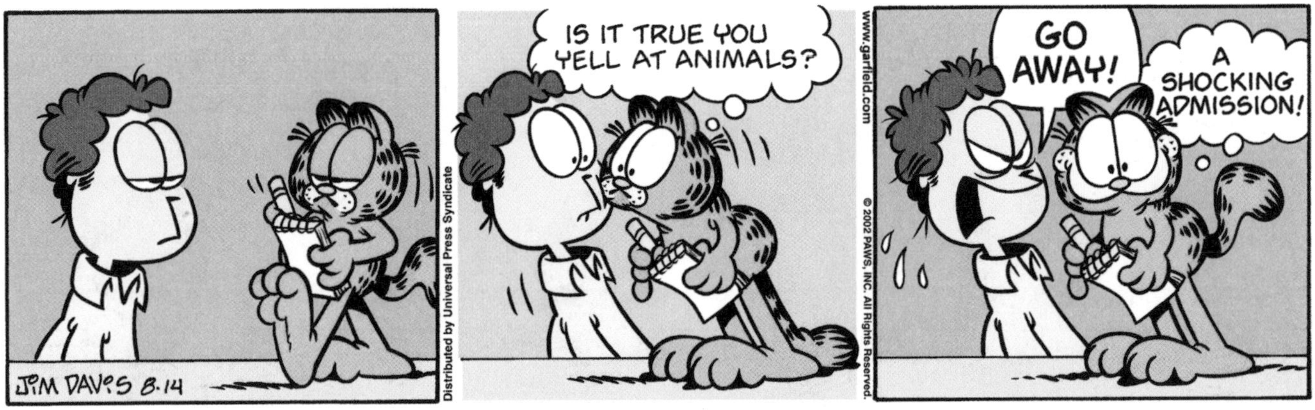
JIM DAVIS 8-14
IS IT TRUE YOU YELL AT ANIMALS?
GO AWAY!
A SHOCKING ADMISSION!
Distributed by Universal Press Syndicate
www.garfield.com
© 2002 PAWS, INC. All Rights Reserved.

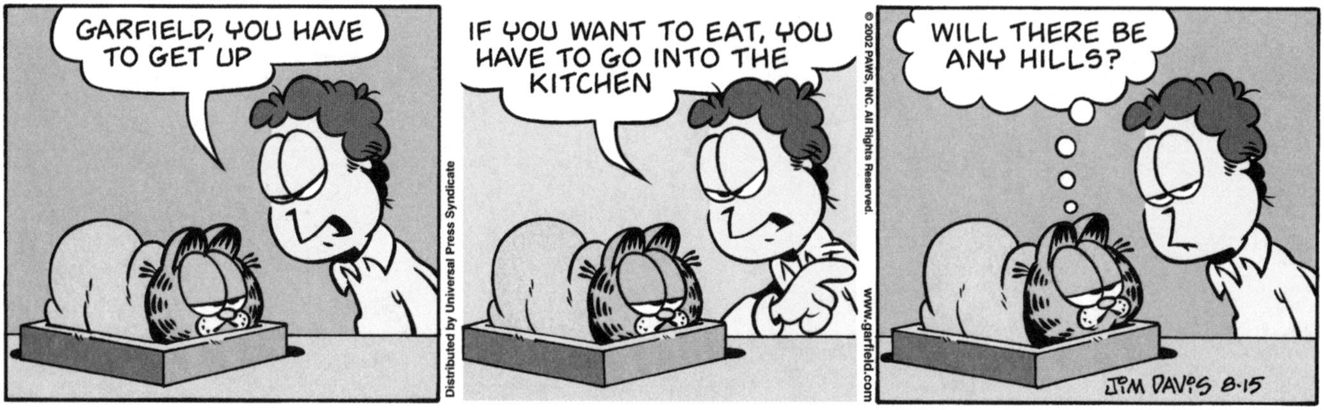
GARFIELD, YOU HAVE TO GET UP
Distributed by Universal Press Syndicate
IF YOU WANT TO EAT, YOU HAVE TO GO INTO THE KITCHEN
© 2002 PAWS, INC. All Rights Reserved.
www.garfield.com
WILL THERE BE ANY HILLS?
JIM DAVIS 8-15

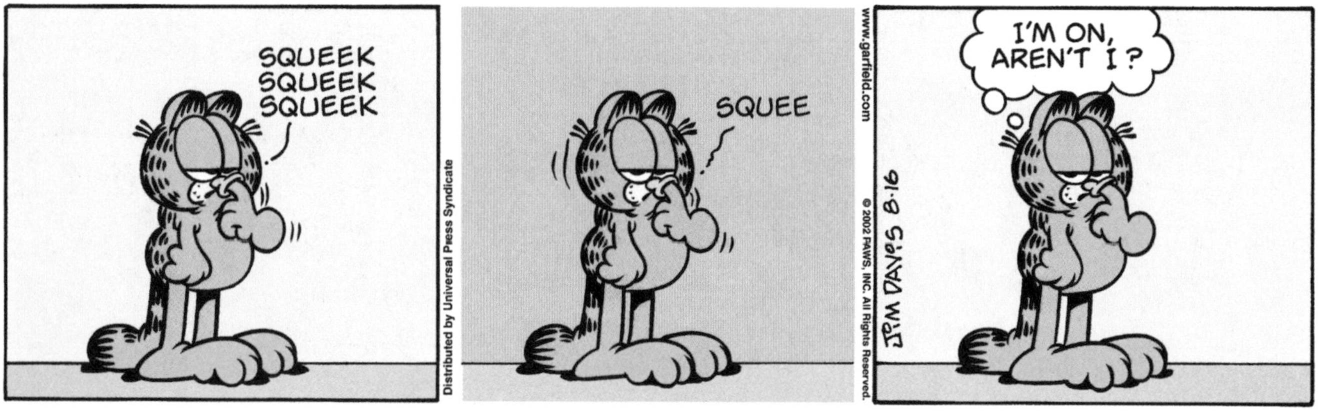
SQUEEK SQUEEK SQUEEK
Distributed by Universal Press Syndicate
SQUEE
www.garfield.com
© 2002 PAWS, INC. All Rights Reserved.
JIM DAVIS 8-16
I'M ON, AREN'T I ?

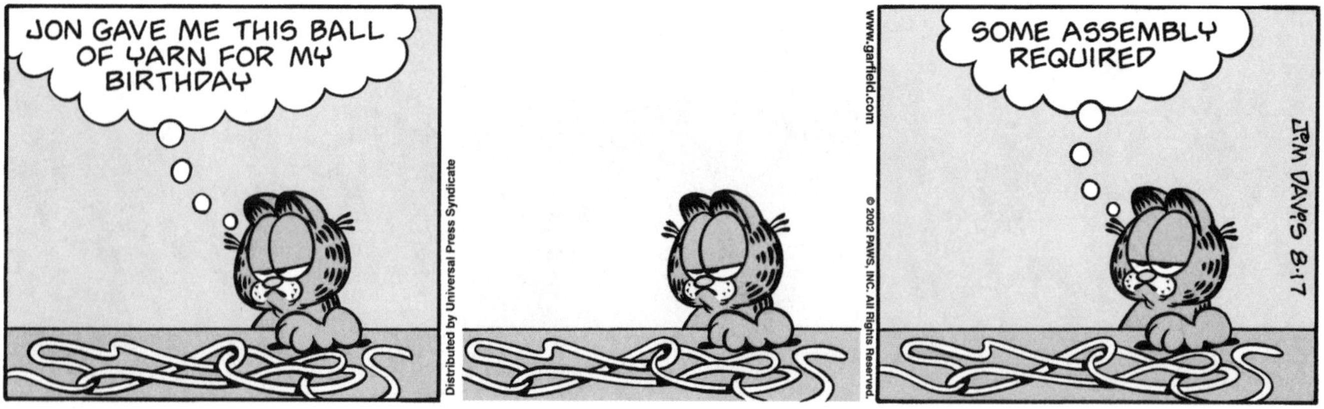
JON GAVE ME THIS BALL OF YARN FOR MY BIRTHDAY
Distributed by Universal Press Syndicate
www.garfield.com
© 2002 PAWS, INC. All Rights Reserved.
SOME ASSEMBLY REQUIRED
JIM DAVIS 8-17

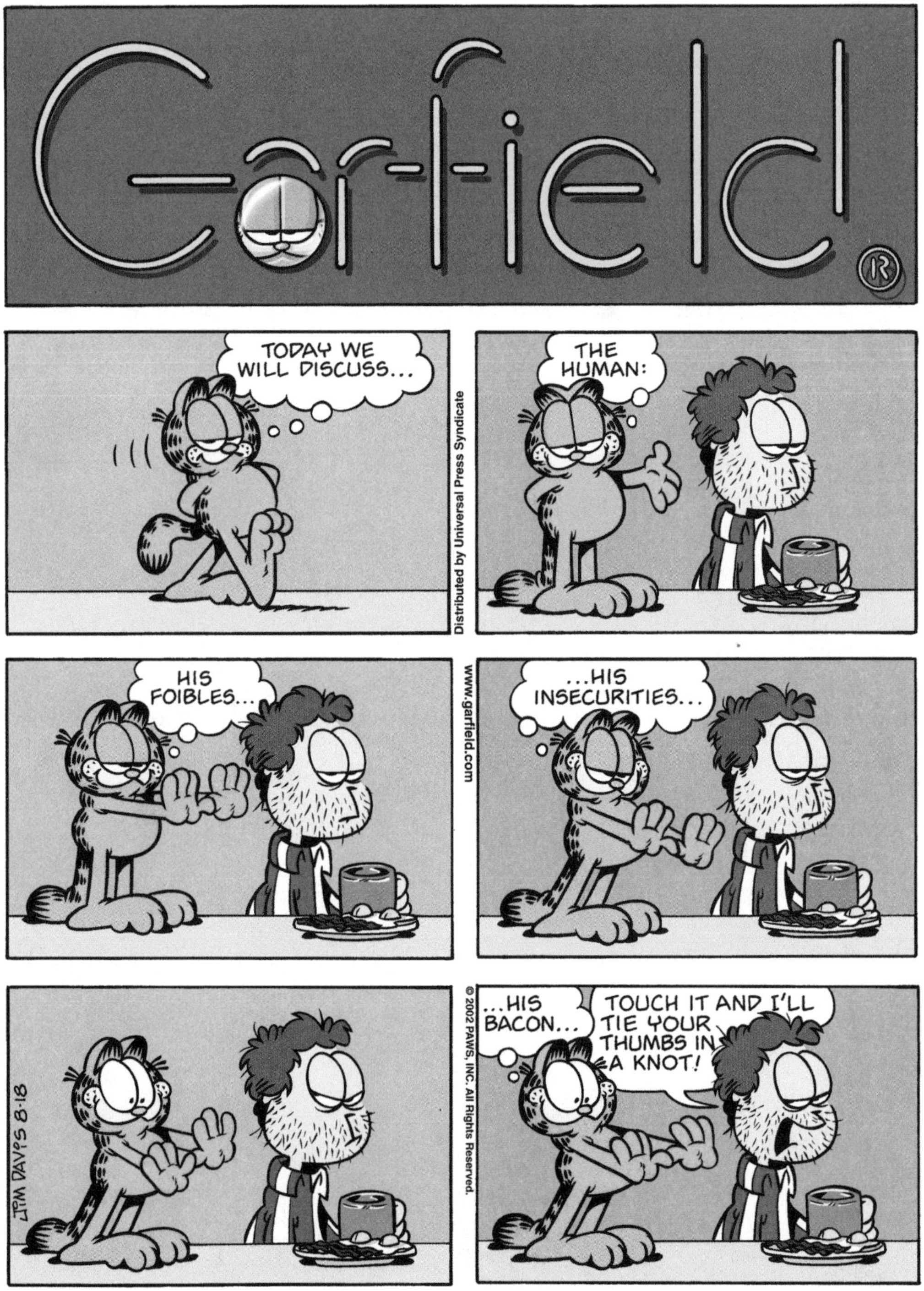
Garfield®
TODAY WE WILL DISCUSS...
THE HUMAN:
HIS FOIBLES...
...HIS INSECURITIES...
...HIS BACON...
TOUCH IT AND I'LL TIE YOUR THUMBS IN A KNOT!
JPM DAVPS 8-18
Distributed by Universal Press Syndicate
www.garfield.com
© 2002 PAWS, INC. All Rights Reserved.

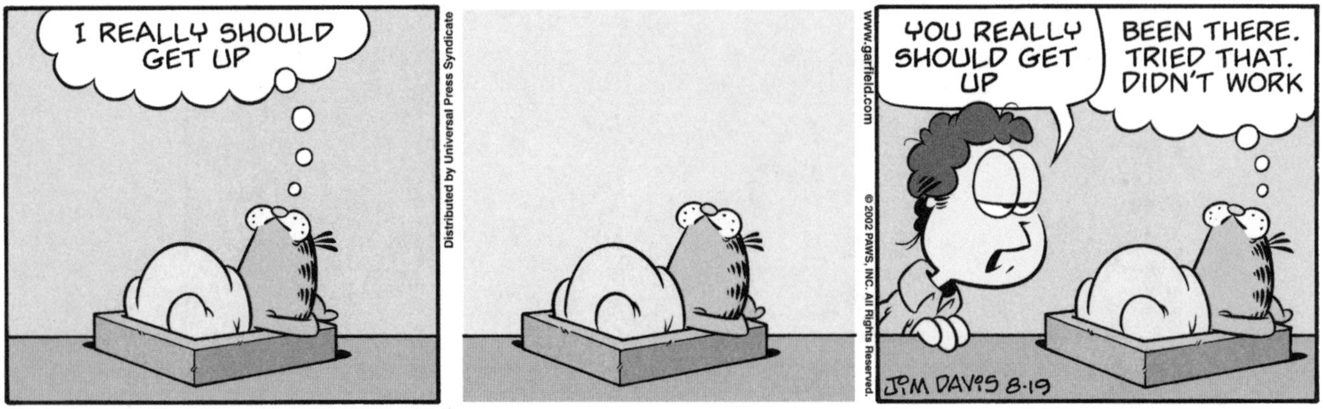
I REALLY SHOULD GET UP
YOU REALLY SHOULD GET UP
BEEN THERE. TRIED THAT. DIDN'T WORK
JIM DAVIS 8-19
Distributed by Universal Press Syndicate
www.garfield.com
© 2002 PAWS, INC. All Rights Reserved.

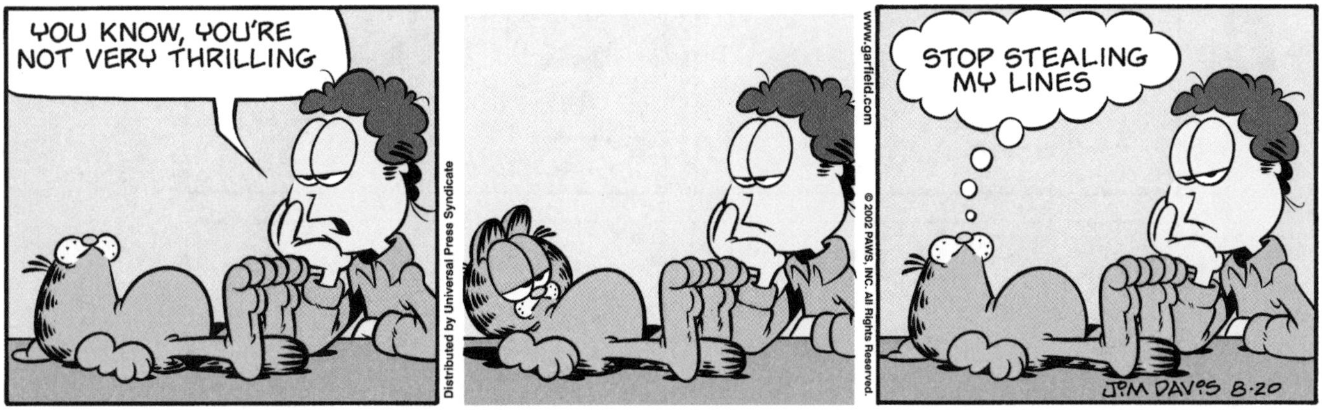
YOU KNOW, YOU'RE NOT VERY THRILLING
STOP STEALING MY LINES
JIM DAVIS 8-20
Distributed by Universal Press Syndicate
www.garfield.com
© 2002 PAWS, INC. All Rights Reserved.

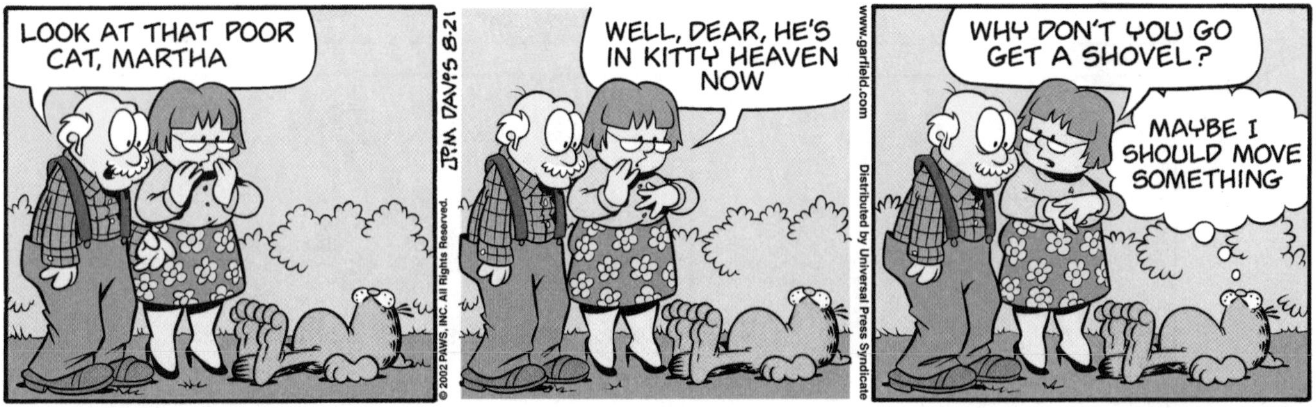
LOOK AT THAT POOR CAT, MARTHA
WELL, DEAR, HE'S IN KITTY HEAVEN NOW
WHY DON'T YOU GO GET A SHOVEL?
MAYBE I SHOULD MOVE SOMETHING
JIM DAVIS 8-21
© 2002 PAWS, INC. All Rights Reserved.
www.garfield.com
Distributed by Universal Press Syndicate

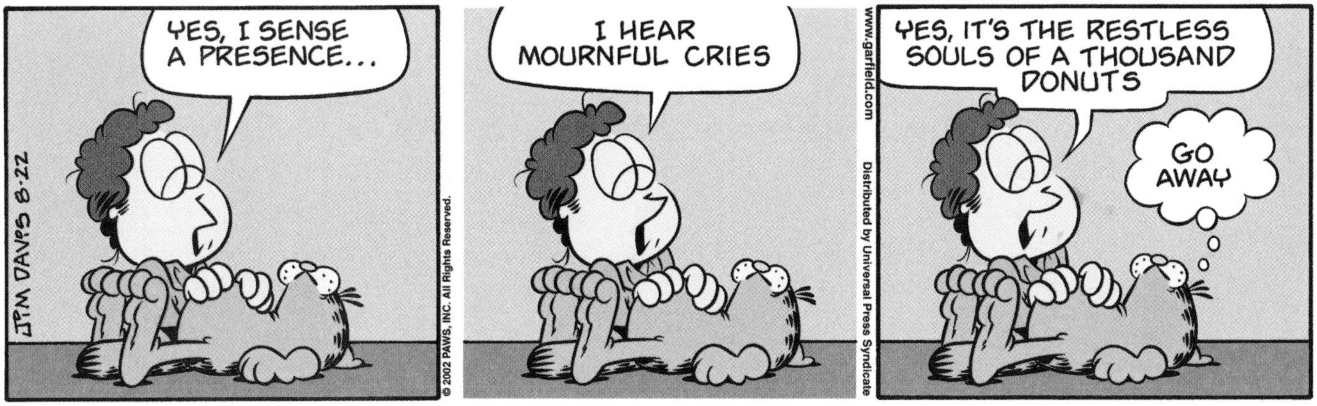
JIM DAVIS 8-22
YES, I SENSE A PRESENCE...
© 2002 PAWS, INC. All Rights Reserved.
I HEAR MOURNFUL CRIES
www.garfield.com Distributed by Universal Press Syndicate
YES, IT'S THE RESTLESS SOULS OF A THOUSAND DONUTS
GO AWAY

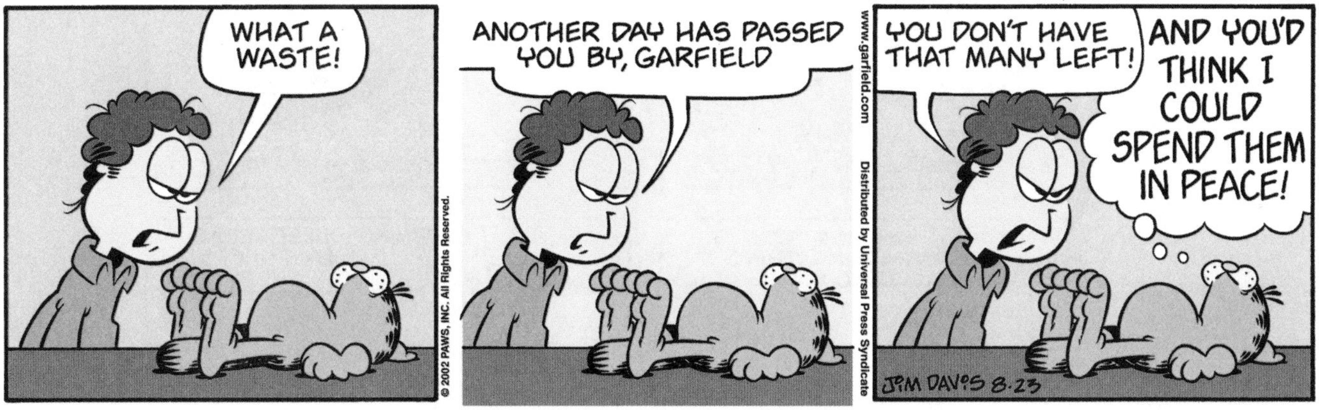
WHAT A WASTE!
© 2002 PAWS, INC. All Rights Reserved.
ANOTHER DAY HAS PASSED YOU BY, GARFIELD
www.garfield.com Distributed by Universal Press Syndicate
YOU DON'T HAVE THAT MANY LEFT!
AND YOU'D THINK I COULD SPEND THEM IN PEACE!
JIM DAVIS 8-23

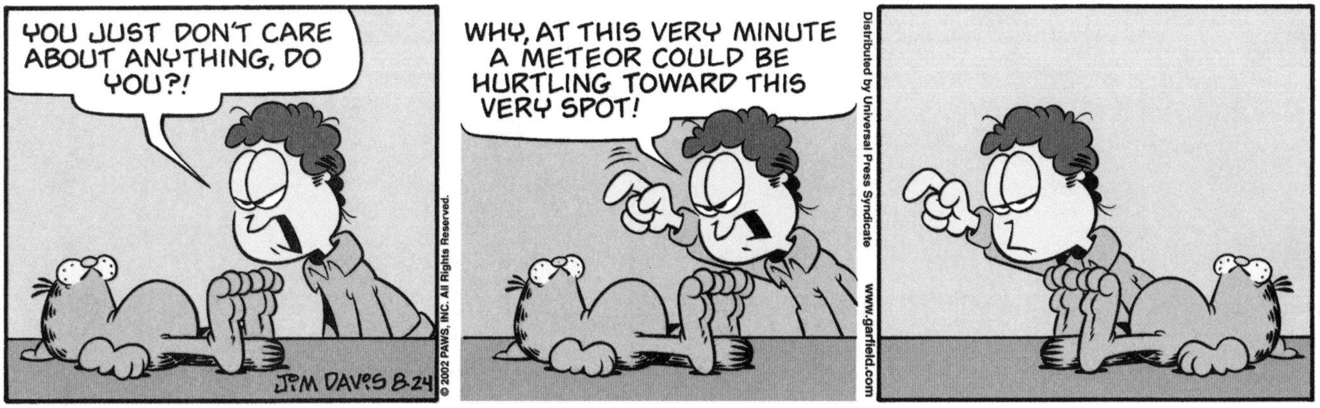
YOU JUST DON'T CARE ABOUT ANYTHING, DO YOU?!
JIM DAVIS 8-24
© 2002 PAWS, INC. All Rights Reserved.
WHY, AT THIS VERY MINUTE A METEOR COULD BE HURTLING TOWARD THIS VERY SPOT!
Distributed by Universal Press Syndicate www.garfield.com

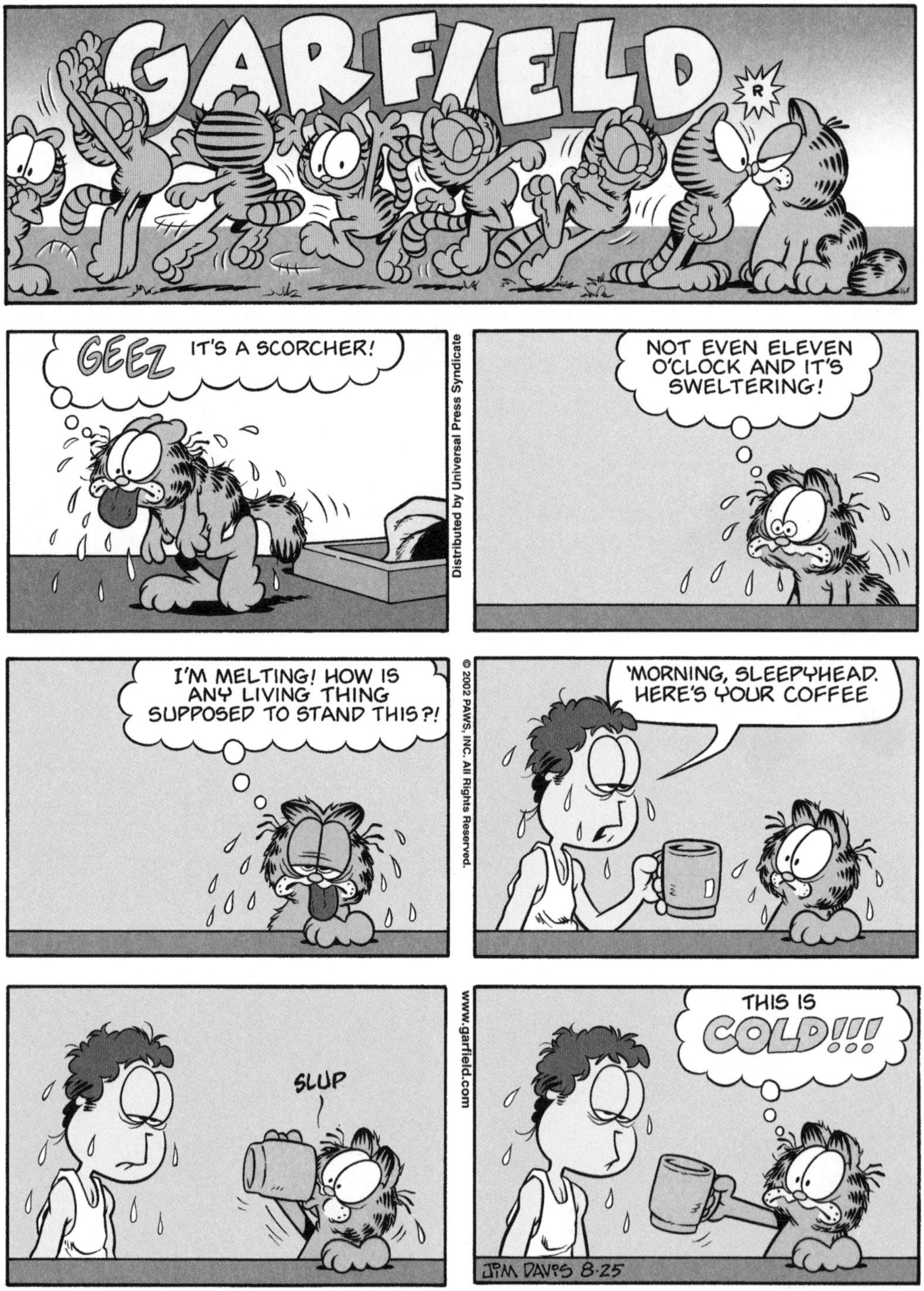
GARFIELD
GEEZ IT'S A SCORCHER!
NOT EVEN ELEVEN O'CLOCK AND IT'S SWELTERING!
I'M MELTING! HOW IS ANY LIVING THING SUPPOSED TO STAND THIS?!
'MORNING, SLEEPYHEAD. HERE'S YOUR COFFEE
SLUP
THIS IS COLD!!!
JIM DAVIS 8·25
Distributed by Universal Press Syndicate
© 2002 PAWS, INC. All Rights Reserved.
www.garfield.com

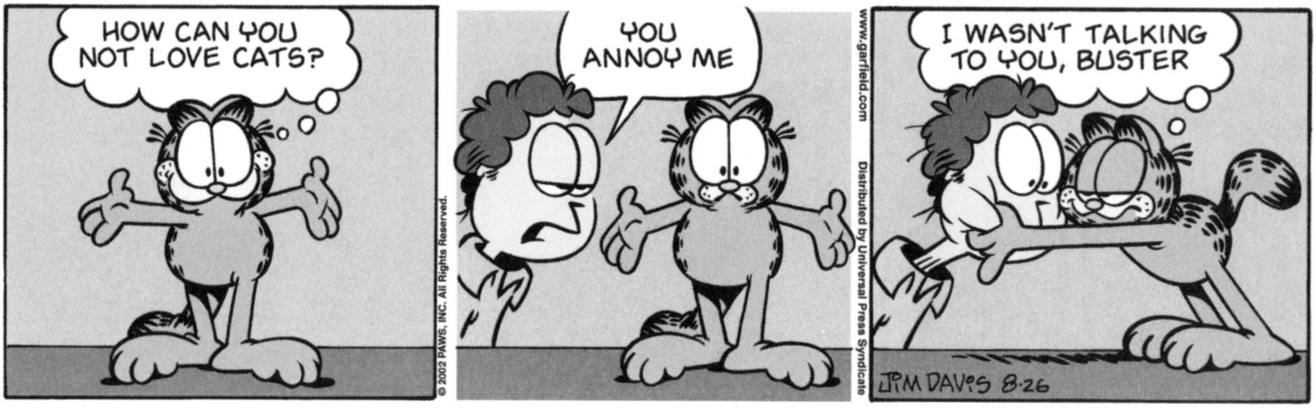
HOW CAN YOU NOT LOVE CATS?
© 2002 PAWS, INC. All Rights Reserved.
YOU ANNOY ME
www.garfield.com
Distributed by Universal Press Syndicate
I WASN'T TALKING TO YOU, BUSTER
JIM DAVIS 8-26

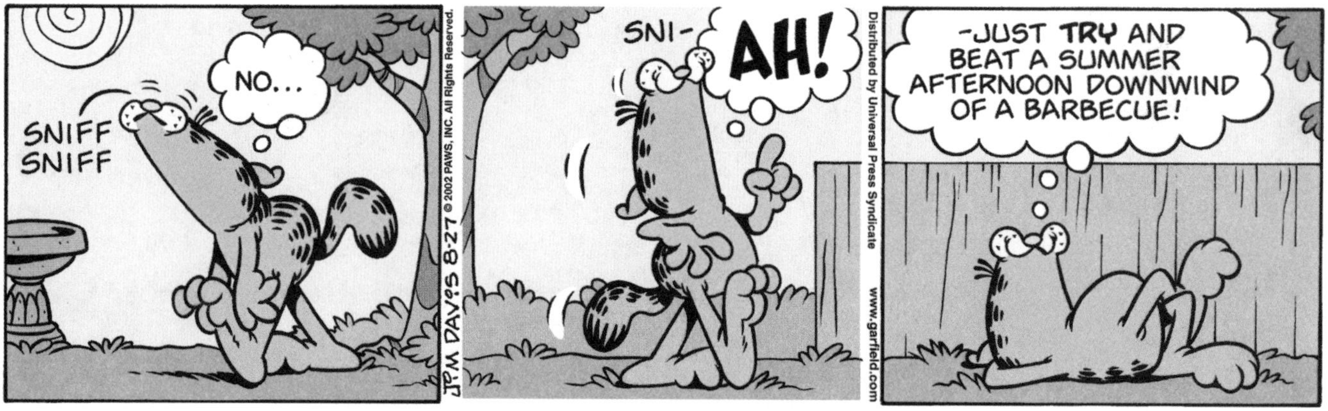
SNIFF SNIFF
NO...
JIM DAVIS 8-27
© 2002 PAWS, INC. All Rights Reserved.
SNI-
AH!
Distributed by Universal Press Syndicate
www.garfield.com
-JUST TRY AND BEAT A SUMMER AFTERNOON DOWNWIND OF A BARBECUE!

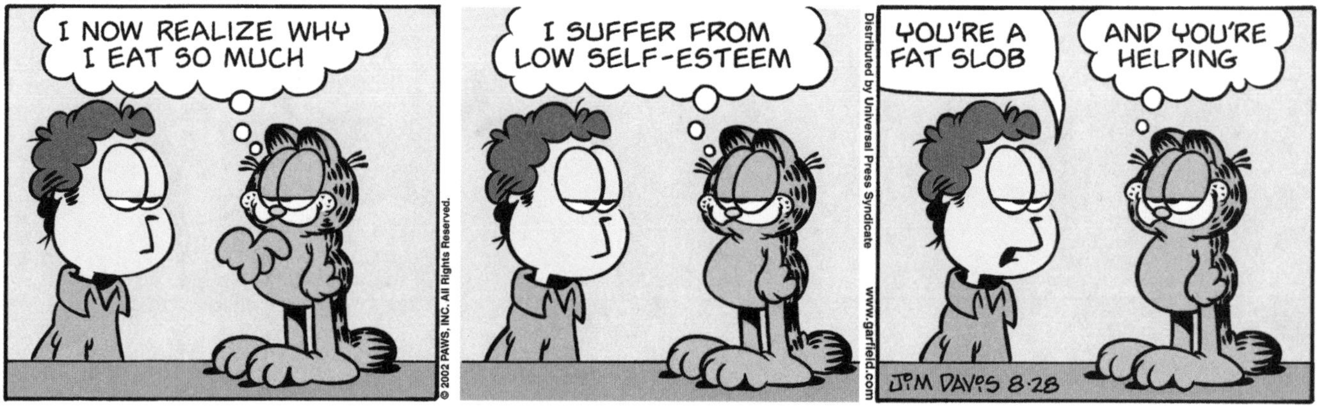
I NOW REALIZE WHY I EAT SO MUCH
© 2002 PAWS, INC. All Rights Reserved.
I SUFFER FROM LOW SELF-ESTEEM
Distributed by Universal Press Syndicate
www.garfield.com
YOU'RE A FAT SLOB
AND YOU'RE HELPING
JIM DAVIS 8-28

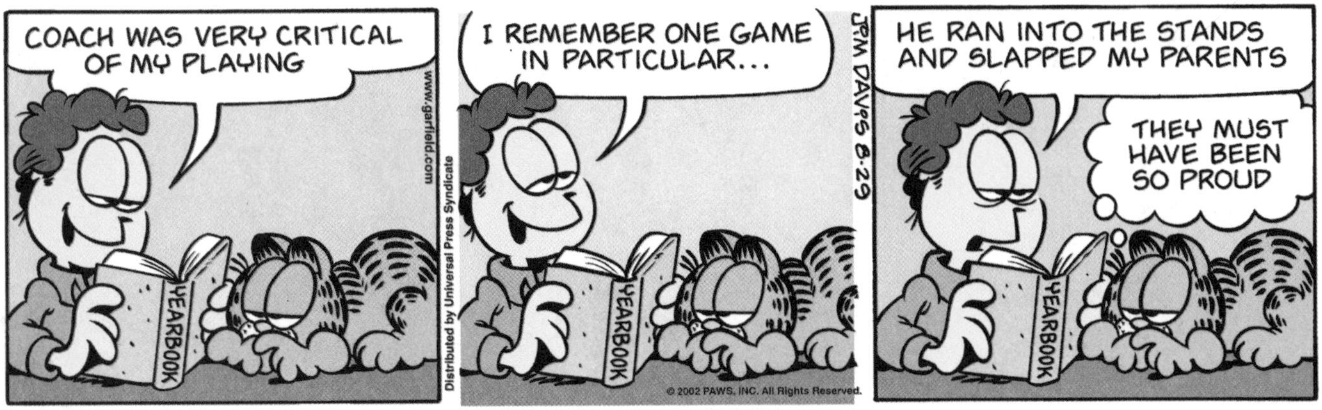
COACH WAS VERY CRITICAL OF MY PLAYING
I REMEMBER ONE GAME IN PARTICULAR...
HE RAN INTO THE STANDS AND SLAPPED MY PARENTS
THEY MUST HAVE BEEN SO PROUD
YEARBOOK
JIM DAVIS 8-29
www.garfield.com
Distributed by Universal Press Syndicate
© 2002 PAWS, INC. All Rights Reserved.

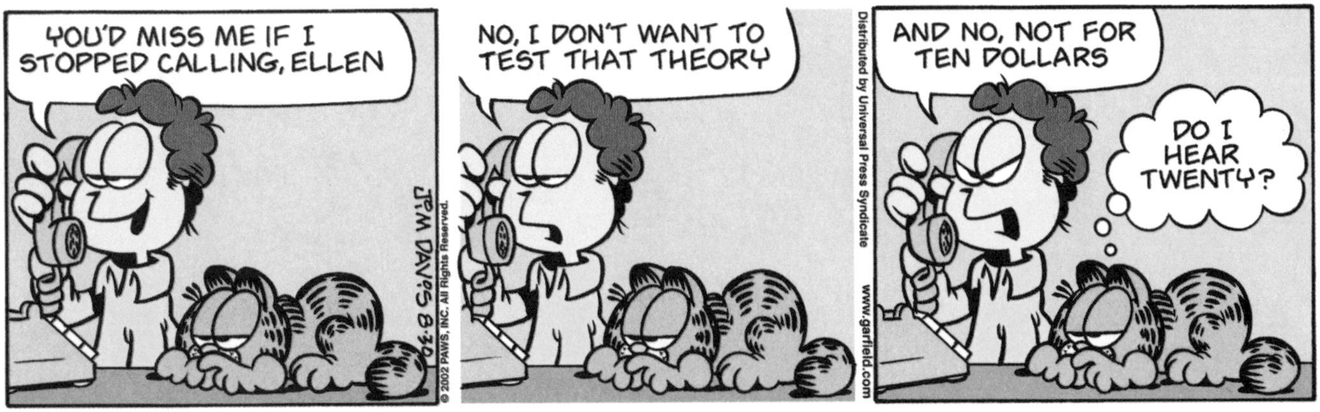
YOU'D MISS ME IF I STOPPED CALLING, ELLEN
NO, I DON'T WANT TO TEST THAT THEORY
AND NO, NOT FOR TEN DOLLARS
DO I HEAR TWENTY?
JIM DAVIS 8-30
© 2002 PAWS, INC. All Rights Reserved.
Distributed by Universal Press Syndicate
www.garfield.com

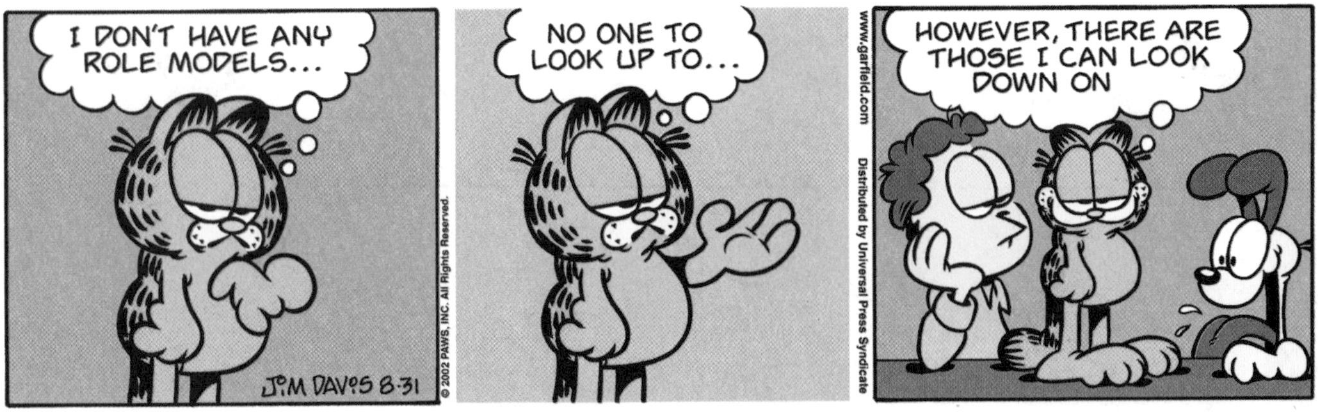
I DON'T HAVE ANY ROLE MODELS...
NO ONE TO LOOK UP TO...
HOWEVER, THERE ARE THOSE I CAN LOOK DOWN ON
JIM DAVIS 8-31
© 2002 PAWS, INC. All Rights Reserved.
www.garfield.com
Distributed by Universal Press Syndicate

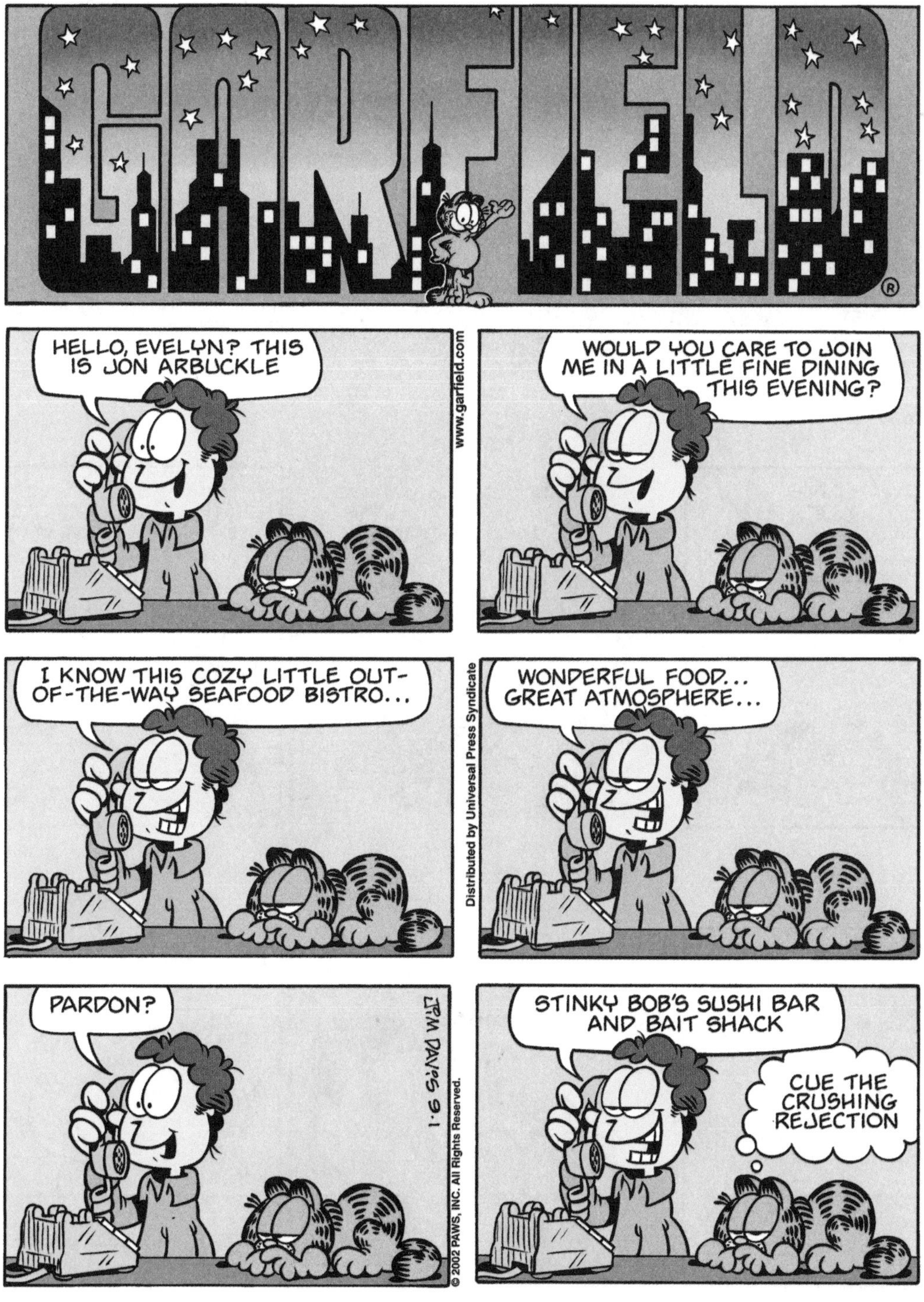
GARFIELD
HELLO, EVELYN? THIS IS JON ARBUCKLE
WOULD YOU CARE TO JOIN ME IN A LITTLE FINE DINING THIS EVENING?
I KNOW THIS COZY LITTLE OUT-OF-THE-WAY SEAFOOD BISTRO...
WONDERFUL FOOD... GREAT ATMOSPHERE...
PARDON?
STINKY BOB'S SUSHI BAR AND BAIT SHACK
CUE THE CRUSHING REJECTION
www.garfield.com
Distributed by Universal Press Syndicate
JIM DAVIS 9-1
© 2002 PAWS, INC. All Rights Reserved.

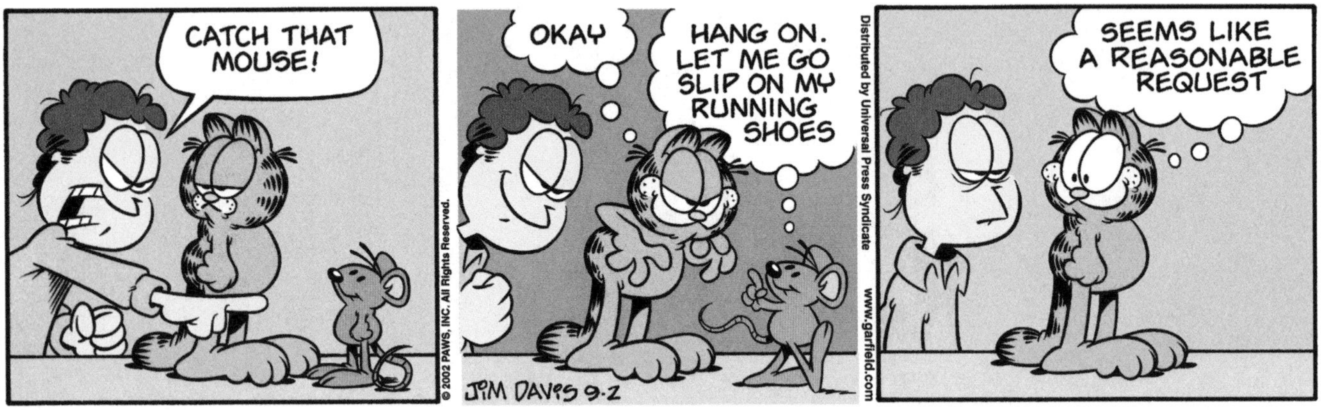
CATCH THAT MOUSE!
OKAY
HANG ON. LET ME GO SLIP ON MY RUNNING SHOES
SEEMS LIKE A REASONABLE REQUEST
© 2002 PAWS, INC. All Rights Reserved.
JIM DAVIS 9-2
Distributed by Universal Press Syndicate
www.garfield.com

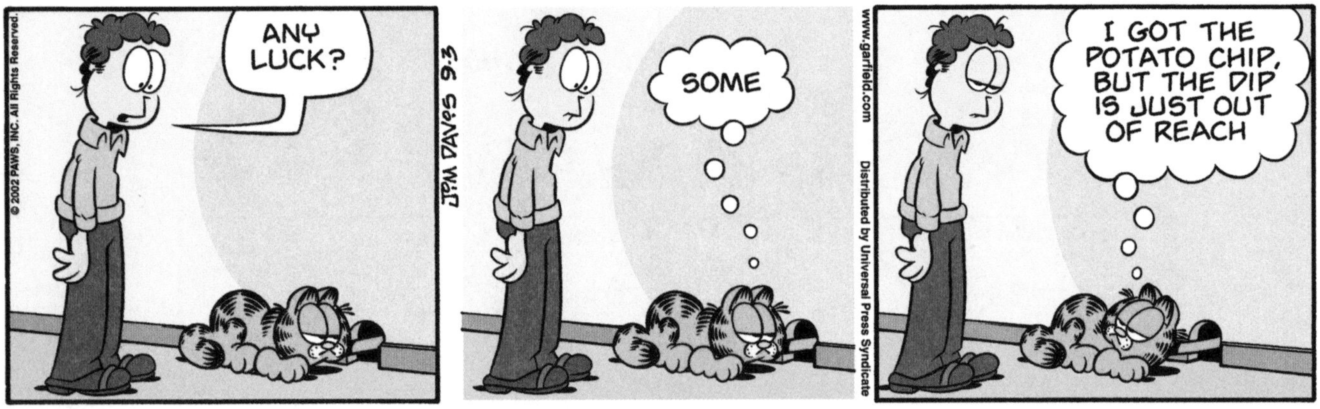
ANY LUCK?
SOME
I GOT THE POTATO CHIP, BUT THE DIP IS JUST OUT OF REACH
© 2002 PAWS, INC. All Rights Reserved.
JIM DAVIS 9-3
www.garfield.com
Distributed by Universal Press Syndicate

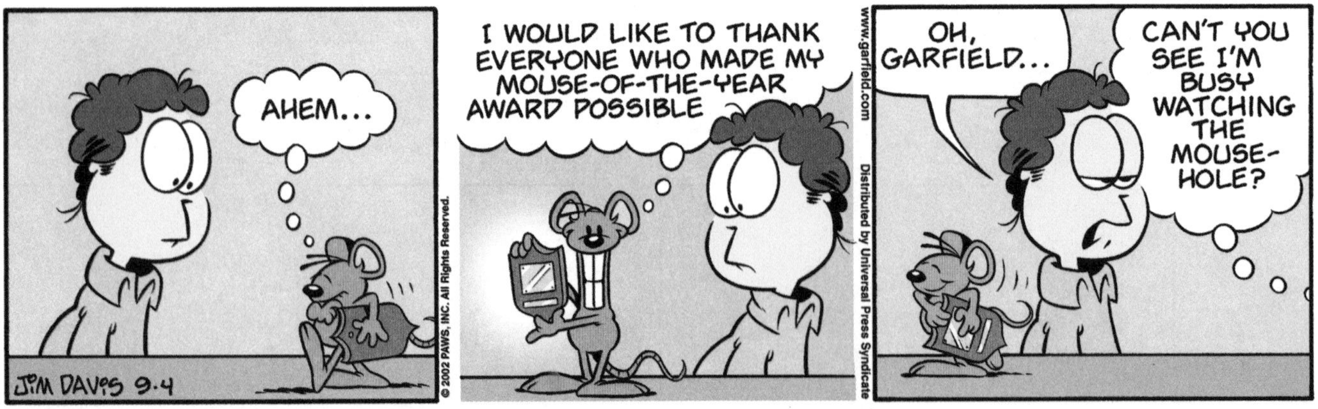
AHEM...
I WOULD LIKE TO THANK EVERYONE WHO MADE MY MOUSE-OF-THE-YEAR AWARD POSSIBLE
OH, GARFIELD...
CAN'T YOU SEE I'M BUSY WATCHING THE MOUSE-HOLE?
JIM DAVIS 9-4
© 2002 PAWS, INC. All Rights Reserved.
www.garfield.com
Distributed by Universal Press Syndicate

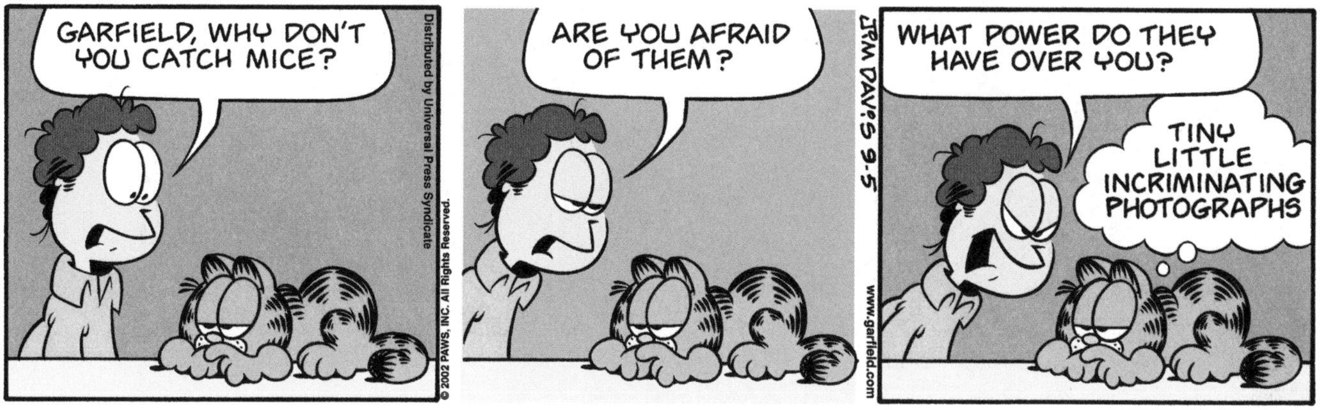
GARFIELD, WHY DON'T YOU CATCH MICE?
ARE YOU AFRAID OF THEM?
JIM DAVIS 9-5
WHAT POWER DO THEY HAVE OVER YOU?
TINY LITTLE INCRIMINATING PHOTOGRAPHS
© 2002 PAWS, INC. All Rights Reserved.
Distributed by Universal Press Syndicate
www.garfield.com

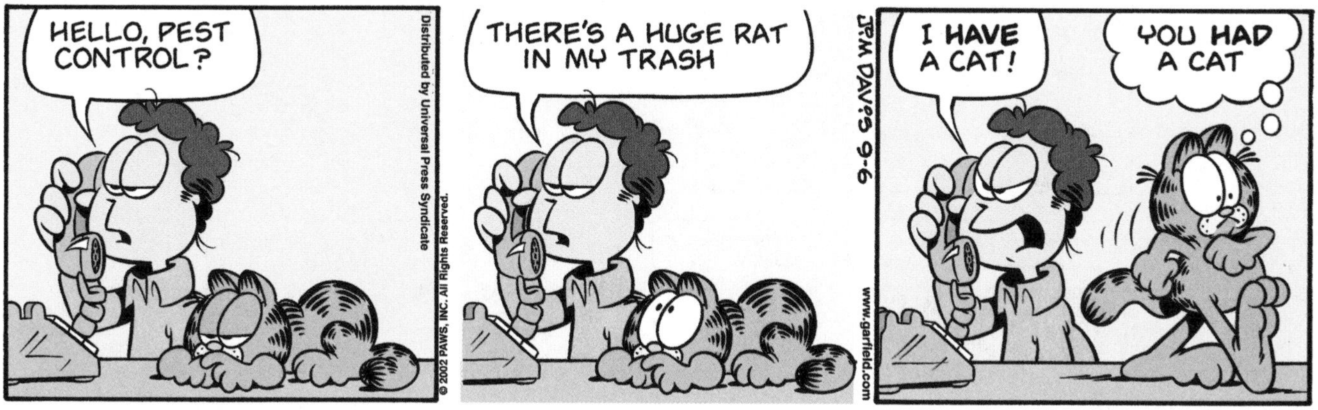
HELLO, PEST CONTROL?
THERE'S A HUGE RAT IN MY TRASH
JIM DAVIS 9-6
I **HAVE** A CAT!
YOU **HAD** A CAT
© 2002 PAWS, INC. All Rights Reserved.
Distributed by Universal Press Syndicate
www.garfield.com

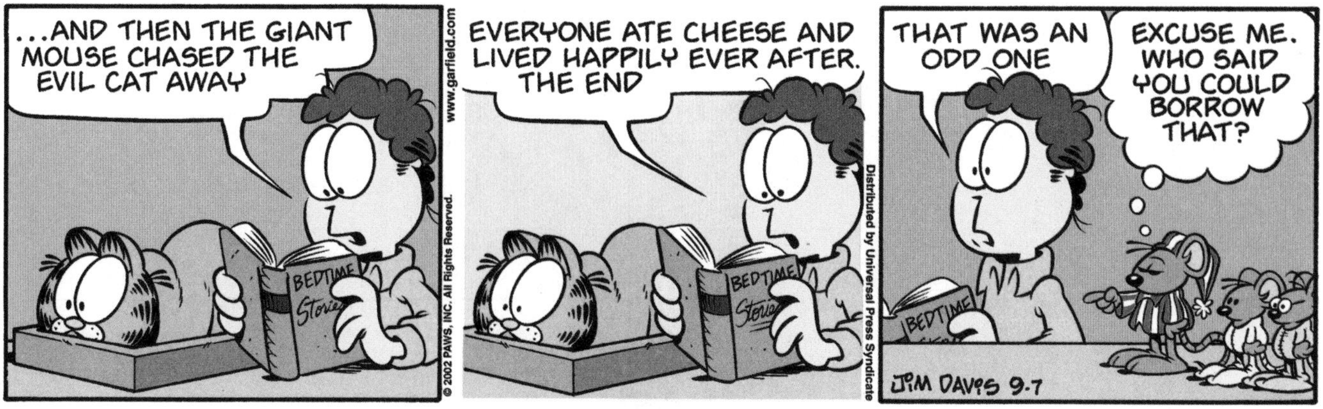
...AND THEN THE GIANT MOUSE CHASED THE EVIL CAT AWAY
BEDTIME Stories
EVERYONE ATE CHEESE AND LIVED HAPPILY EVER AFTER. THE END
THAT WAS AN ODD ONE
EXCUSE ME. WHO SAID YOU COULD BORROW THAT?
JIM DAVIS 9-7
© 2002 PAWS, INC. All Rights Reserved.
www.garfield.com
Distributed by Universal Press Syndicate

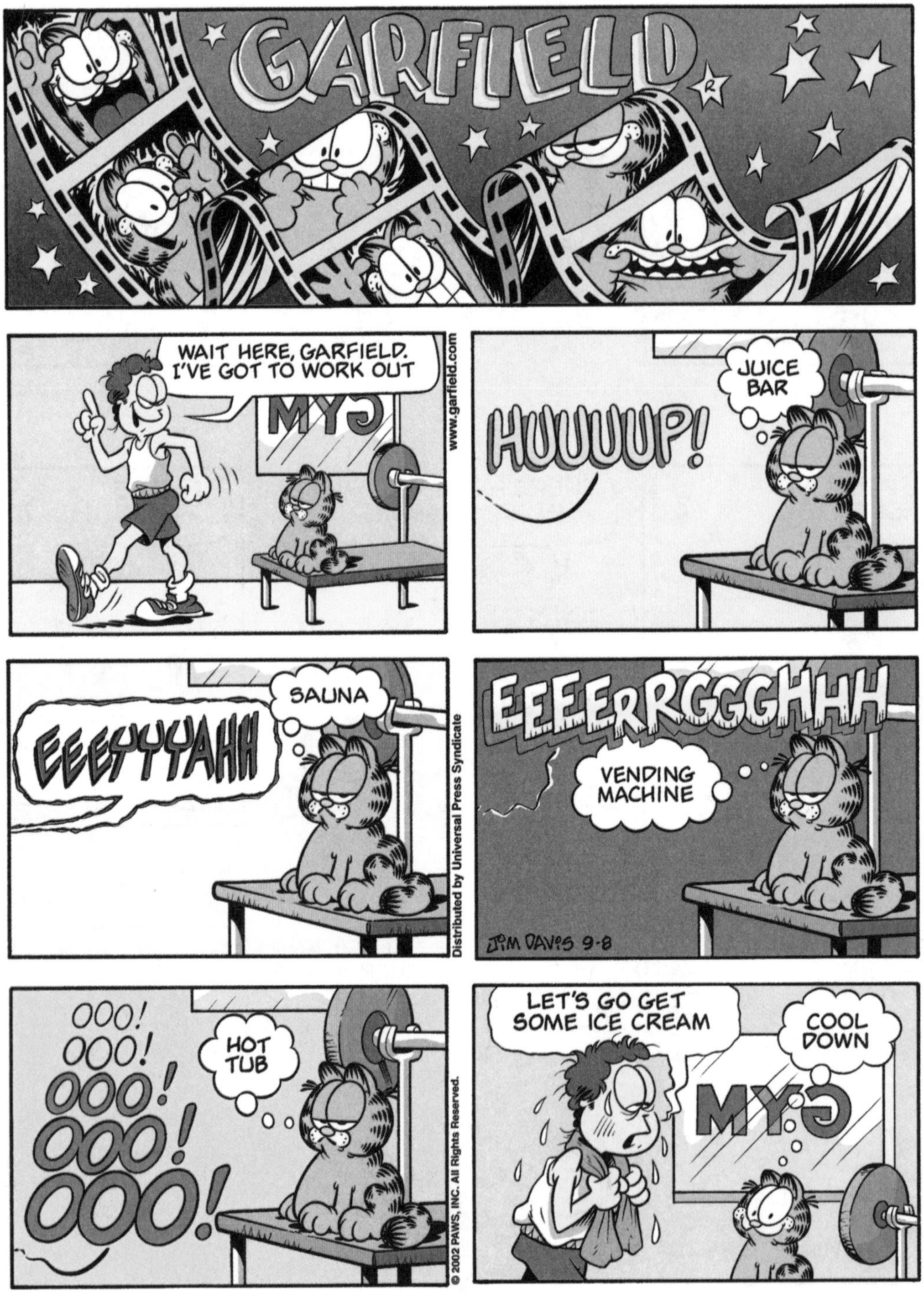
GARFIELD
WAIT HERE, GARFIELD. I'VE GOT TO WORK OUT
MYG
www.garfield.com
HUUUUP!
JUICE BAR
EEEYYYAHH
SAUNA
Distributed by Universal Press Syndicate
EEEERRGGGHHH
VENDING MACHINE
JIM DAVIS 9-8
OOO! OOO! OOO! OOO! OOO!
HOT TUB
© 2002 PAWS, INC. All Rights Reserved.
LET'S GO GET SOME ICE CREAM
COOL DOWN
MYG

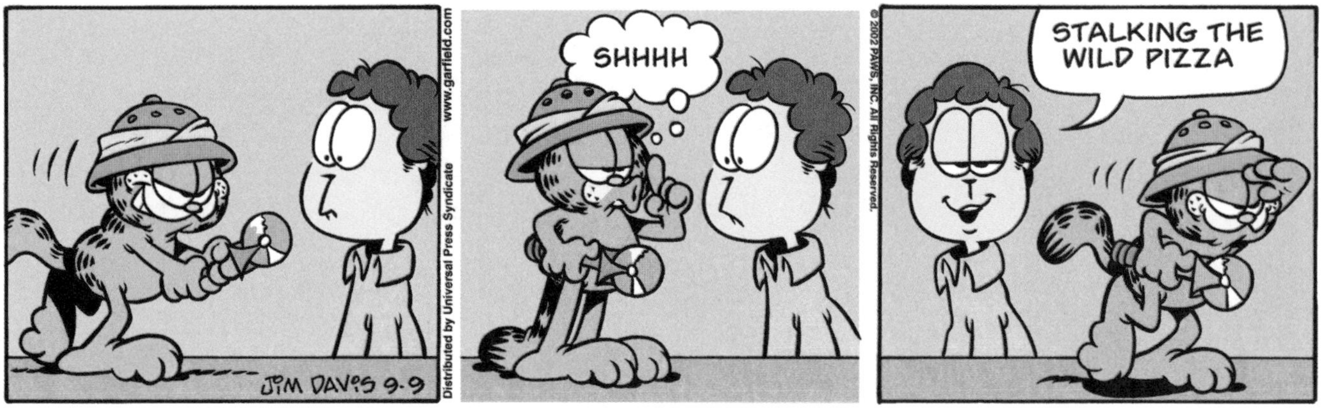
JIM DAVIS 9-9
www.garfield.com
Distributed by Universal Press Syndicate
SHHHH
© 2002 PAWS, INC. All Rights Reserved.
STALKING THE WILD PIZZA

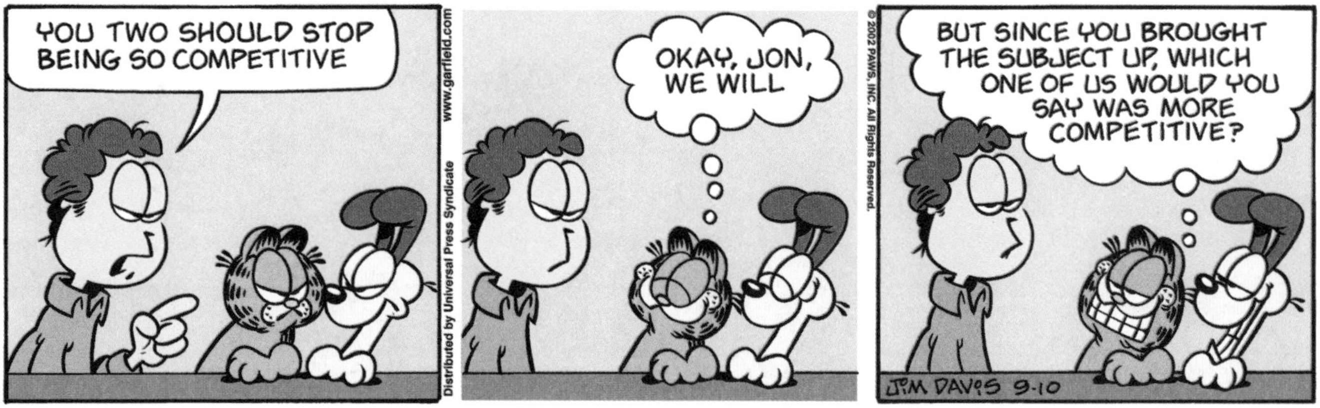
YOU TWO SHOULD STOP BEING SO COMPETITIVE
www.garfield.com
Distributed by Universal Press Syndicate
OKAY, JON, WE WILL
© 2002 PAWS, INC. All Rights Reserved.
BUT SINCE YOU BROUGHT THE SUBJECT UP, WHICH ONE OF US WOULD YOU SAY WAS MORE COMPETITIVE?
JIM DAVIS 9-10

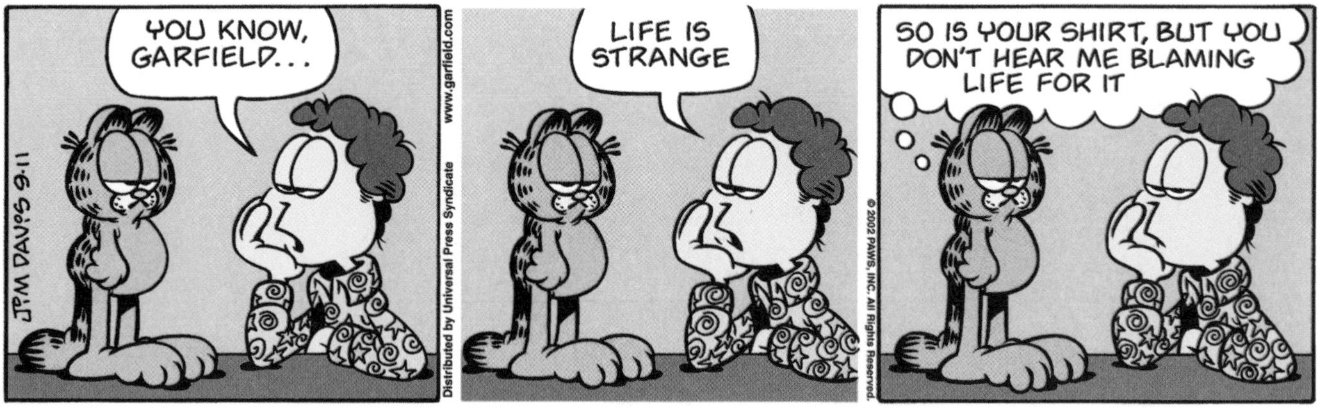
YOU KNOW, GARFIELD...
JIM DAVIS 9-11
www.garfield.com
Distributed by Universal Press Syndicate
LIFE IS STRANGE
© 2002 PAWS, INC. All Rights Reserved.
SO IS YOUR SHIRT, BUT YOU DON'T HEAR ME BLAMING LIFE FOR IT

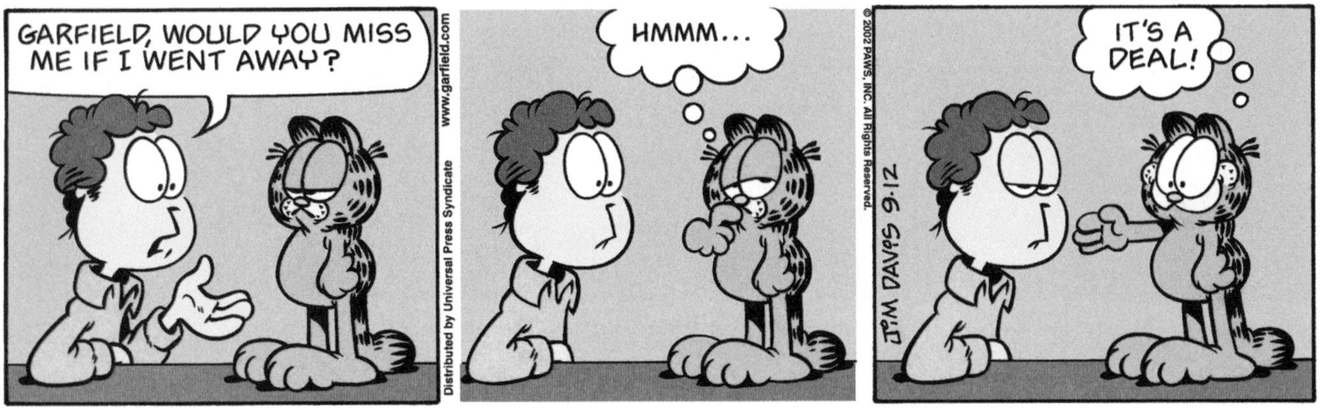
GARFIELD, WOULD YOU MISS ME IF I WENT AWAY?
HMMM...
IT'S A DEAL!
Distributed by Universal Press Syndicate www.garfield.com
© 2002 PAWS, INC. All Rights Reserved.
JIM DAVIS 9-12

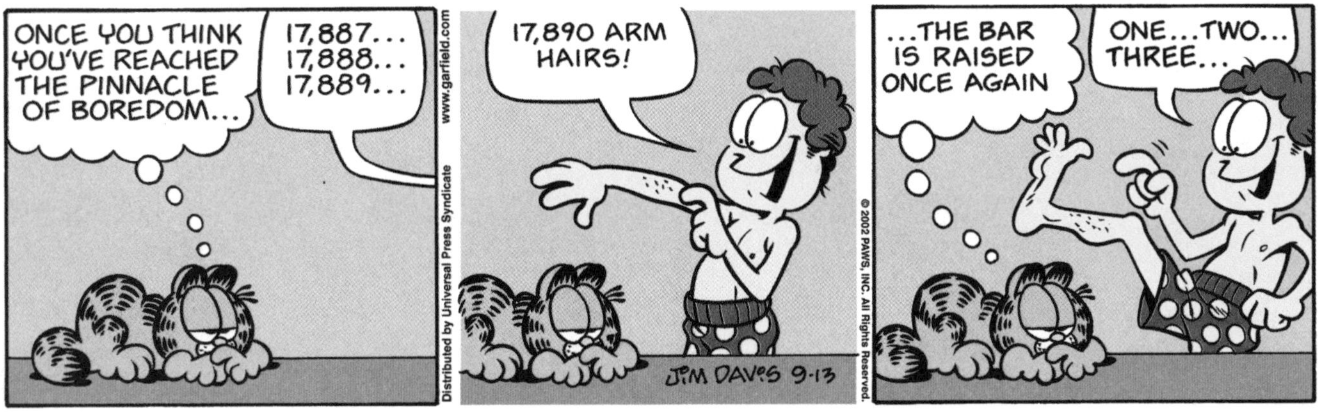
ONCE YOU THINK YOU'VE REACHED THE PINNACLE OF BOREDOM...
17,887... 17,888... 17,889...
17,890 ARM HAIRS!
...THE BAR IS RAISED ONCE AGAIN
ONE...TWO... THREE...
Distributed by Universal Press Syndicate www.garfield.com
© 2002 PAWS, INC. All Rights Reserved.
JIM DAVIS 9-13

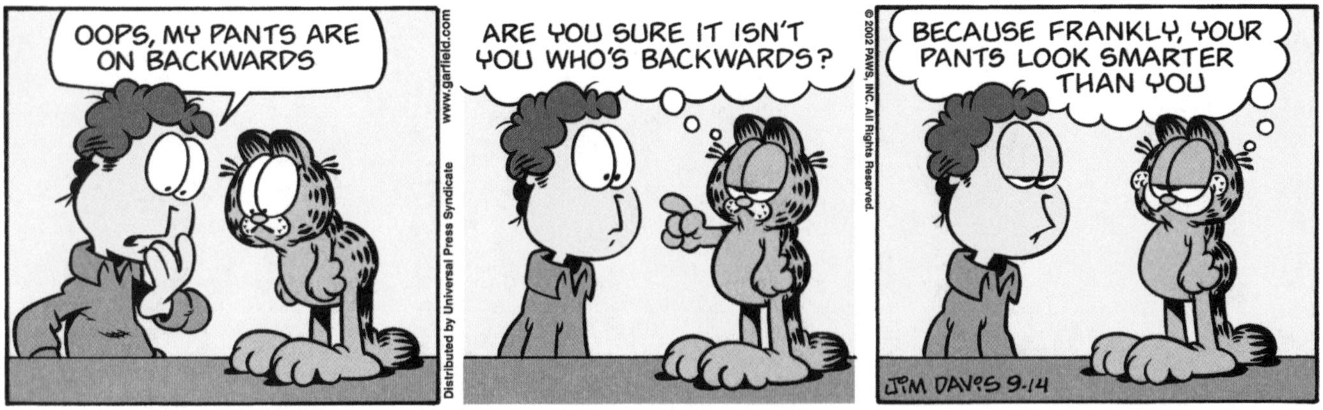
OOPS, MY PANTS ARE ON BACKWARDS
ARE YOU SURE IT ISN'T YOU WHO'S BACKWARDS?
BECAUSE FRANKLY, YOUR PANTS LOOK SMARTER THAN YOU
Distributed by Universal Press Syndicate www.garfield.com
© 2002 PAWS, INC. All Rights Reserved.
JIM DAVIS 9-14

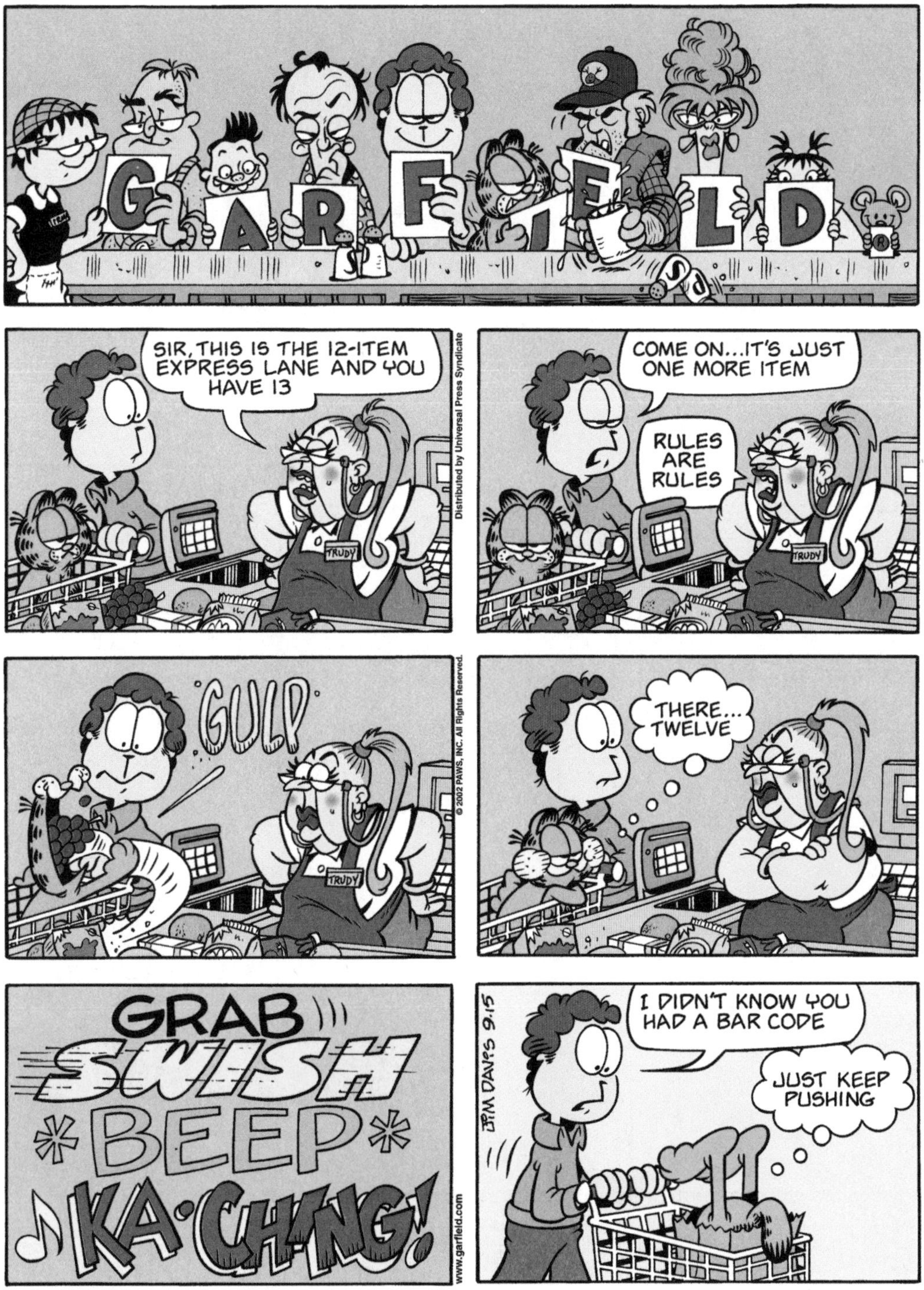
GARFIELD
SIR, THIS IS THE 12-ITEM EXPRESS LANE AND YOU HAVE 13
TRUDY
COME ON...IT'S JUST ONE MORE ITEM
RULES ARE RULES
TRUDY
GULP
TRUDY
THERE... TWELVE
GRAB
SWISH
BEEP
KA-CHING!
I DIDN'T KNOW YOU HAD A BAR CODE
JUST KEEP PUSHING
JIM DAVIS 9.15
Distributed by Universal Press Syndicate
© 2002 PAWS, INC. All Rights Reserved.
www.garfield.com

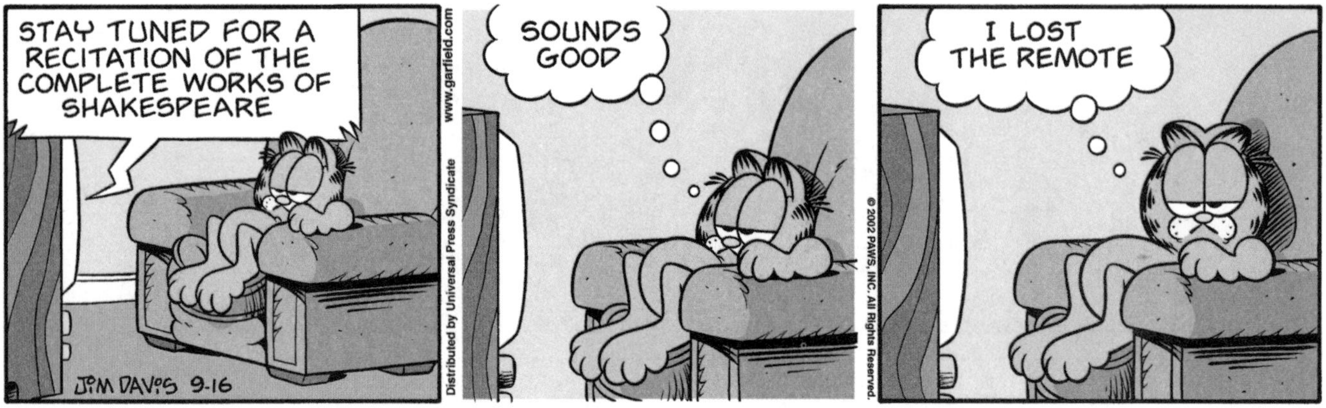
STAY TUNED FOR A RECITATION OF THE COMPLETE WORKS OF SHAKESPEARE
SOUNDS GOOD
I LOST THE REMOTE
JIM DAVIS 9-16

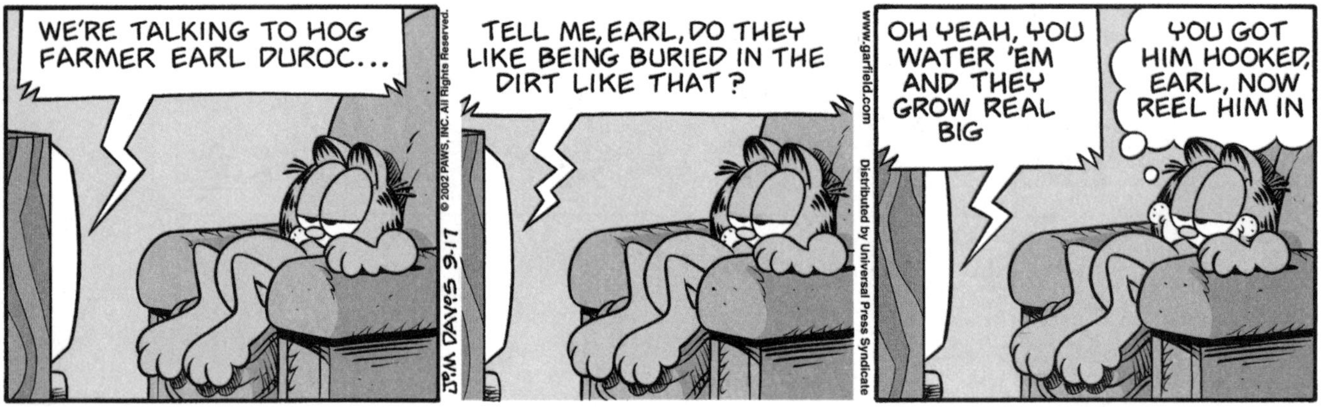
WE'RE TALKING TO HOG FARMER EARL DUROC...
TELL ME, EARL, DO THEY LIKE BEING BURIED IN THE DIRT LIKE THAT?
OH YEAH, YOU WATER 'EM AND THEY GROW REAL BIG
YOU GOT HIM HOOKED, EARL, NOW REEL HIM IN
JIM DAVIS 9-17

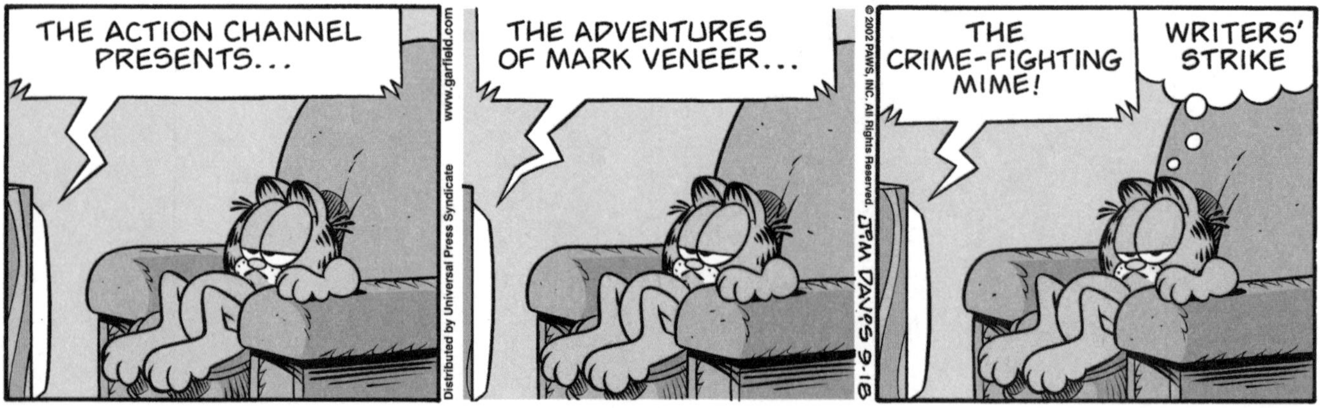
THE ACTION CHANNEL PRESENTS...
THE ADVENTURES OF MARK VENEER...
THE CRIME-FIGHTING MIME!
WRITERS' STRIKE
JIM DAVIS 9-18

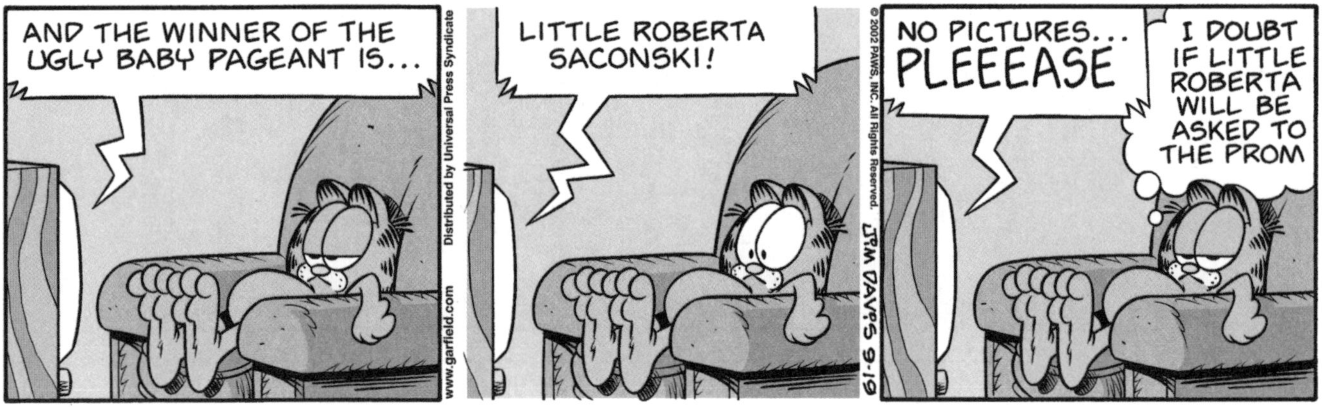
AND THE WINNER OF THE UGLY BABY PAGEANT IS...
LITTLE ROBERTA SACONSKI!
NO PICTURES... PLEEEASE
I DOUBT IF LITTLE ROBERTA WILL BE ASKED TO THE PROM
www.garfield.com Distributed by Universal Press Syndicate
© 2002 PAWS, INC. All Rights Reserved.
JIM DAVIS 9-19

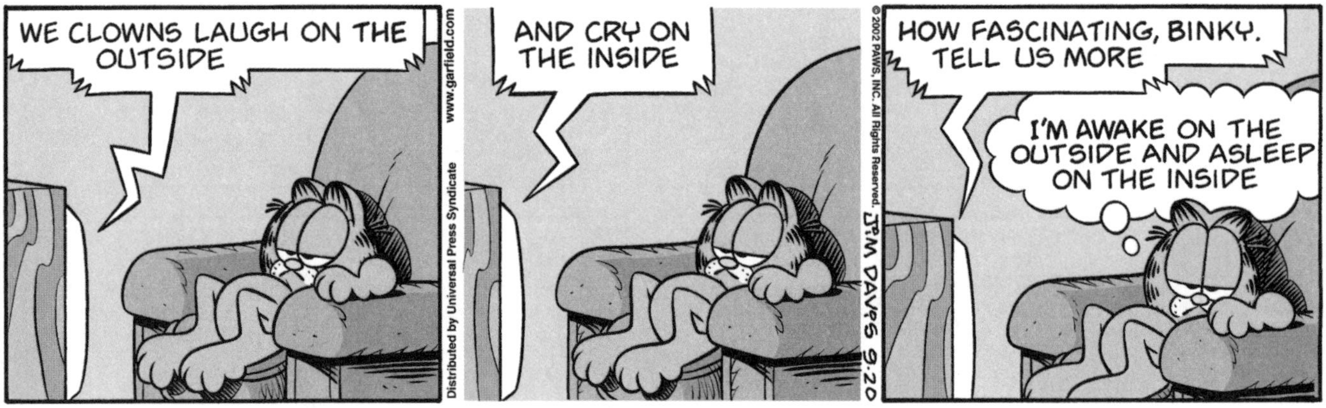
WE CLOWNS LAUGH ON THE OUTSIDE
AND CRY ON THE INSIDE
HOW FASCINATING, BINKY. TELL US MORE
I'M AWAKE ON THE OUTSIDE AND ASLEEP ON THE INSIDE
Distributed by Universal Press Syndicate www.garfield.com
© 2002 PAWS, INC. All Rights Reserved.
JIM DAVIS 9-20

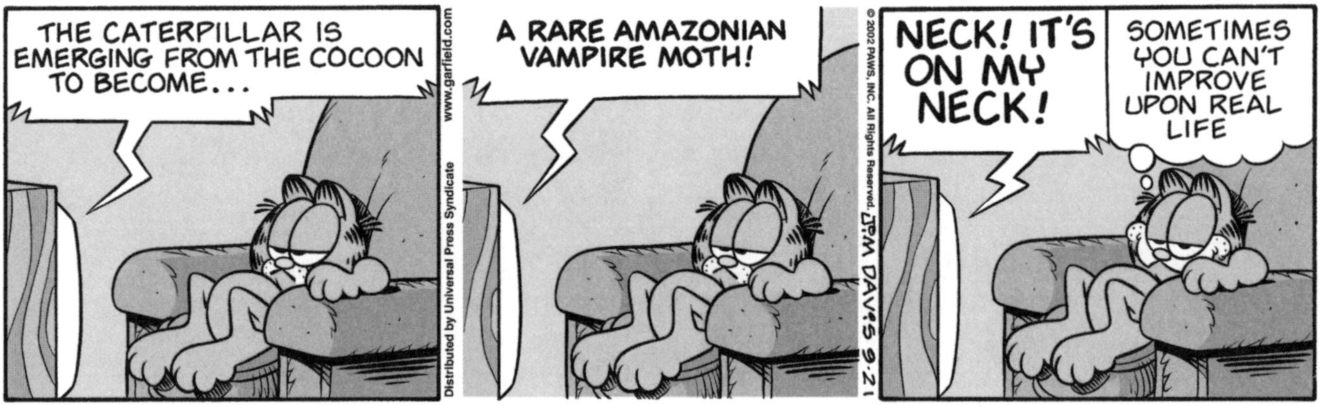
THE CATERPILLAR IS EMERGING FROM THE COCOON TO BECOME...
A RARE AMAZONIAN VAMPIRE MOTH!
NECK! IT'S ON MY NECK!
SOMETIMES YOU CAN'T IMPROVE UPON REAL LIFE
Distributed by Universal Press Syndicate www.garfield.com
© 2002 PAWS, INC. All Rights Reserved.
JIM DAVIS 9-21

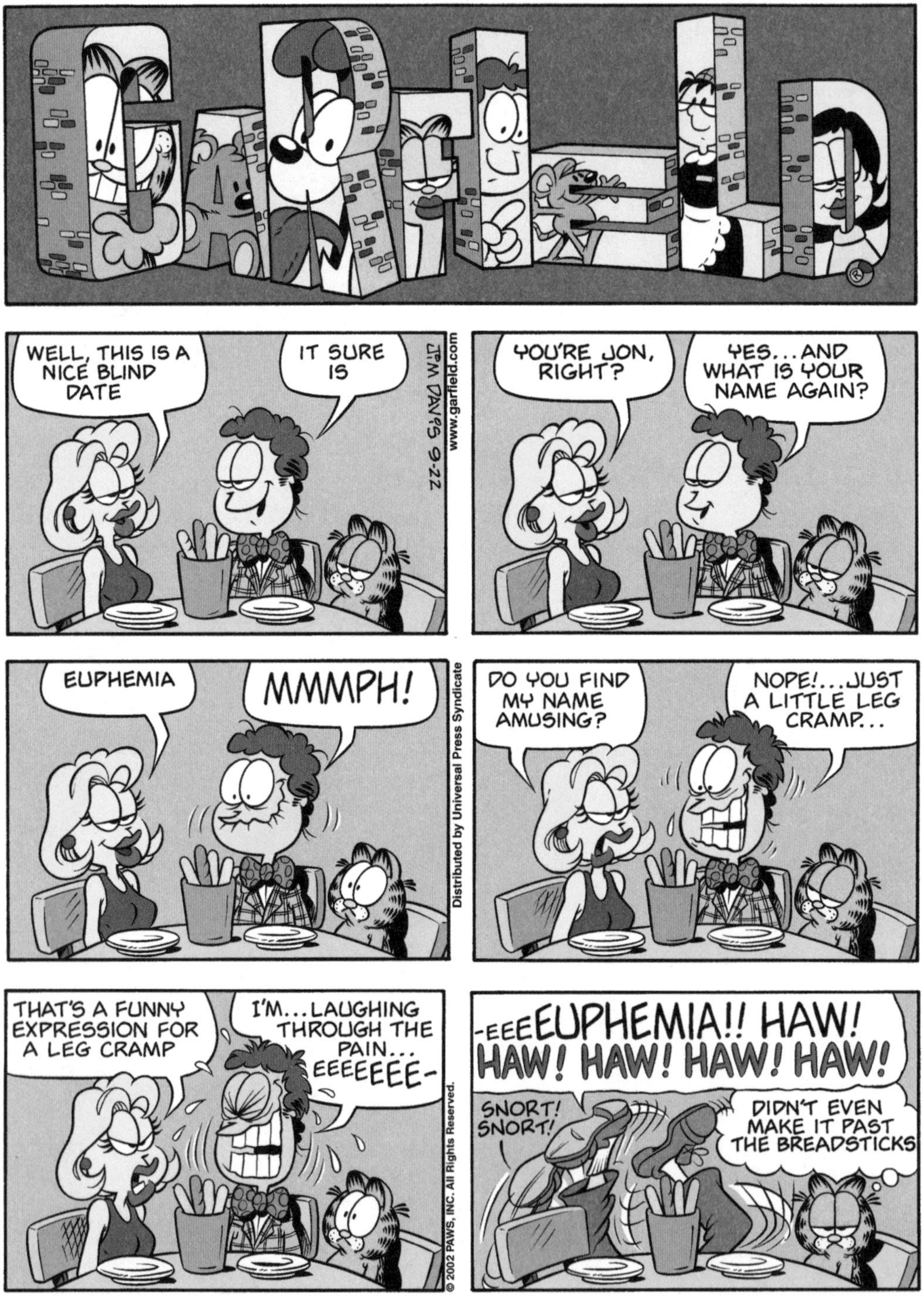
GARFIELD
JIM DAVIS 9-22
www.garfield.com
WELL, THIS IS A NICE BLIND DATE
IT SURE IS
YOU'RE JON, RIGHT?
YES... AND WHAT IS YOUR NAME AGAIN?
Distributed by Universal Press Syndicate
EUPHEMIA
MMMPH!
DO YOU FIND MY NAME AMUSING?
NOPE!... JUST A LITTLE LEG CRAMP...
© 2002 PAWS, INC. All Rights Reserved.
THAT'S A FUNNY EXPRESSION FOR A LEG CRAMP
I'M... LAUGHING THROUGH THE PAIN... EEEEEEE-
-EEEEUPHEMIA!! HAW! HAW! HAW! HAW! HAW!
SNORT! SNORT!
DIDN'T EVEN MAKE IT PAST THE BREADSTICKS

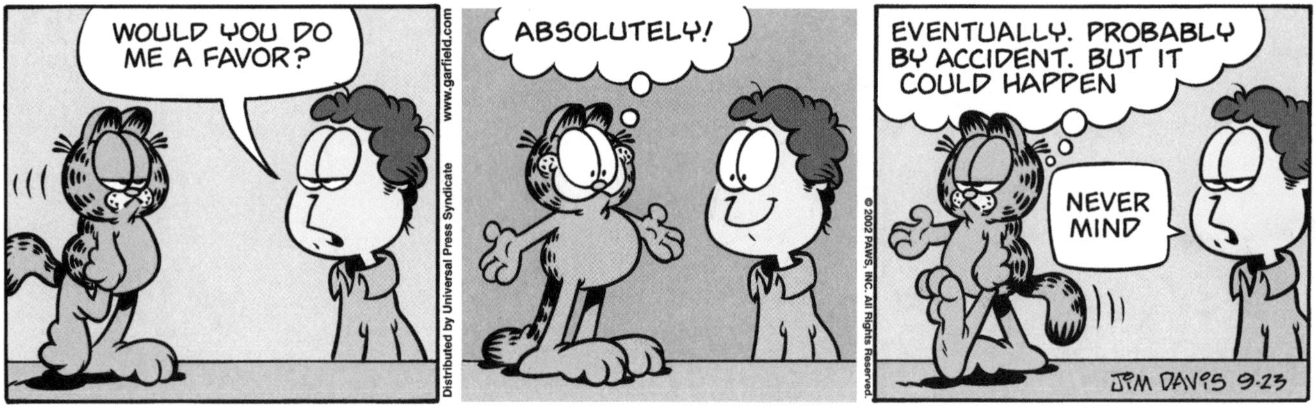
WOULD YOU DO ME A FAVOR?
ABSOLUTELY!
EVENTUALLY. PROBABLY BY ACCIDENT. BUT IT COULD HAPPEN
NEVER MIND
JIM DAVIS 9-23
www.garfield.com
Distributed by Universal Press Syndicate
© 2002 PAWS, INC. All Rights Reserved.

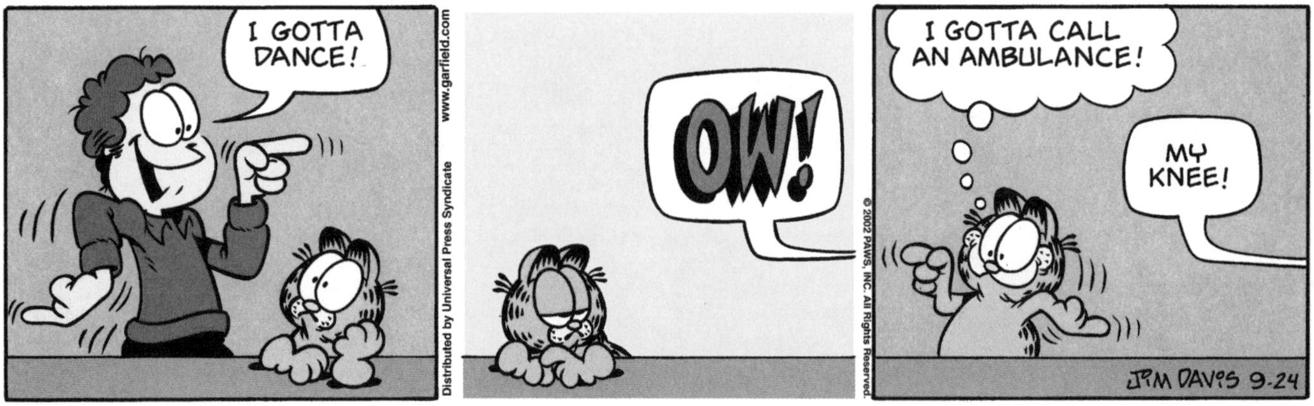
I GOTTA DANCE!
OW!
I GOTTA CALL AN AMBULANCE!
MY KNEE!
JIM DAVIS 9-24
www.garfield.com
Distributed by Universal Press Syndicate
© 2002 PAWS, INC. All Rights Reserved.

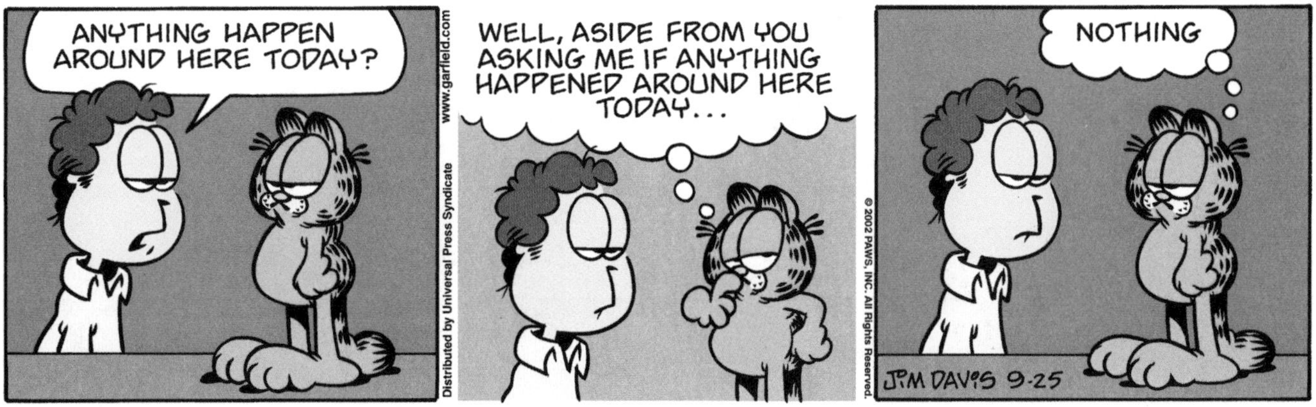
ANYTHING HAPPEN AROUND HERE TODAY?
WELL, ASIDE FROM YOU ASKING ME IF ANYTHING HAPPENED AROUND HERE TODAY...
NOTHING
JIM DAVIS 9-25
www.garfield.com
Distributed by Universal Press Syndicate
© 2002 PAWS, INC. All Rights Reserved.

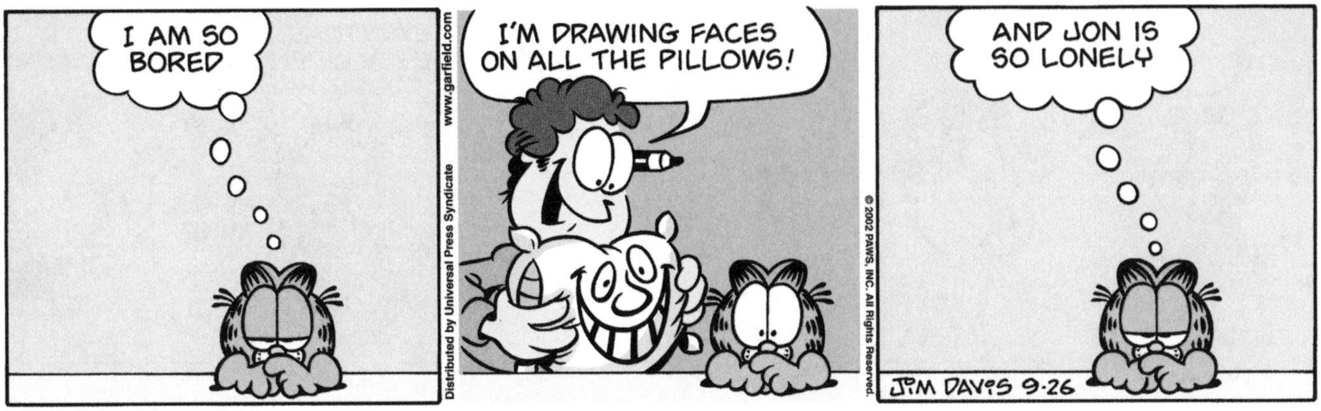
I AM SO BORED
I'M DRAWING FACES ON ALL THE PILLOWS!
AND JON IS SO LONELY
JIM DAVIS 9-26
www.garfield.com
Distributed by Universal Press Syndicate
© 2002 PAWS, INC. All Rights Reserved.

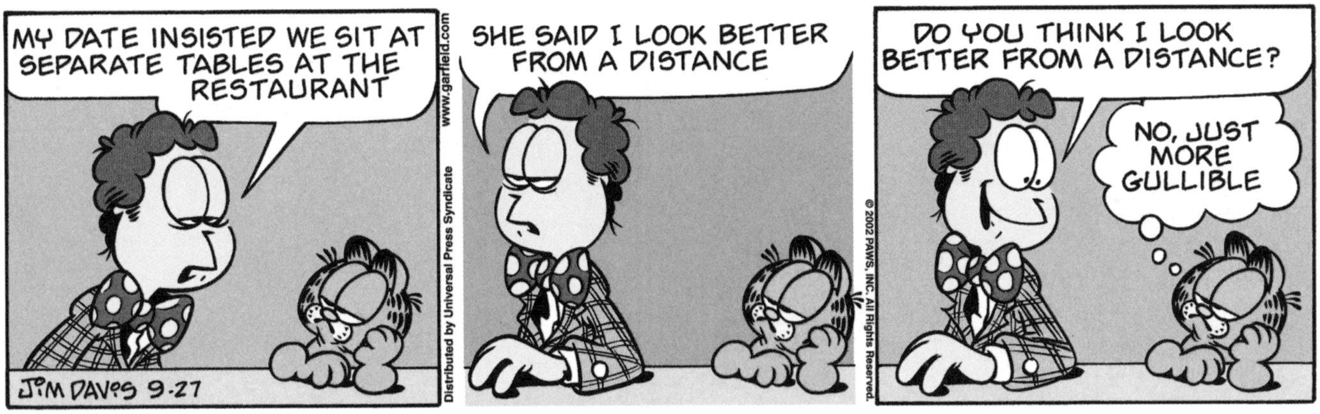
MY DATE INSISTED WE SIT AT SEPARATE TABLES AT THE RESTAURANT
SHE SAID I LOOK BETTER FROM A DISTANCE
DO YOU THINK I LOOK BETTER FROM A DISTANCE?
NO, JUST MORE GULLIBLE
JIM DAVIS 9-27
www.garfield.com
Distributed by Universal Press Syndicate
© 2002 PAWS, INC. All Rights Reserved.

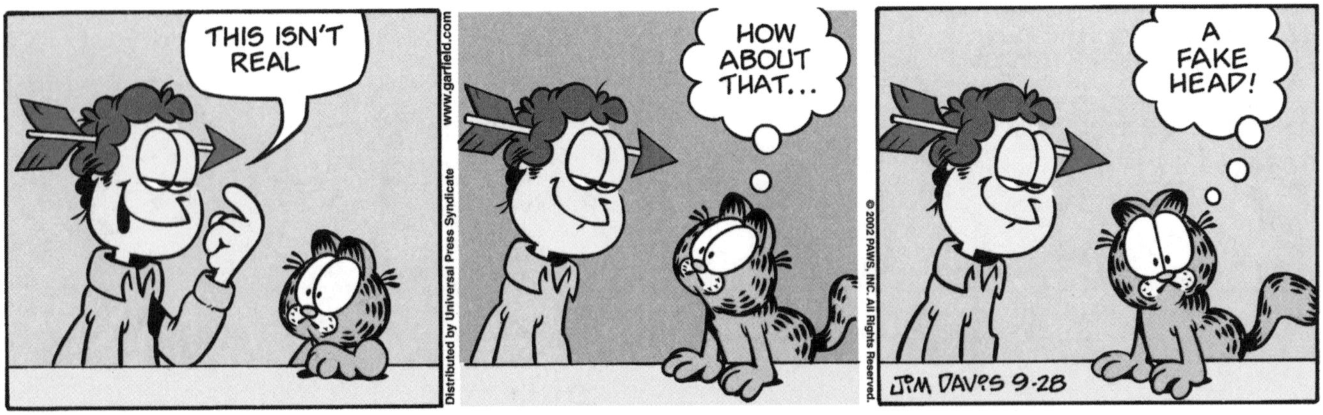
THIS ISN'T REAL
HOW ABOUT THAT...
A FAKE HEAD!
JIM DAVIS 9-28
www.garfield.com
Distributed by Universal Press Syndicate
© 2002 PAWS, INC. All Rights Reserved.

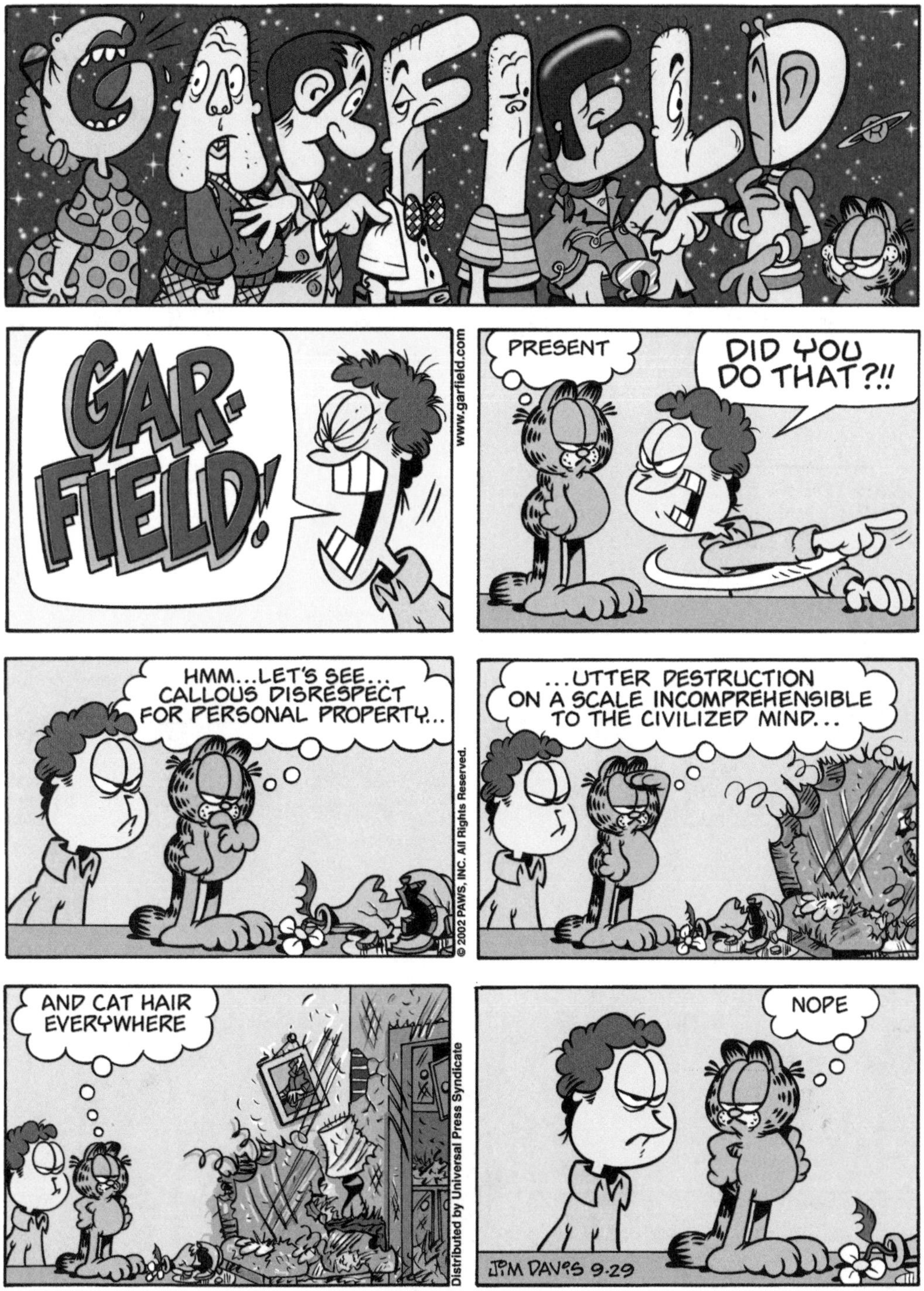
GARFIELD
GAR-FIELD!
www.garfield.com
PRESENT
DID YOU DO THAT?!!
HMM...LET'S SEE... CALLOUS DISRESPECT FOR PERSONAL PROPERTY...
© 2002 PAWS, INC. All Rights Reserved.
...UTTER DESTRUCTION ON A SCALE INCOMPREHENSIBLE TO THE CIVILIZED MIND...
AND CAT HAIR EVERYWHERE
Distributed by Universal Press Syndicate
NOPE
JIM DAVIS 9-29

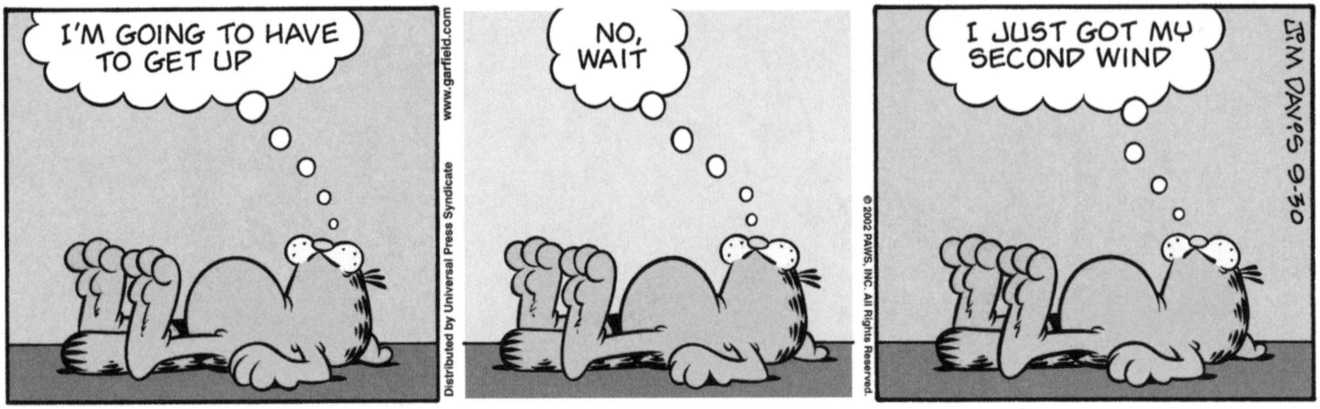
I'M GOING TO HAVE TO GET UP
www.garfield.com
Distributed by Universal Press Syndicate
NO, WAIT
© 2002 PAWS, INC. All Rights Reserved.
I JUST GOT MY SECOND WIND

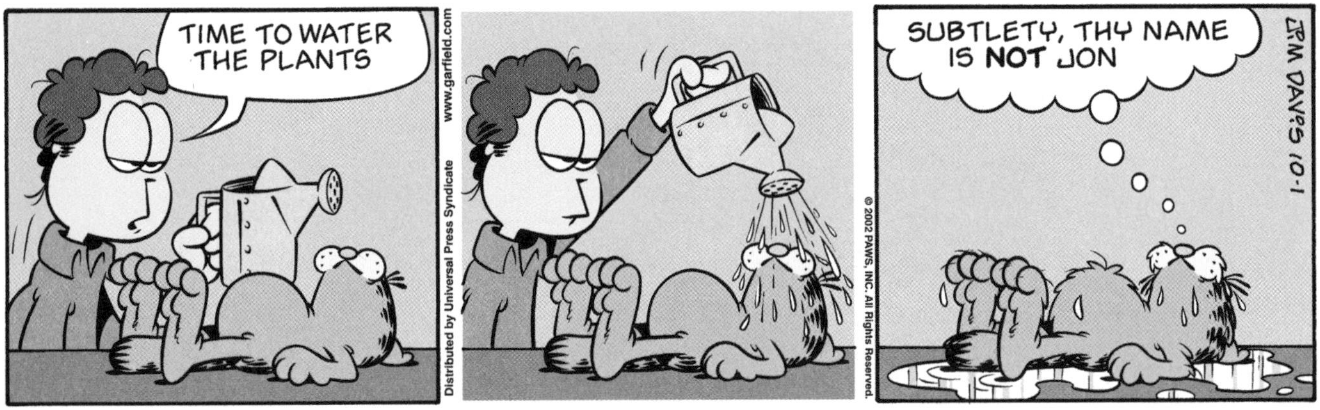
TIME TO WATER THE PLANTS
www.garfield.com
Distributed by Universal Press Syndicate
© 2002 PAWS, INC. All Rights Reserved.
SUBTLETY, THY NAME IS **NOT** JON

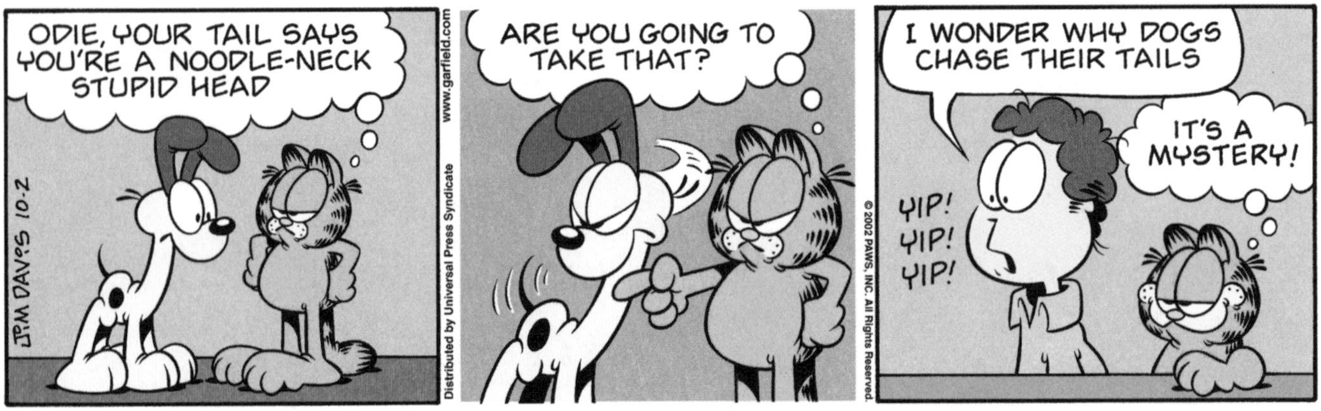
ODIE, YOUR TAIL SAYS YOU'RE A NOODLE-NECK STUPID HEAD
www.garfield.com
Distributed by Universal Press Syndicate
ARE YOU GOING TO TAKE THAT?
© 2002 PAWS, INC. All Rights Reserved.
I WONDER WHY DOGS CHASE THEIR TAILS
YIP! YIP! YIP!
IT'S A MYSTERY!

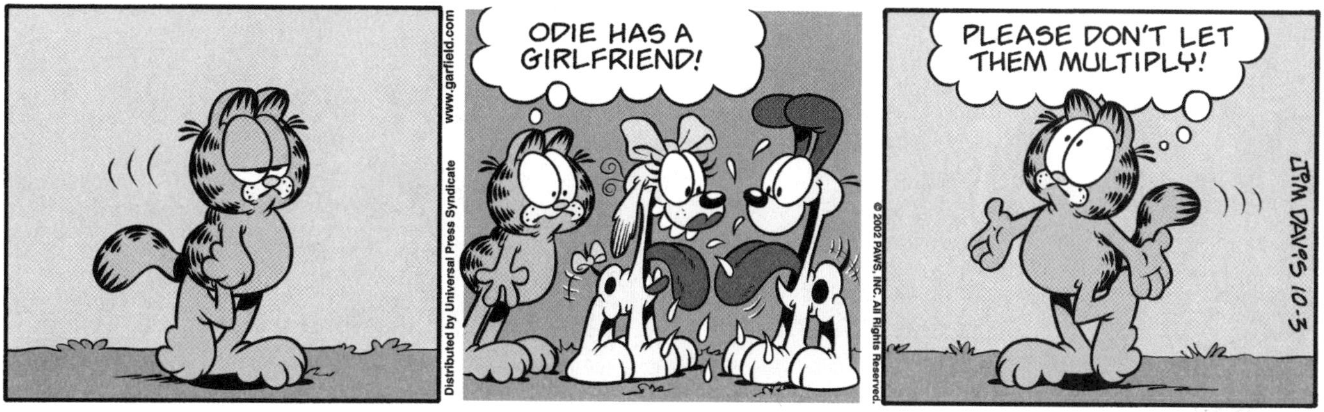
ODIE HAS A GIRLFRIEND!
PLEASE DON'T LET THEM MULTIPLY!
JIM DAVIS 10-3
www.garfield.com
Distributed by Universal Press Syndicate
© 2002 PAWS, INC. All Rights Reserved.

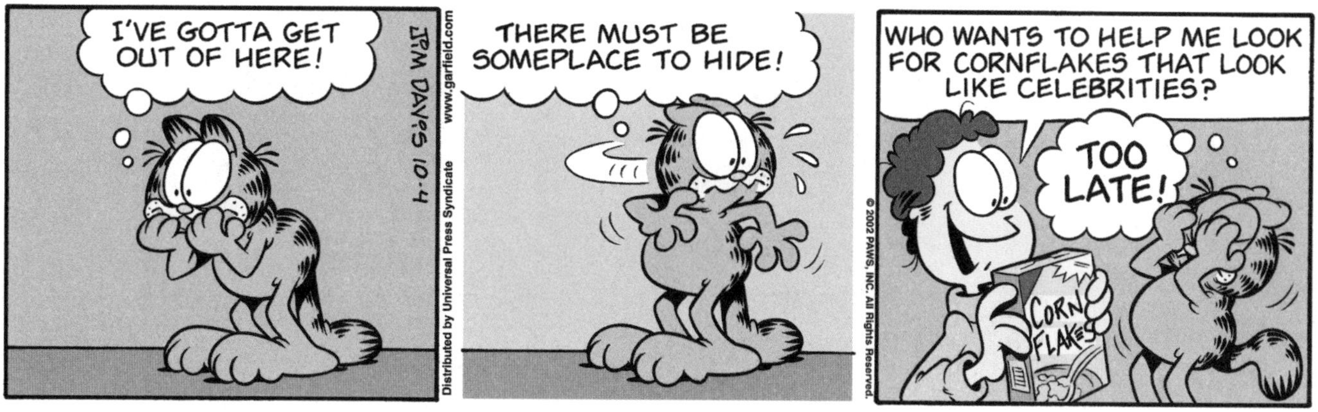
I'VE GOTTA GET OUT OF HERE!
JIM DAVIS 10-4
THERE MUST BE SOMEPLACE TO HIDE!
WHO WANTS TO HELP ME LOOK FOR CORNFLAKES THAT LOOK LIKE CELEBRITIES?
TOO LATE!
CORN FLAKES
www.garfield.com
Distributed by Universal Press Syndicate
© 2002 PAWS, INC. All Rights Reserved.

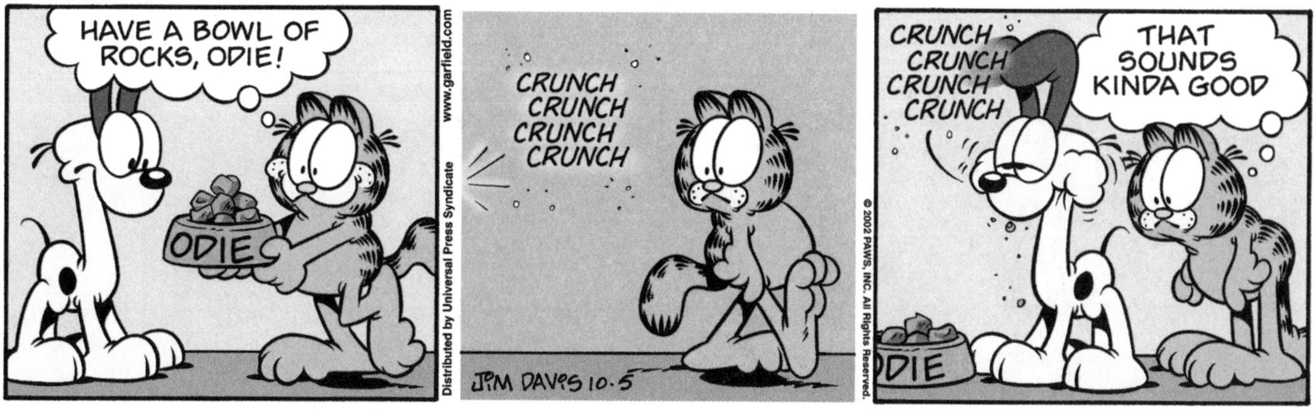
HAVE A BOWL OF ROCKS, ODIE!
ODIE
CRUNCH CRUNCH CRUNCH CRUNCH
JIM DAVIS 10-5
CRUNCH CRUNCH CRUNCH CRUNCH
THAT SOUNDS KINDA GOOD
DIE
www.garfield.com
Distributed by Universal Press Syndicate
© 2002 PAWS, INC. All Rights Reserved.

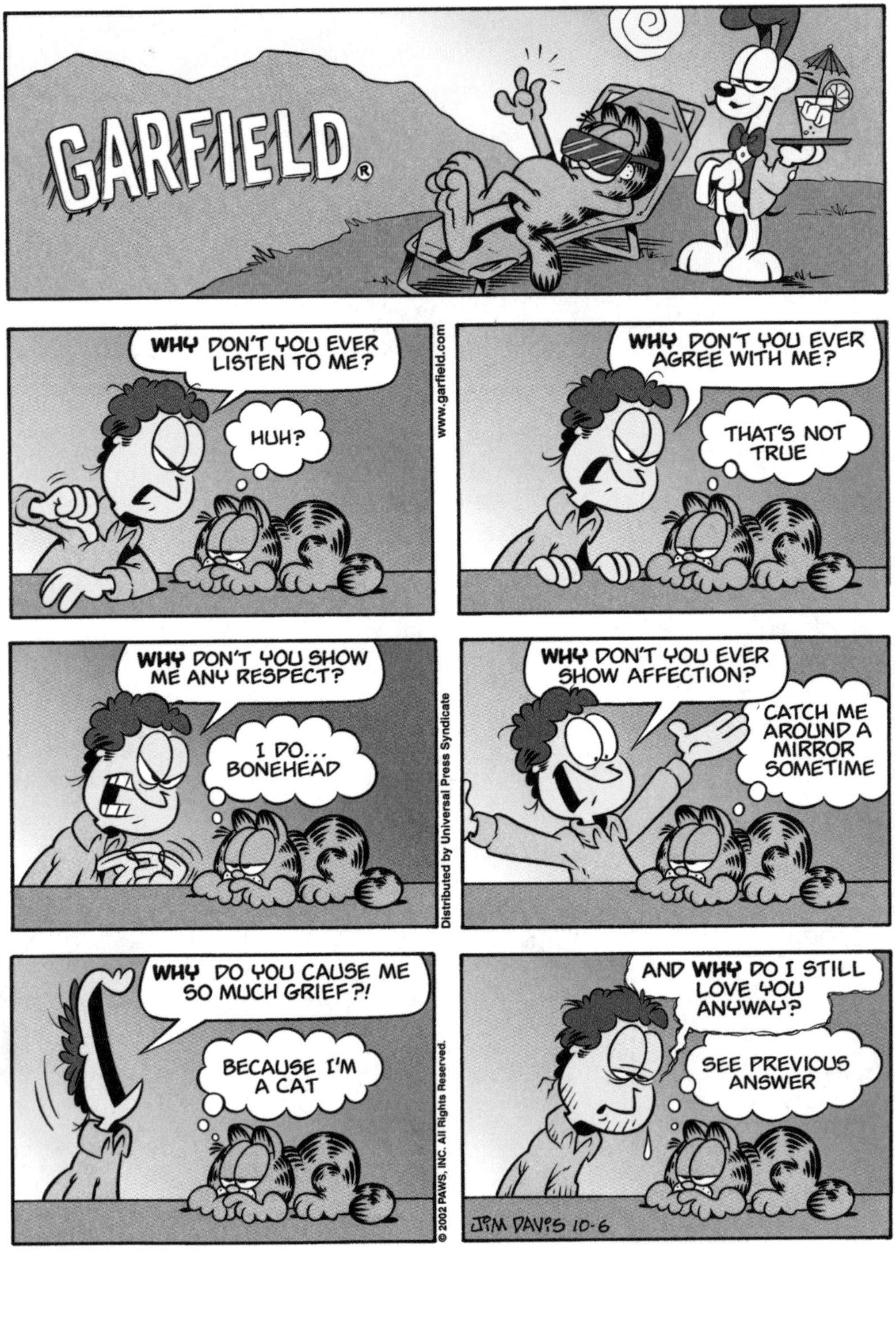

GARFIELD®
WHY DON'T YOU EVER LISTEN TO ME?
HUH?
WHY DON'T YOU EVER AGREE WITH ME?
THAT'S NOT TRUE
WHY DON'T YOU SHOW ME ANY RESPECT?
I DO... BONEHEAD
WHY DON'T YOU EVER SHOW AFFECTION?
CATCH ME AROUND A MIRROR SOMETIME
WHY DO YOU CAUSE ME SO MUCH GRIEF?!
BECAUSE I'M A CAT
AND WHY DO I STILL LOVE YOU ANYWAY?
SEE PREVIOUS ANSWER
JIM DAVIS 10-6

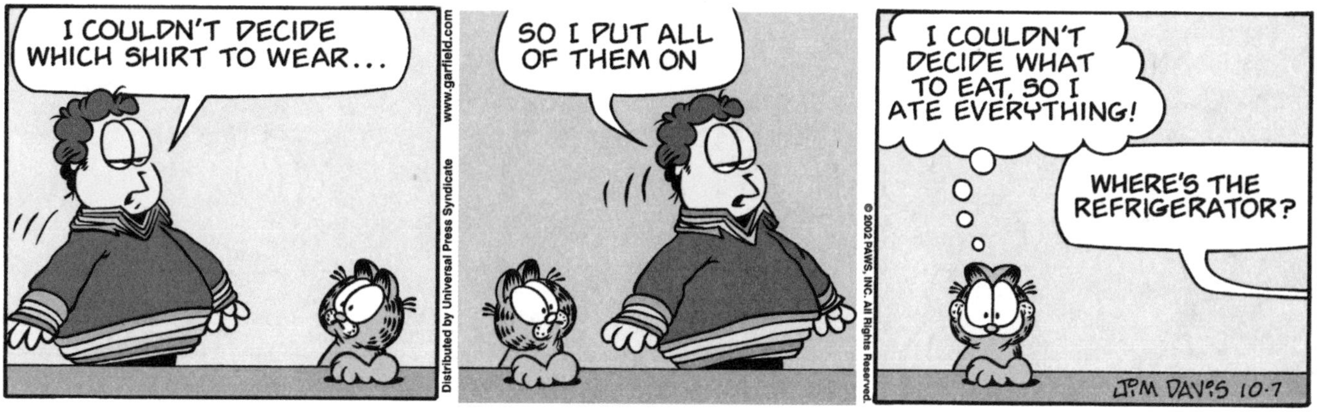
I COULDN'T DECIDE WHICH SHIRT TO WEAR...
SO I PUT ALL OF THEM ON
I COULDN'T DECIDE WHAT TO EAT, SO I ATE EVERYTHING!
WHERE'S THE REFRIGERATOR?
JIM DAVIS 10-7
Distributed by Universal Press Syndicate www.garfield.com
© 2002 PAWS, INC. All Rights Reserved.

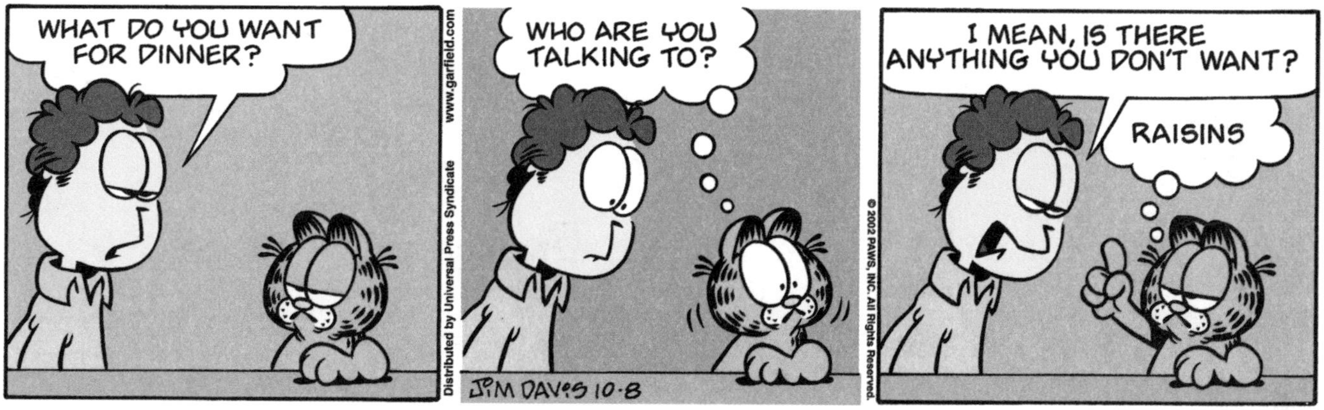
WHAT DO YOU WANT FOR DINNER?
WHO ARE YOU TALKING TO?
I MEAN, IS THERE ANYTHING YOU DON'T WANT?
RAISINS
JIM DAVIS 10-8
Distributed by Universal Press Syndicate www.garfield.com
© 2002 PAWS, INC. All Rights Reserved.

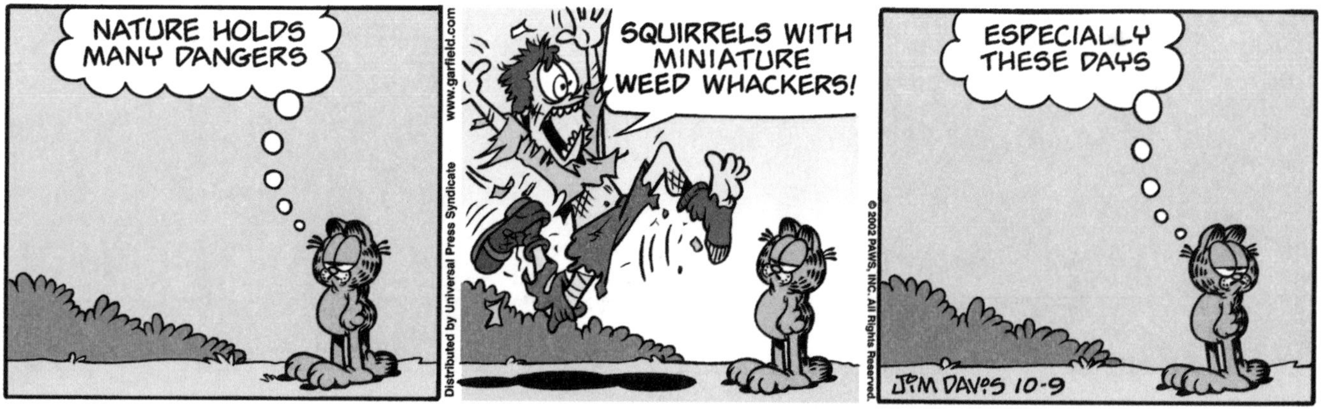
NATURE HOLDS MANY DANGERS
SQUIRRELS WITH MINIATURE WEED WHACKERS!
ESPECIALLY THESE DAYS
JIM DAVIS 10-9
Distributed by Universal Press Syndicate www.garfield.com
© 2002 PAWS, INC. All Rights Reserved.

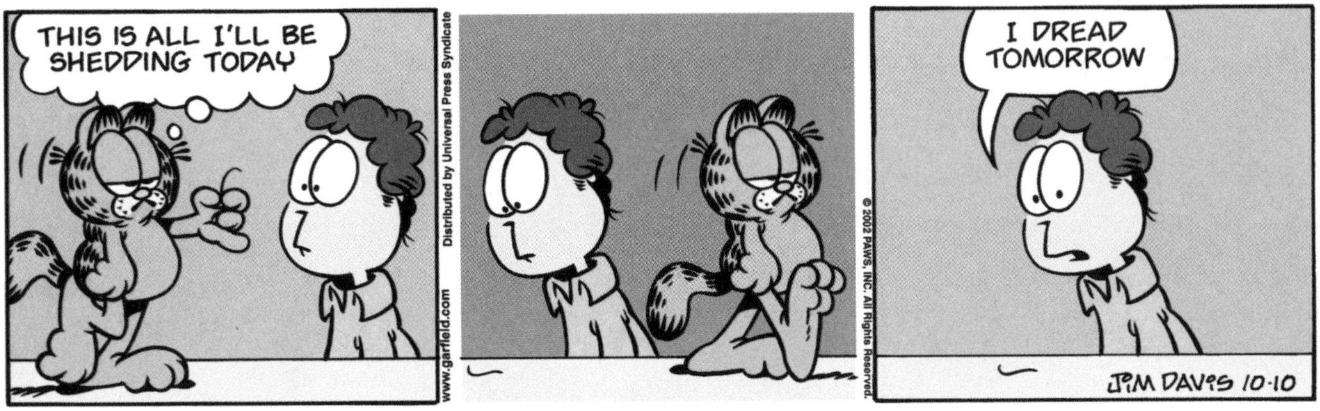
THIS IS ALL I'LL BE SHEDDING TODAY
www.garfield.com
Distributed by Universal Press Syndicate
© 2002 PAWS, INC. All Rights Reserved.
I DREAD TOMORROW
JIM DAVIS 10·10

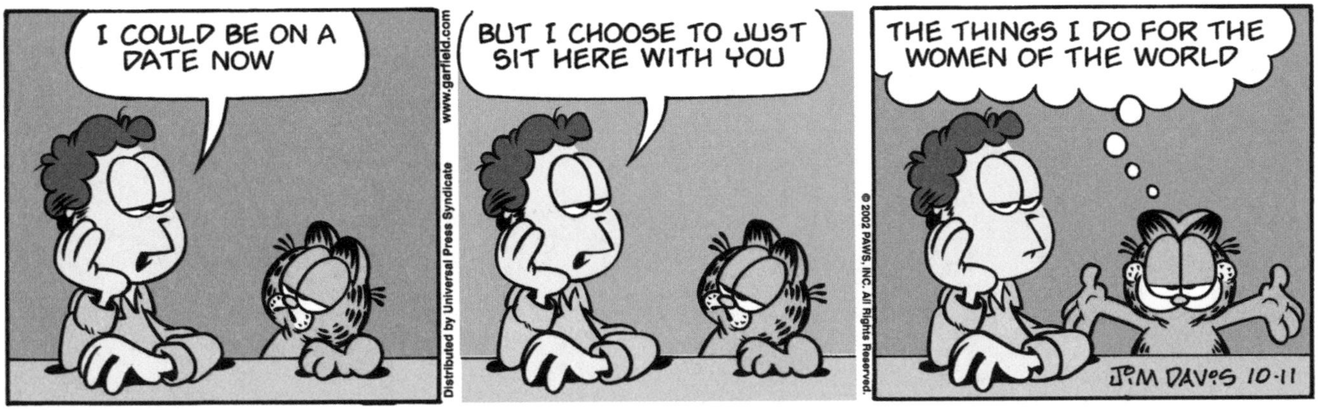
I COULD BE ON A DATE NOW
Distributed by Universal Press Syndicate
www.garfield.com
BUT I CHOOSE TO JUST SIT HERE WITH YOU
© 2002 PAWS, INC. All Rights Reserved.
THE THINGS I DO FOR THE WOMEN OF THE WORLD
JIM DAVIS 10·11

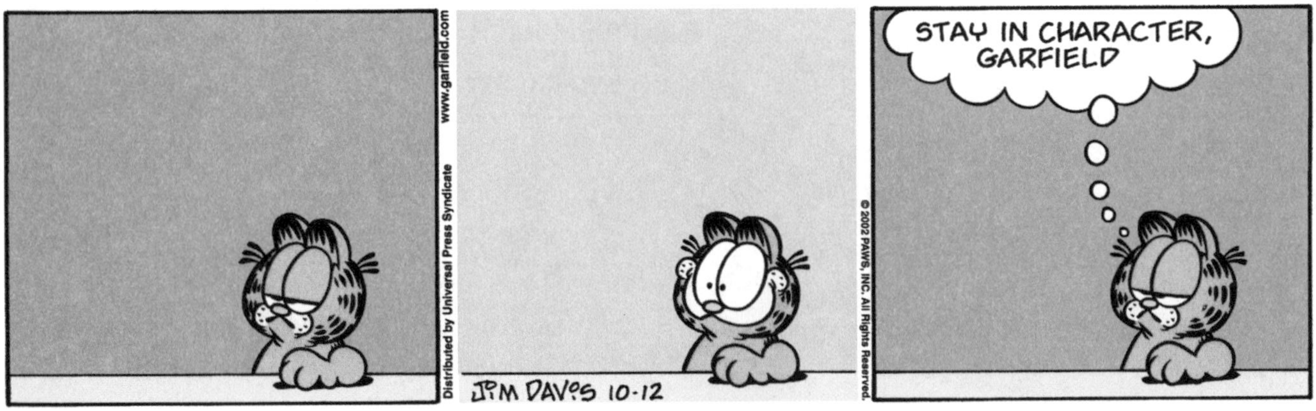
Distributed by Universal Press Syndicate
www.garfield.com
JIM DAVIS 10-12
© 2002 PAWS, INC. All Rights Reserved.
STAY IN CHARACTER, GARFIELD

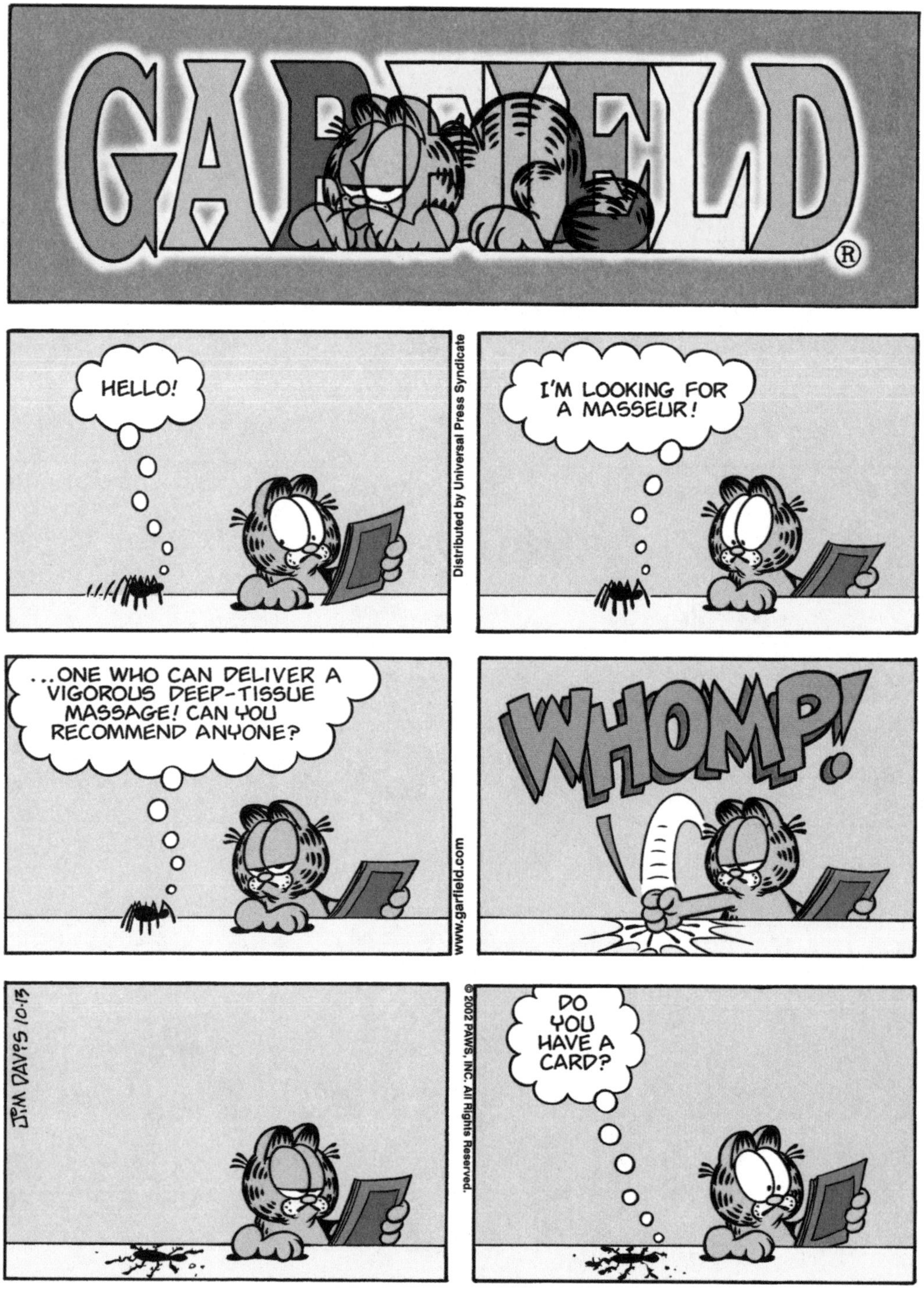
GARFIELD®
HELLO!
I'M LOOKING FOR A MASSEUR!
Distributed by Universal Press Syndicate
...ONE WHO CAN DELIVER A VIGOROUS DEEP-TISSUE MASSAGE! CAN YOU RECOMMEND ANYONE?
WHOMP!
www.garfield.com
JIM DAVIS 10-13
© 2002 PAWS, INC. All Rights Reserved.
DO YOU HAVE A CARD?

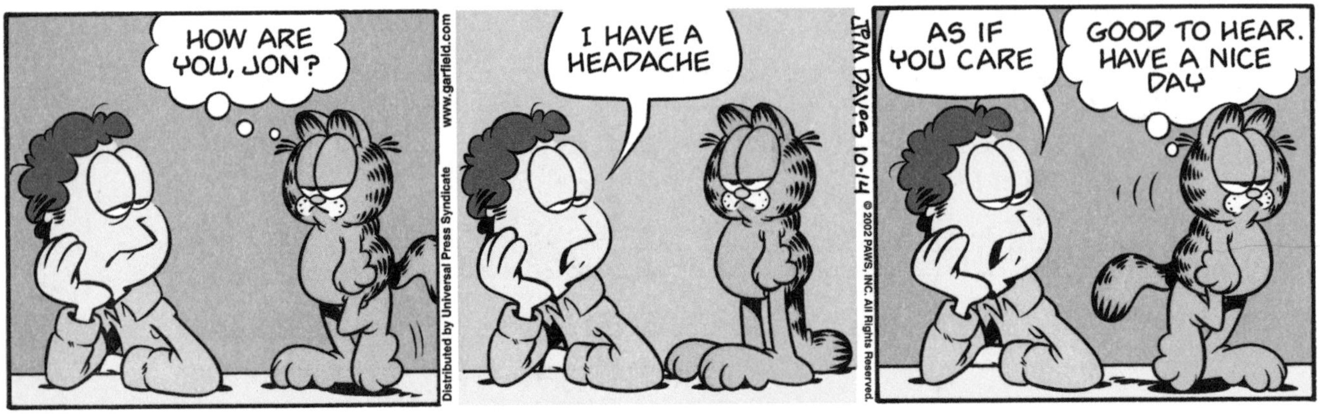
HOW ARE YOU, JON?
I HAVE A HEADACHE
AS IF YOU CARE
GOOD TO HEAR. HAVE A NICE DAY
JIM DAVIS 10-14
Distributed by Universal Press Syndicate www.garfield.com
© 2002 PAWS, INC. All Rights Reserved.

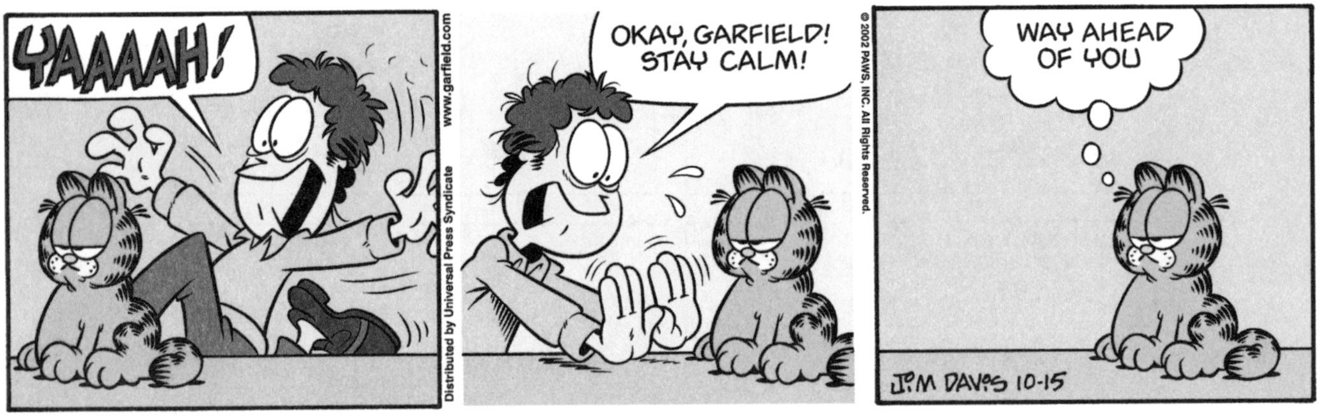
YAAAAH!
OKAY, GARFIELD! STAY CALM!
WAY AHEAD OF YOU
JIM DAVIS 10-15
Distributed by Universal Press Syndicate www.garfield.com
© 2002 PAWS, INC. All Rights Reserved.

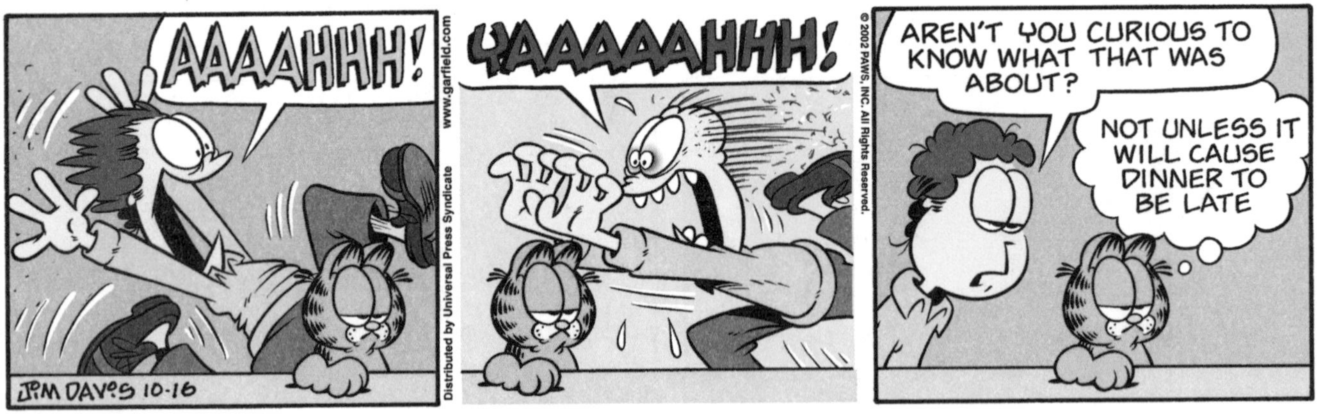
AAAAHHH!
YAAAAAHHH!
AREN'T YOU CURIOUS TO KNOW WHAT THAT WAS ABOUT?
NOT UNLESS IT WILL CAUSE DINNER TO BE LATE
JIM DAVIS 10-16
Distributed by Universal Press Syndicate www.garfield.com
© 2002 PAWS, INC. All Rights Reserved.

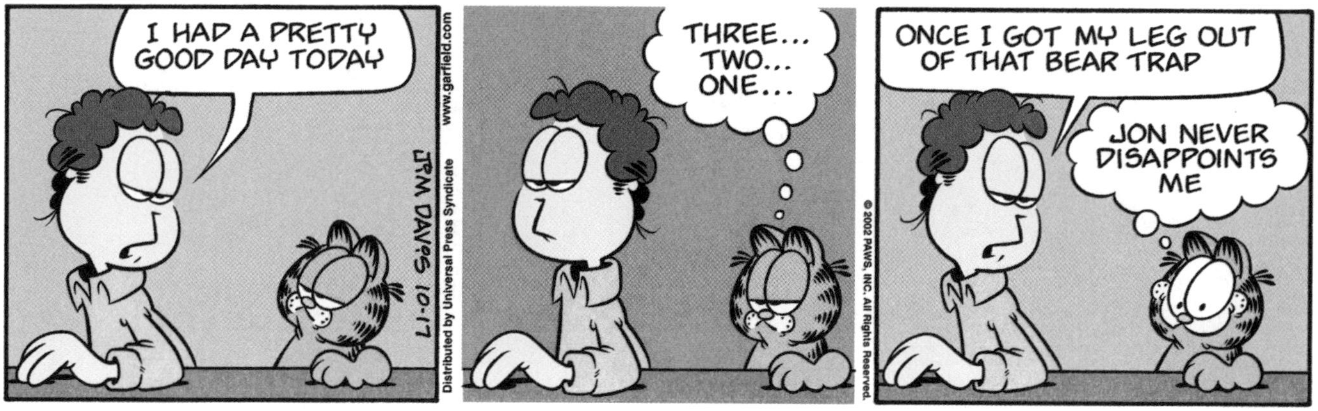
I HAD A PRETTY GOOD DAY TODAY
JIM DAVIS 10-17
Distributed by Universal Press Syndicate www.garfield.com
THREE... TWO... ONE...
© 2002 PAWS, INC. All Rights Reserved.
ONCE I GOT MY LEG OUT OF THAT BEAR TRAP
JON NEVER DISAPPOINTS ME

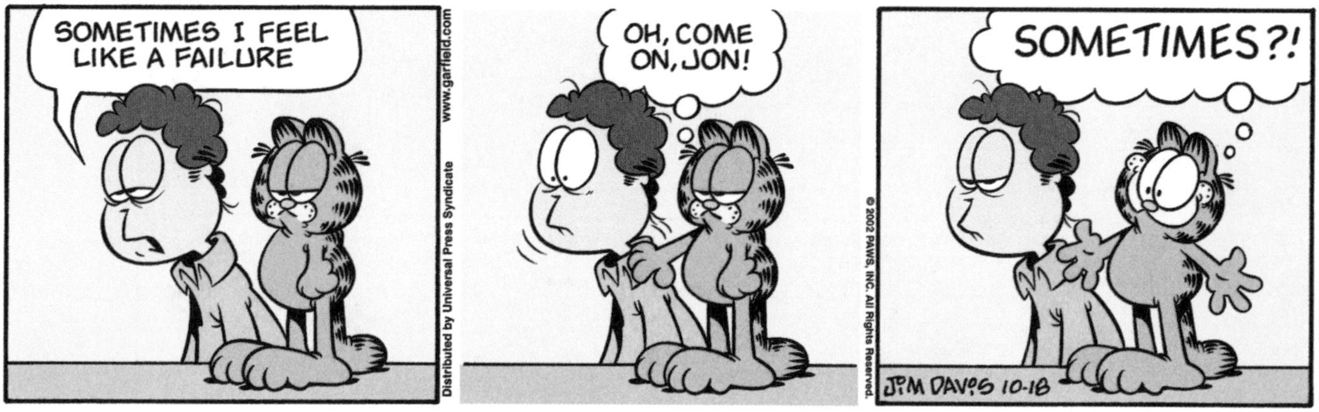
SOMETIMES I FEEL LIKE A FAILURE
Distributed by Universal Press Syndicate www.garfield.com
OH, COME ON, JON!
© 2002 PAWS, INC. All Rights Reserved.
SOMETIMES?!
JIM DAVIS 10-18

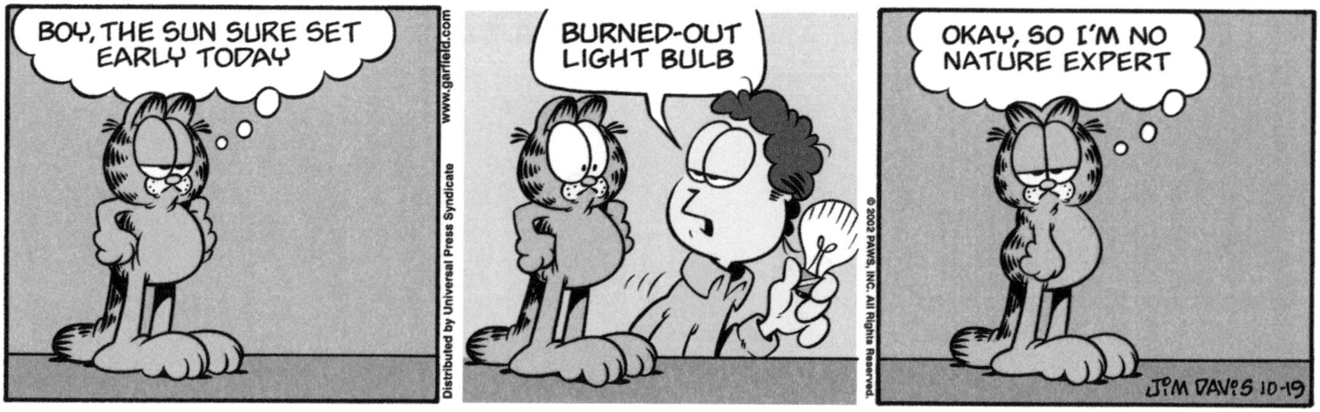
BOY, THE SUN SURE SET EARLY TODAY
Distributed by Universal Press Syndicate www.garfield.com
BURNED-OUT LIGHT BULB
© 2002 PAWS, INC. All Rights Reserved.
OKAY, SO I'M NO NATURE EXPERT
JIM DAVIS 10-19

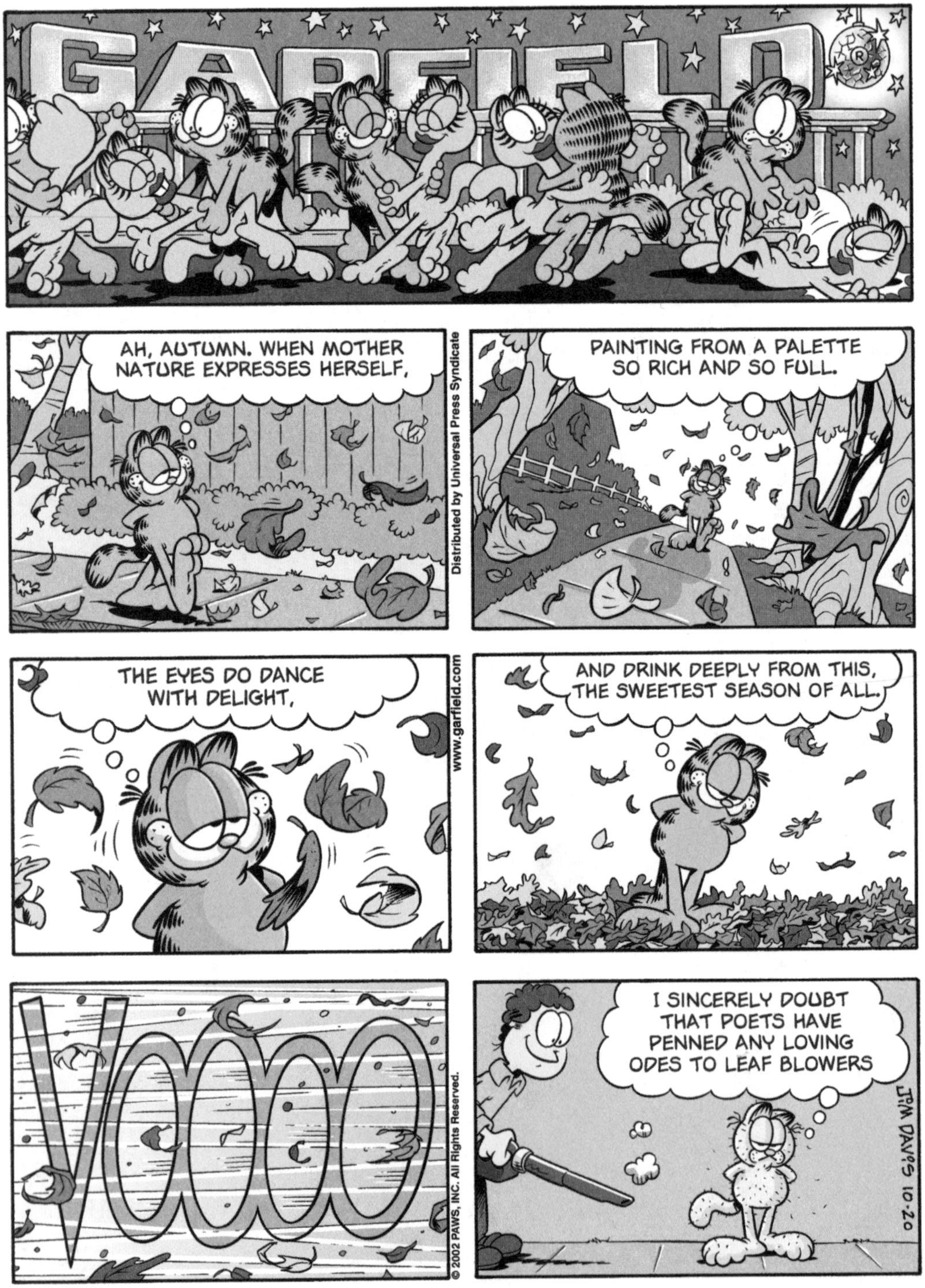
GARFIELD
AH, AUTUMN. WHEN MOTHER NATURE EXPRESSES HERSELF,
PAINTING FROM A PALETTE SO RICH AND SO FULL.
THE EYES DO DANCE WITH DELIGHT,
AND DRINK DEEPLY FROM THIS, THE SWEETEST SEASON OF ALL.
VOOOO
I SINCERELY DOUBT THAT POETS HAVE PENNED ANY LOVING ODES TO LEAF BLOWERS
JIM DAVIS 10-20
Distributed by Universal Press Syndicate
www.garfield.com
© 2002 PAWS, INC. All Rights Reserved.

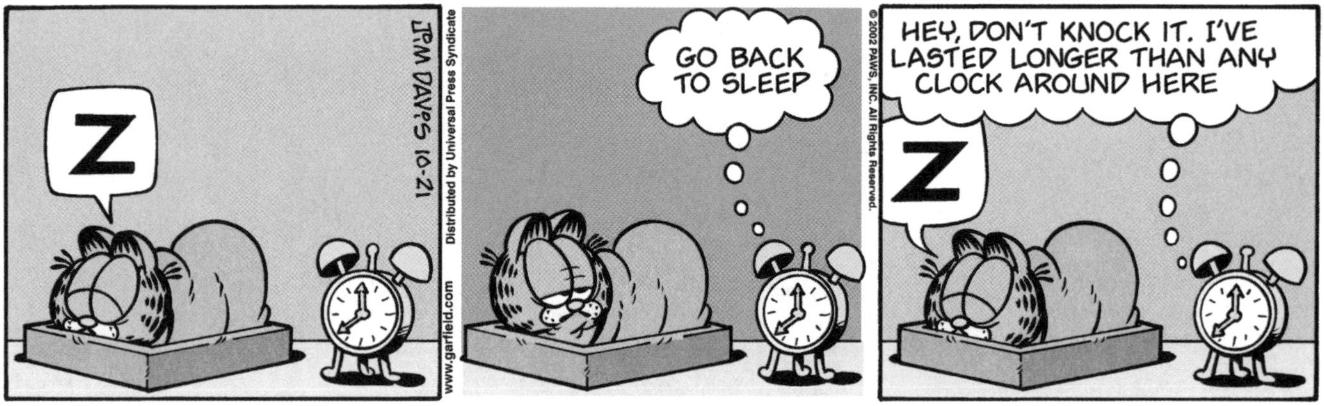
Z
JIM DAVIS 10-21
Distributed by Universal Press Syndicate
www.garfield.com
GO BACK TO SLEEP
© 2002 PAWS, INC. All Rights Reserved.
HEY, DON'T KNOCK IT. I'VE LASTED LONGER THAN ANY CLOCK AROUND HERE
Z

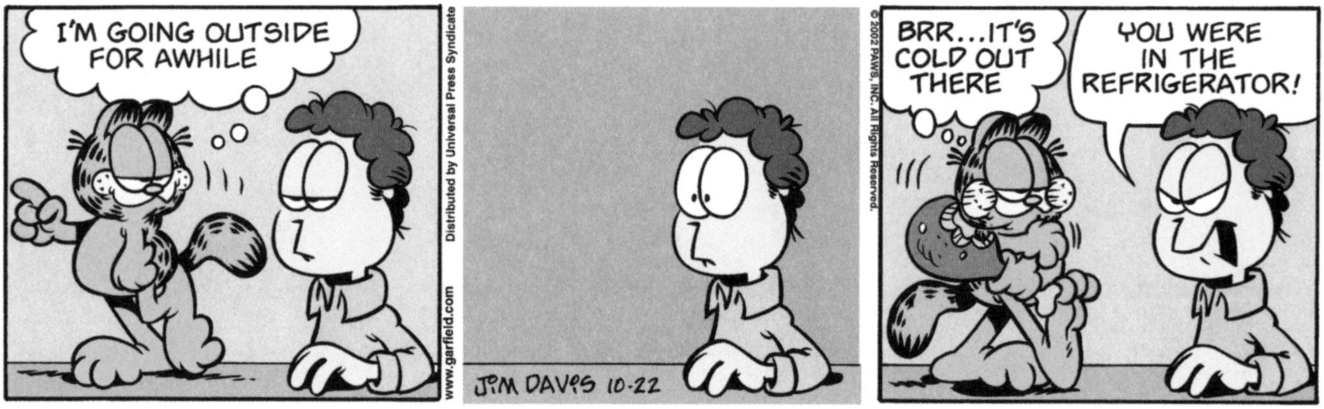
I'M GOING OUTSIDE FOR AWHILE
Distributed by Universal Press Syndicate
www.garfield.com
JIM DAVIS 10-22
© 2002 PAWS, INC. All Rights Reserved.
BRR...IT'S COLD OUT THERE
YOU WERE IN THE REFRIGERATOR!

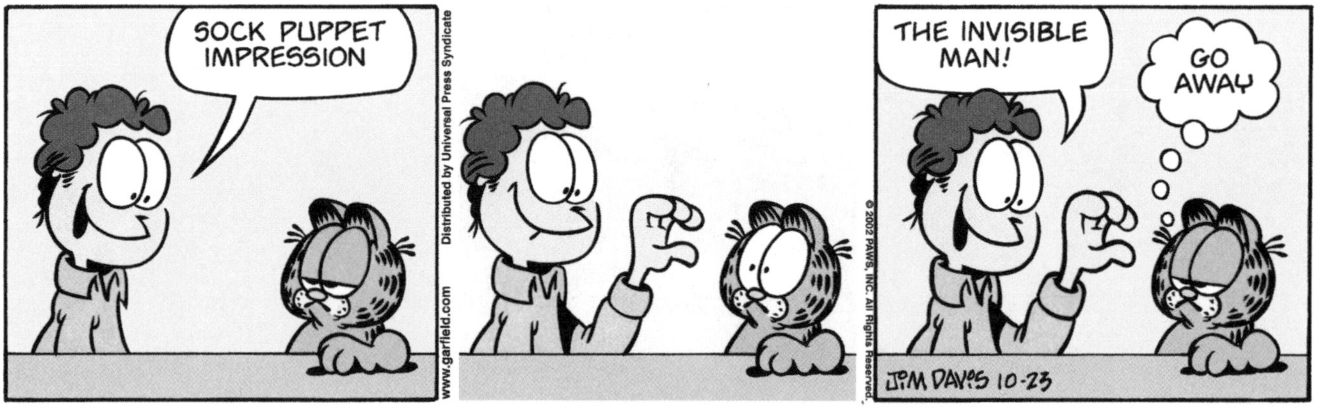
SOCK PUPPET IMPRESSION
Distributed by Universal Press Syndicate
www.garfield.com
© 2002 PAWS, INC. All Rights Reserved.
THE INVISIBLE MAN!
GO AWAY
JIM DAVIS 10-23

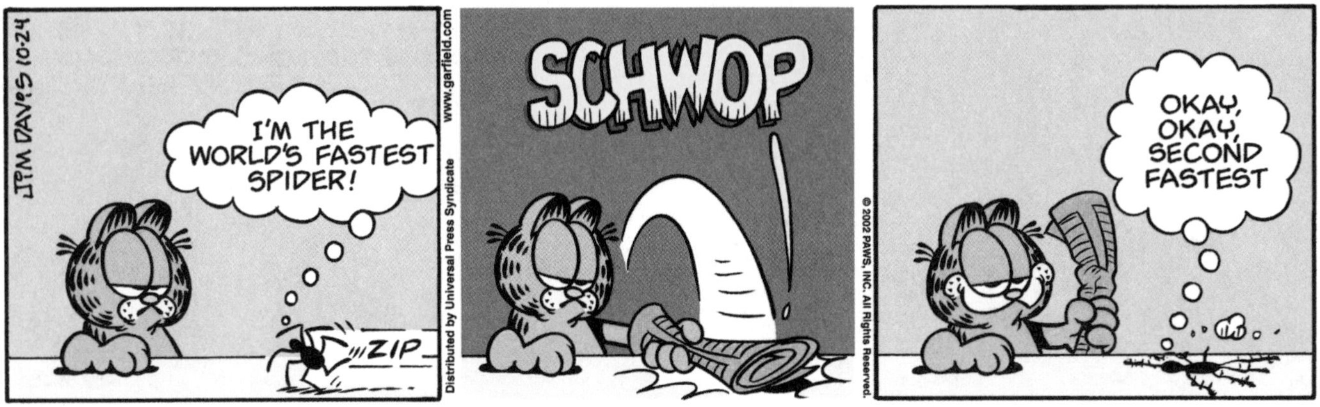
JIM DAVIS 10-24
I'M THE WORLD'S FASTEST SPIDER!
ZIP
Distributed by Universal Press Syndicate www.garfield.com
SCHWOP
© 2002 PAWS, INC. All Rights Reserved.
OKAY, OKAY, SECOND FASTEST

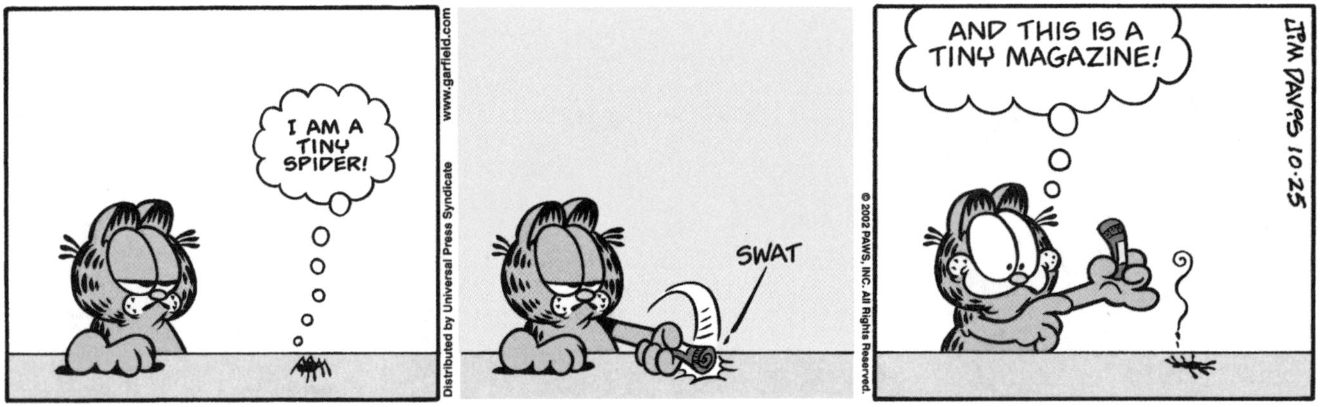
I AM A TINY SPIDER!
Distributed by Universal Press Syndicate www.garfield.com
SWAT
© 2002 PAWS, INC. All Rights Reserved.
AND THIS IS A TINY MAGAZINE!
JIM DAVIS 10-25

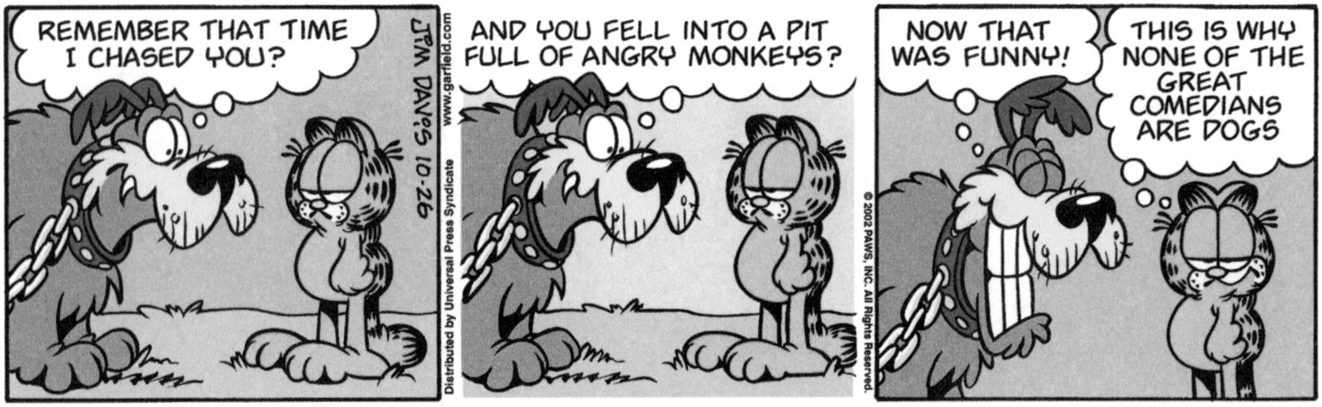
REMEMBER THAT TIME I CHASED YOU?
JIM DAVIS 10-26
Distributed by Universal Press Syndicate www.garfield.com
AND YOU FELL INTO A PIT FULL OF ANGRY MONKEYS?
© 2002 PAWS, INC. All Rights Reserved.
NOW THAT WAS FUNNY!
THIS IS WHY NONE OF THE GREAT COMEDIANS ARE DOGS

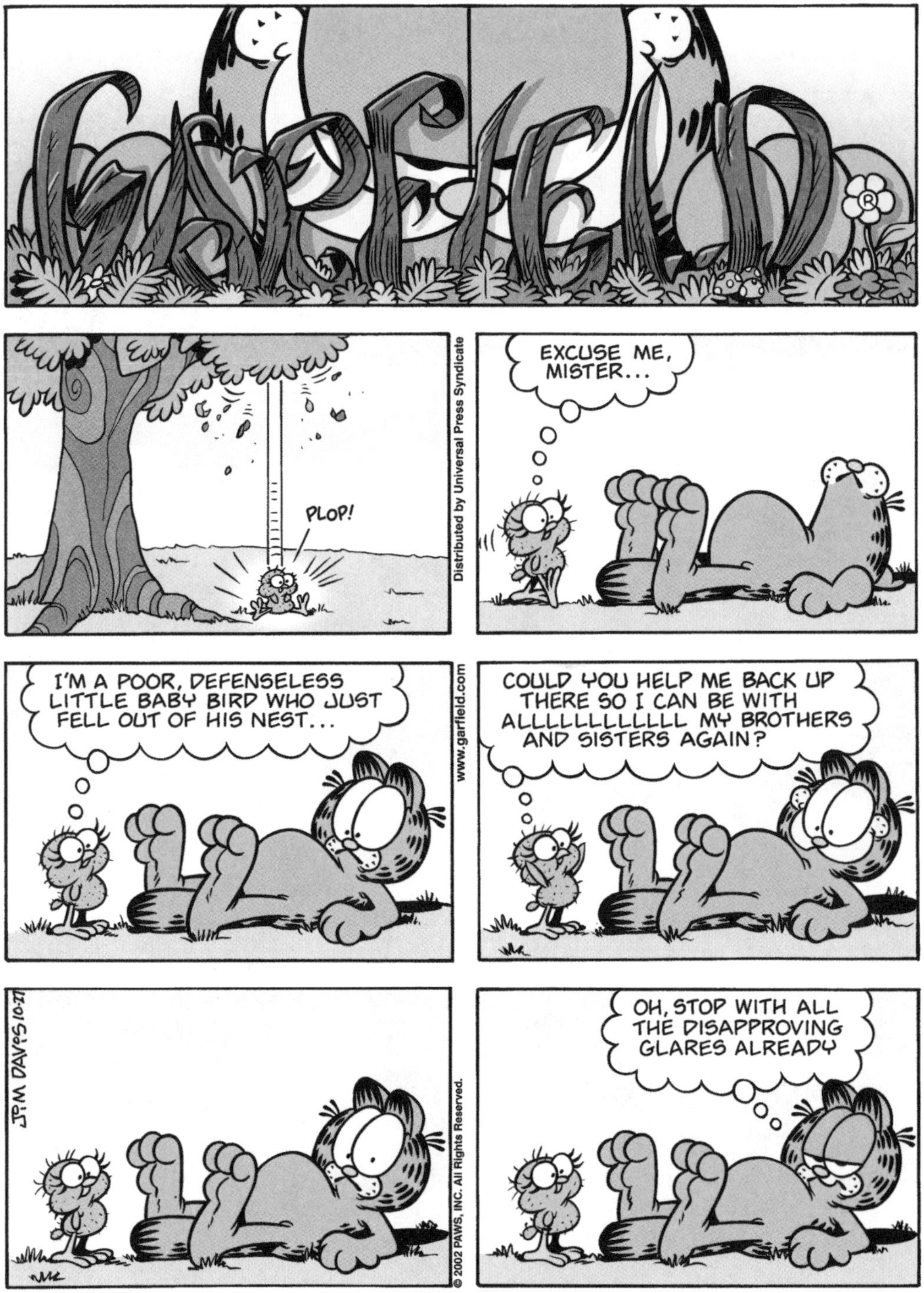
GARFIELD
PLOP!
EXCUSE ME, MISTER...
I'M A POOR, DEFENSELESS LITTLE BABY BIRD WHO JUST FELL OUT OF HIS NEST...
COULD YOU HELP ME BACK UP THERE SO I CAN BE WITH ALLLLLLLLLLLL MY BROTHERS AND SISTERS AGAIN?
OH, STOP WITH ALL THE DISAPPROVING GLARES ALREADY
JIM DAVIS 10-27

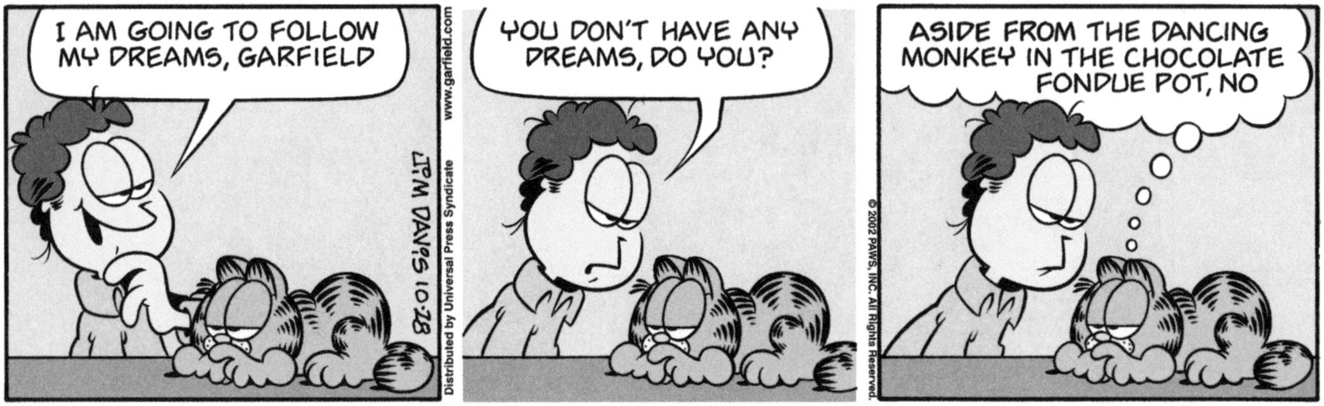
I AM GOING TO FOLLOW MY DREAMS, GARFIELD
JIM DAVIS 10-28
www.garfield.com
Distributed by Universal Press Syndicate
YOU DON'T HAVE ANY DREAMS, DO YOU?
© 2002 PAWS, INC. All Rights Reserved.
ASIDE FROM THE DANCING MONKEY IN THE CHOCOLATE FONDUE POT, NO

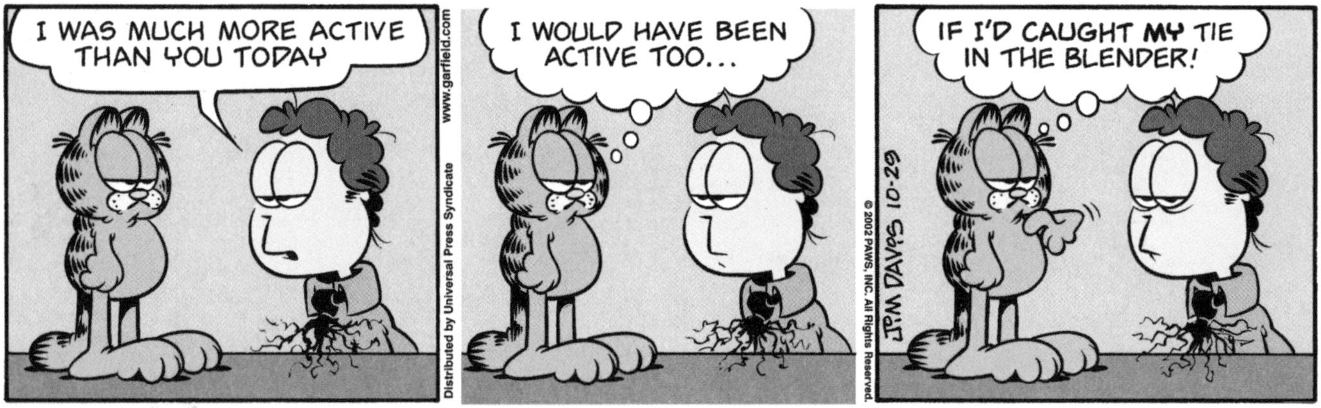
I WAS MUCH MORE ACTIVE THAN YOU TODAY
www.garfield.com
Distributed by Universal Press Syndicate
I WOULD HAVE BEEN ACTIVE TOO...
JIM DAVIS 10-29
© 2002 PAWS, INC. All Rights Reserved.
IF I'D CAUGHT **MY** TIE IN THE BLENDER!

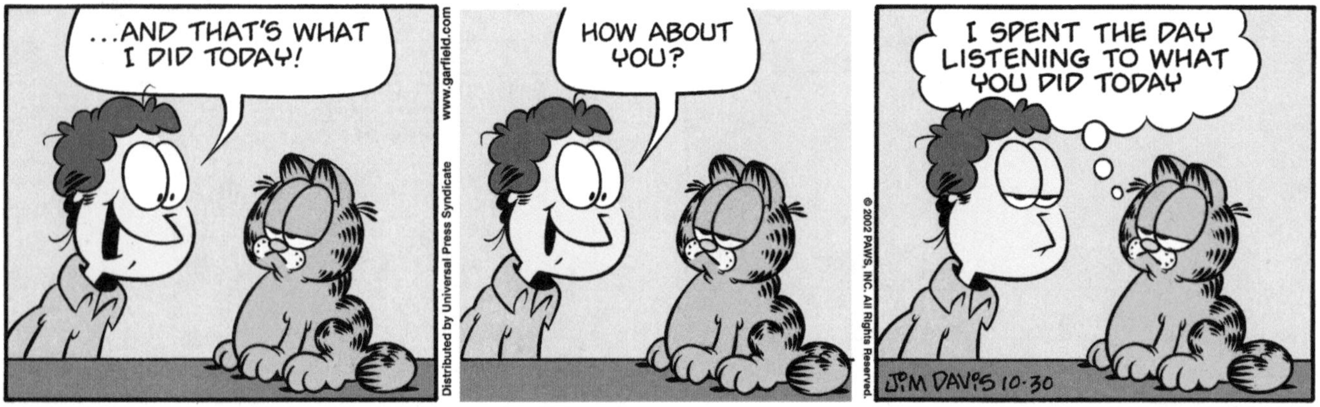
...AND THAT'S WHAT I DID TODAY!
www.garfield.com
Distributed by Universal Press Syndicate
HOW ABOUT YOU?
© 2002 PAWS, INC. All Rights Reserved.
I SPENT THE DAY LISTENING TO WHAT YOU DID TODAY
JIM DAVIS 10-30

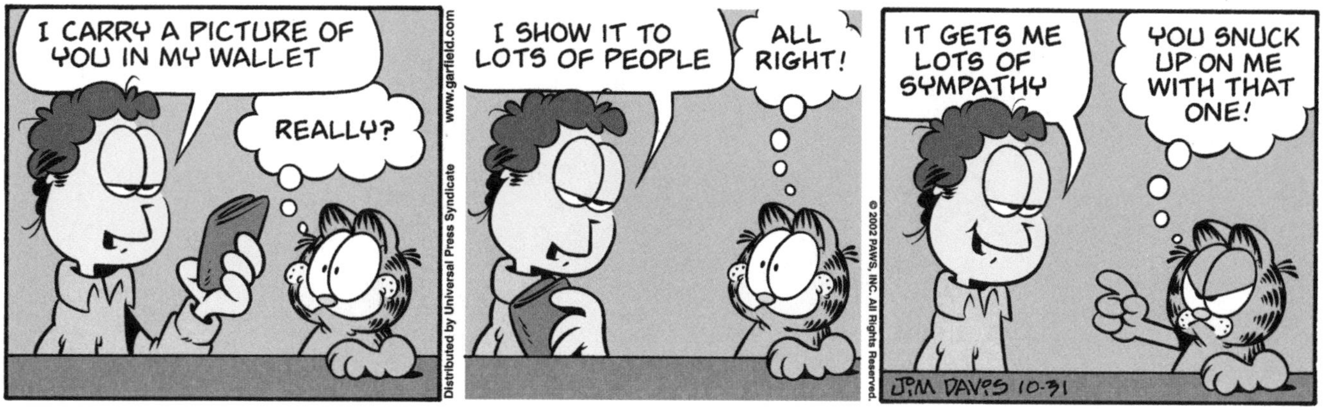
I CARRY A PICTURE OF YOU IN MY WALLET
REALLY?
www.garfield.com
Distributed by Universal Press Syndicate
I SHOW IT TO LOTS OF PEOPLE
ALL RIGHT!
© 2002 PAWS, INC. All Rights Reserved.
IT GETS ME LOTS OF SYMPATHY
YOU SNUCK UP ON ME WITH THAT ONE!
JIM DAVIS 10-31

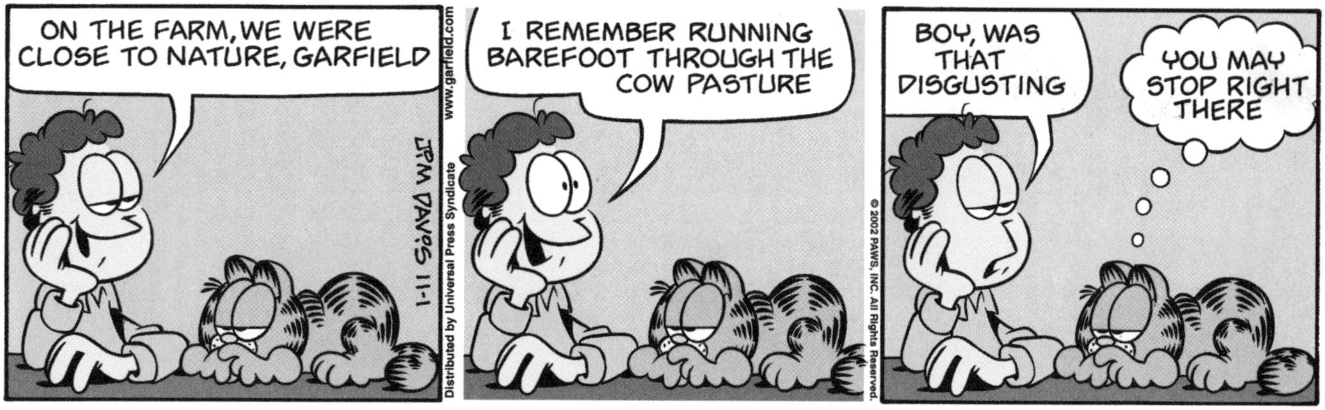
ON THE FARM, WE WERE CLOSE TO NATURE, GARFIELD
JIM DAVIS 11-1
www.garfield.com
Distributed by Universal Press Syndicate
I REMEMBER RUNNING BAREFOOT THROUGH THE COW PASTURE
© 2002 PAWS, INC. All Rights Reserved.
BOY, WAS THAT DISGUSTING
YOU MAY STOP RIGHT THERE

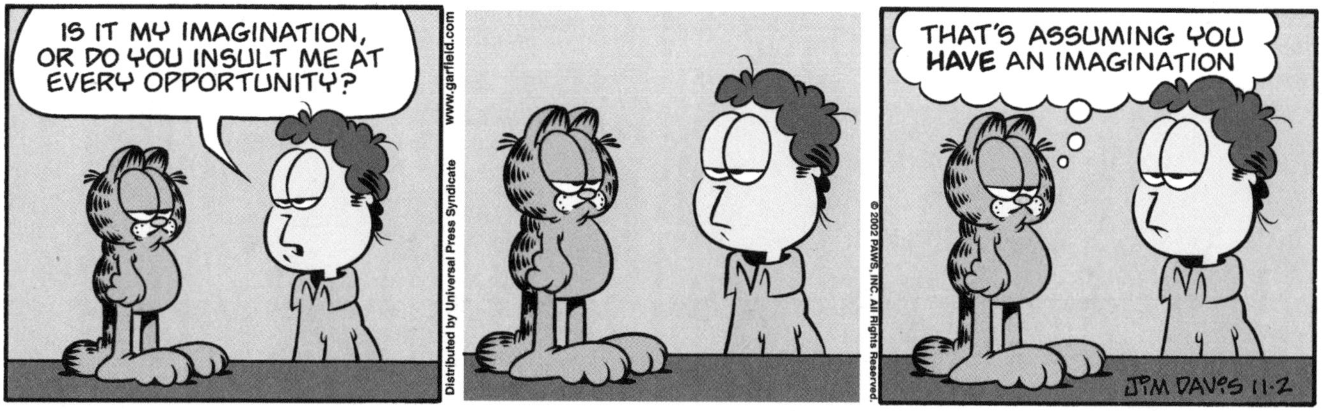
IS IT MY IMAGINATION, OR DO YOU INSULT ME AT EVERY OPPORTUNITY?
www.garfield.com
Distributed by Universal Press Syndicate
© 2002 PAWS, INC. All Rights Reserved.
THAT'S ASSUMING YOU **HAVE** AN IMAGINATION
JIM DAVIS 11-2

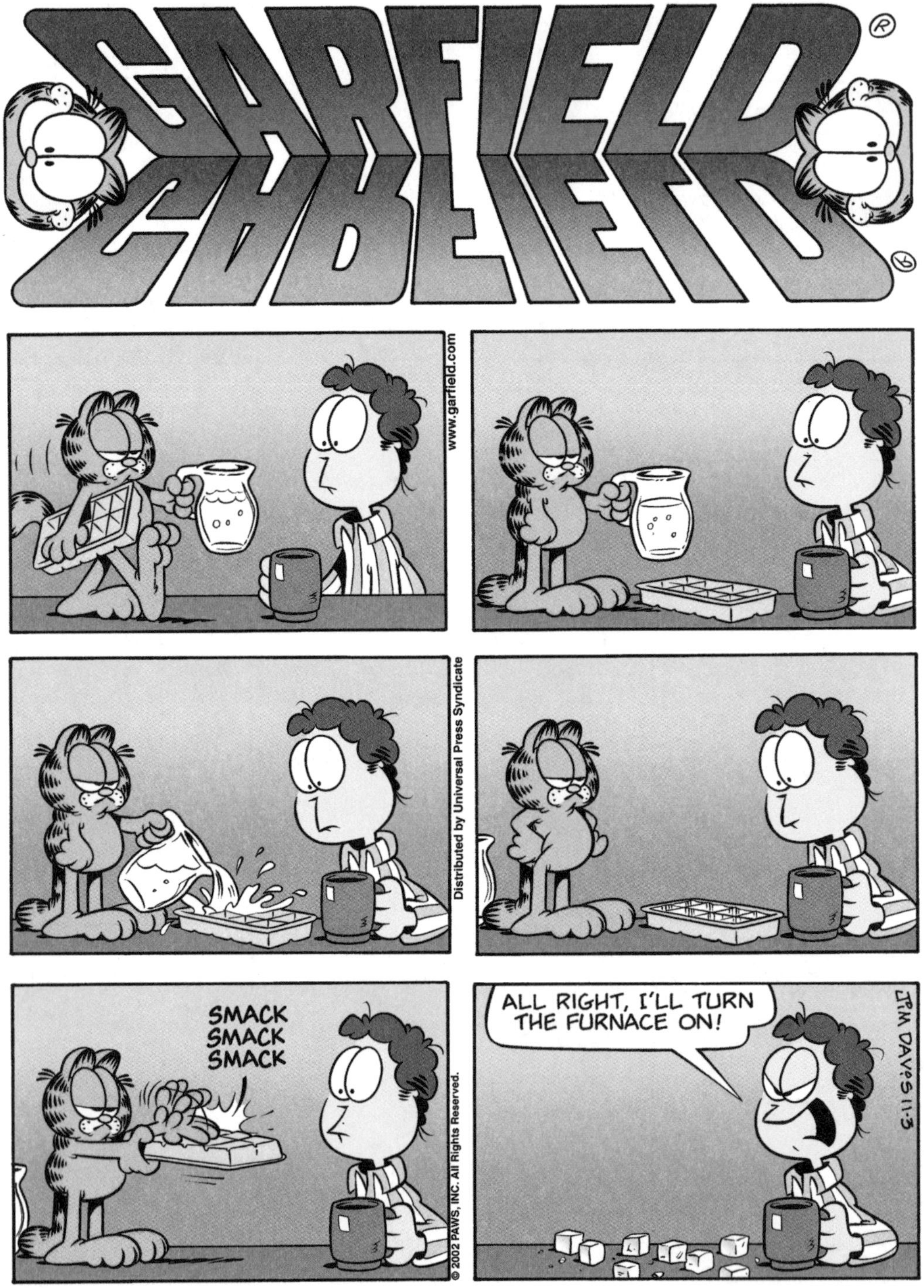
GARFIELD
www.garfield.com
Distributed by Universal Press Syndicate
© 2002 PAWS, INC. All Rights Reserved.
SMACK
SMACK
SMACK
ALL RIGHT, I'LL TURN THE FURNACE ON!
JIM DAVIS 11-3

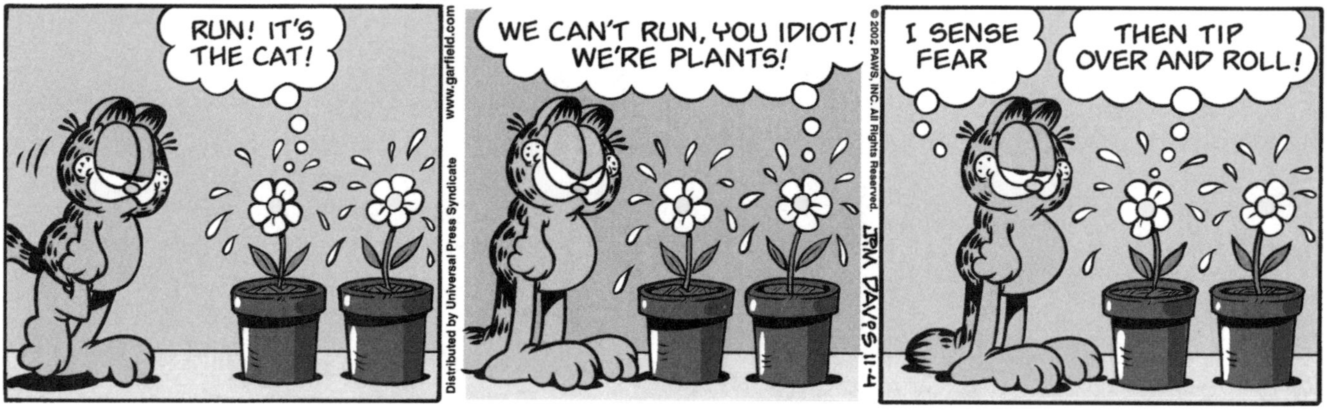
RUN! IT'S THE CAT!
www.garfield.com
Distributed by Universal Press Syndicate
WE CAN'T RUN, YOU IDIOT! WE'RE PLANTS!
© 2002 PAWS, INC. All Rights Reserved.
JIM DAVIS 11-4
I SENSE FEAR
THEN TIP OVER AND ROLL!

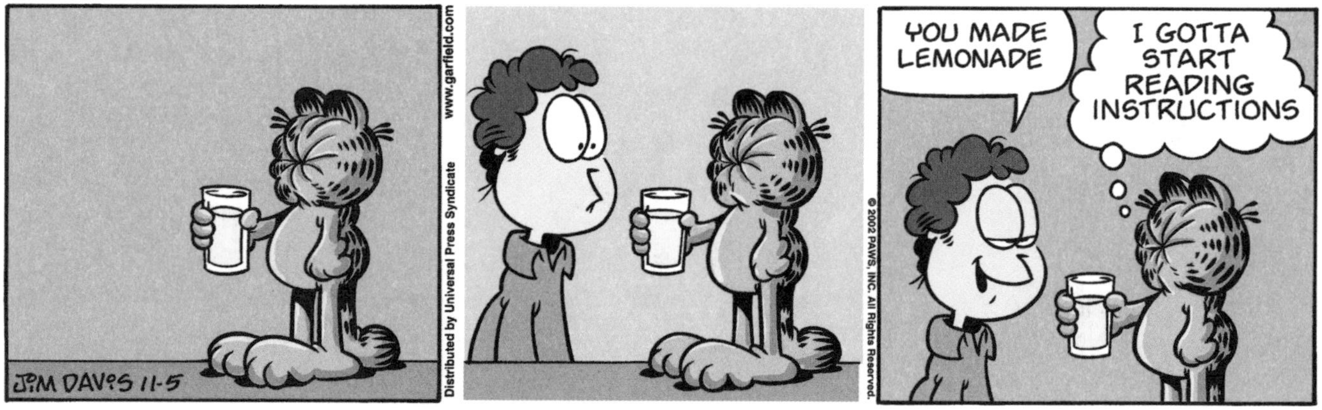
JIM DAVIS 11-5
www.garfield.com
Distributed by Universal Press Syndicate
© 2002 PAWS, INC. All Rights Reserved.
YOU MADE LEMONADE
I GOTTA START READING INSTRUCTIONS

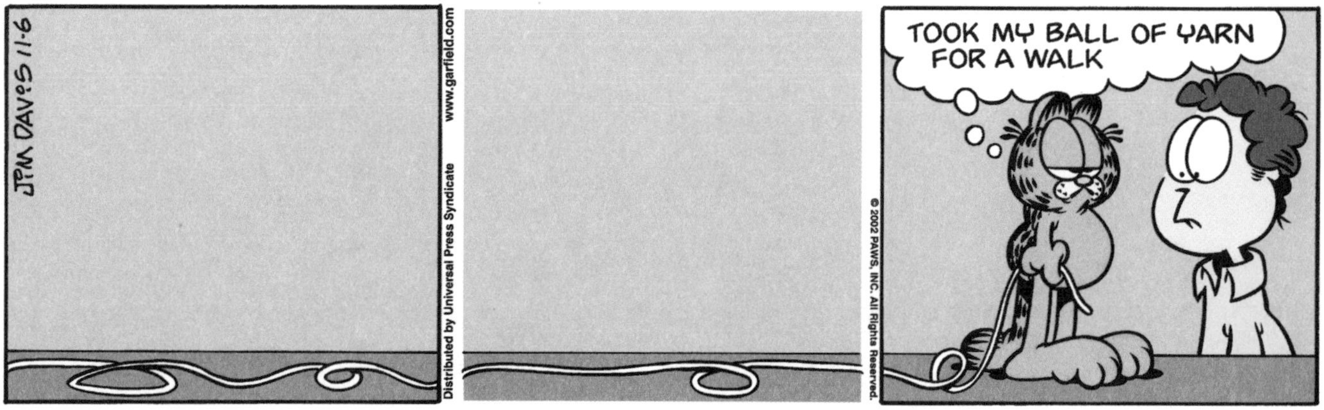
JIM DAVIS 11-6
www.garfield.com
Distributed by Universal Press Syndicate
© 2002 PAWS, INC. All Rights Reserved.
TOOK MY BALL OF YARN FOR A WALK

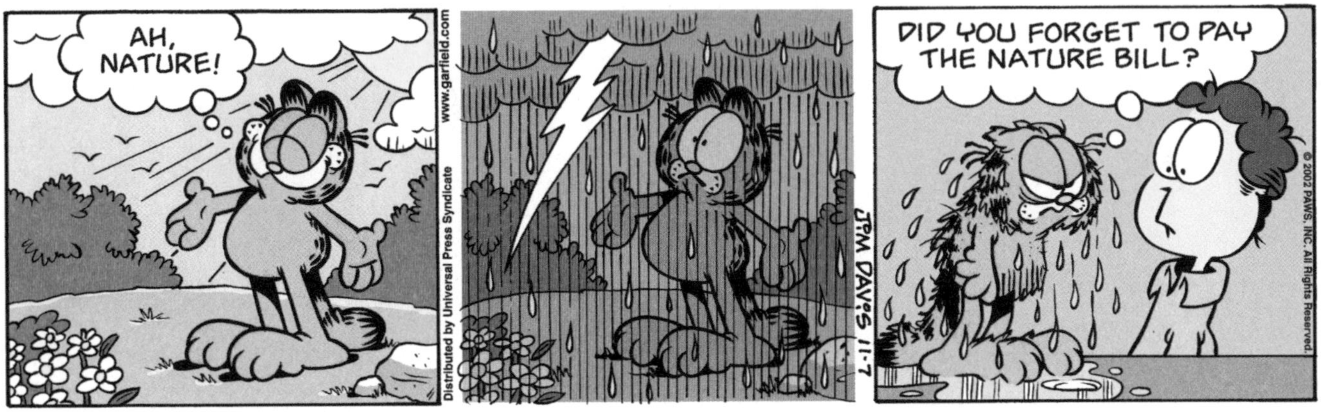
AH, NATURE!
www.garfield.com
Distributed by Universal Press Syndicate
JIM DAVIS 11-7
DID YOU FORGET TO PAY THE NATURE BILL?
© 2002 PAWS, INC. All Rights Reserved.

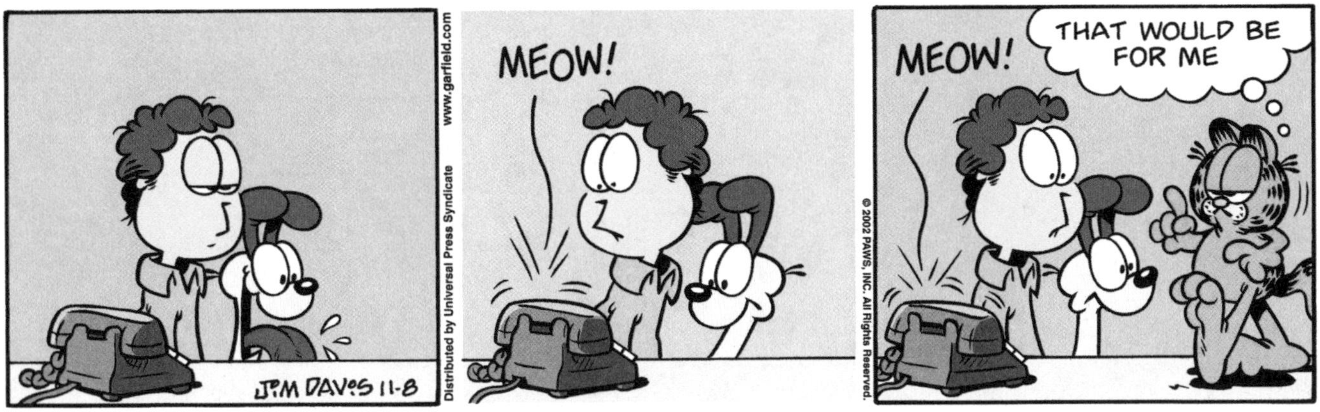
JIM DAVIS 11-8
www.garfield.com
Distributed by Universal Press Syndicate
MEOW!
© 2002 PAWS, INC. All Rights Reserved.
MEOW!
THAT WOULD BE FOR ME

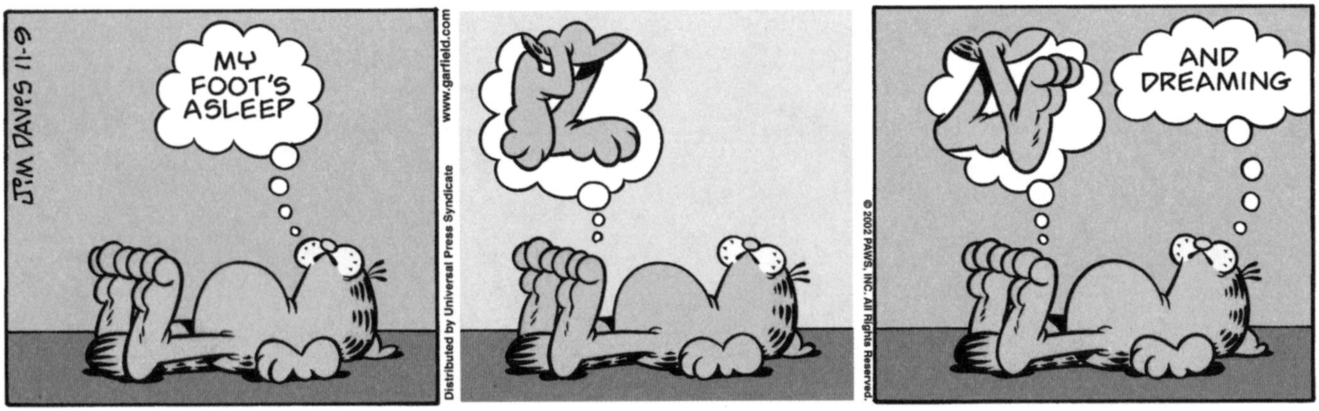
JIM DAVIS 11-9
MY FOOT'S ASLEEP
www.garfield.com
Distributed by Universal Press Syndicate
© 2002 PAWS, INC. All Rights Reserved.
AND DREAMING

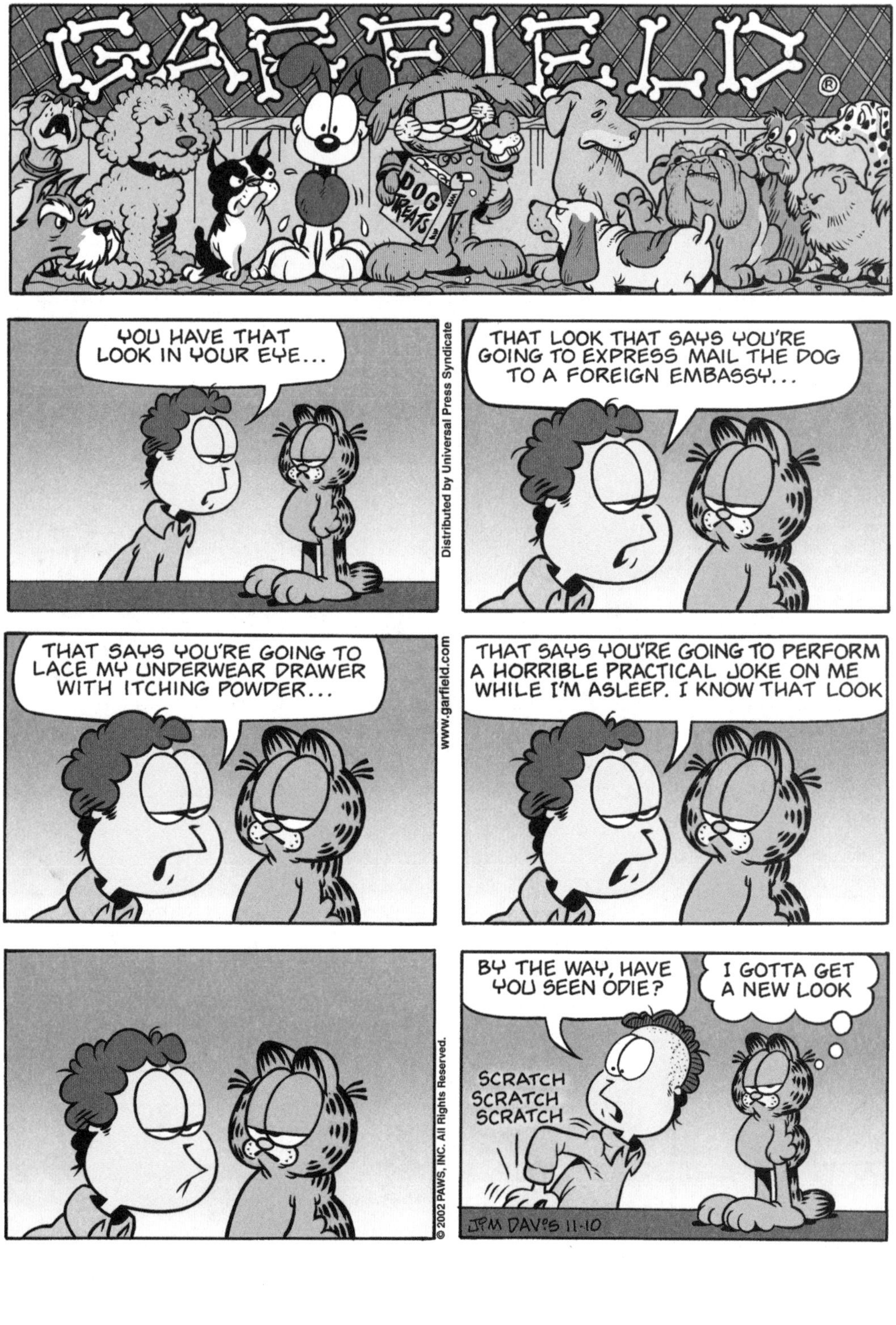
GARFIELD ®
DOG TREATS
YOU HAVE THAT LOOK IN YOUR EYE...
Distributed by Universal Press Syndicate
THAT LOOK THAT SAYS YOU'RE GOING TO EXPRESS MAIL THE DOG TO A FOREIGN EMBASSY...
THAT SAYS YOU'RE GOING TO LACE MY UNDERWEAR DRAWER WITH ITCHING POWDER...
www.garfield.com
THAT SAYS YOU'RE GOING TO PERFORM A HORRIBLE PRACTICAL JOKE ON ME WHILE I'M ASLEEP. I KNOW THAT LOOK
© 2002 PAWS, INC. All Rights Reserved.
BY THE WAY, HAVE YOU SEEN ODIE?
I GOTTA GET A NEW LOOK
SCRATCH SCRATCH SCRATCH
JIM DAVIS 11-10

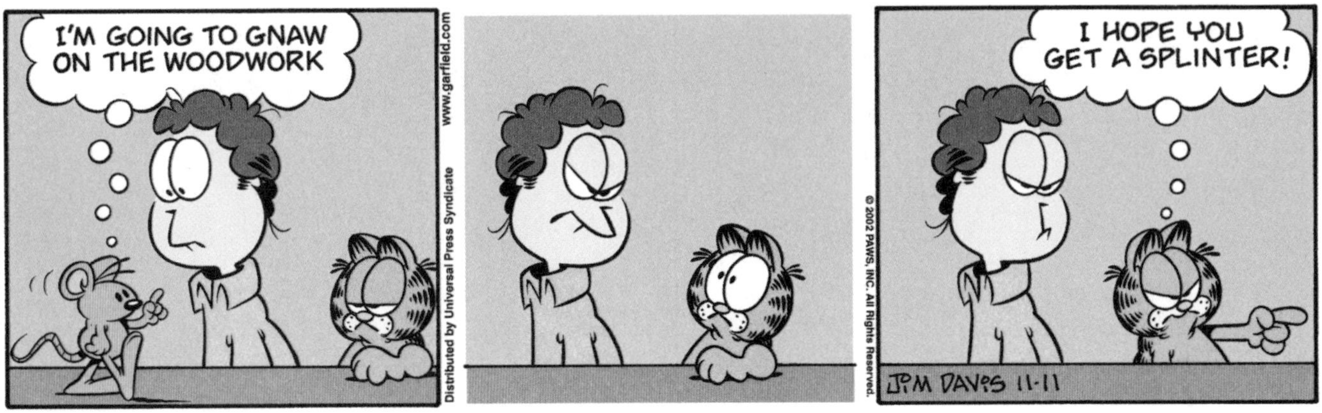
I'M GOING TO GNAW ON THE WOODWORK
Distributed by Universal Press Syndicate www.garfield.com
I HOPE YOU GET A SPLINTER!
© 2002 PAWS, INC. All Rights Reserved.
JIM DAVIS 11-11

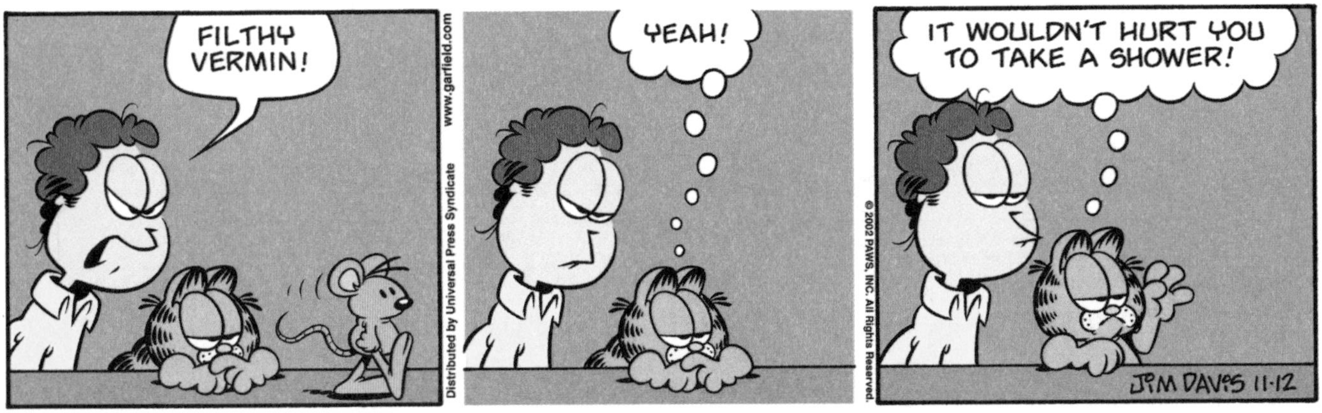
FILTHY VERMIN!
Distributed by Universal Press Syndicate www.garfield.com
YEAH!
IT WOULDN'T HURT YOU TO TAKE A SHOWER!
© 2002 PAWS, INC. All Rights Reserved.
JIM DAVIS 11-12

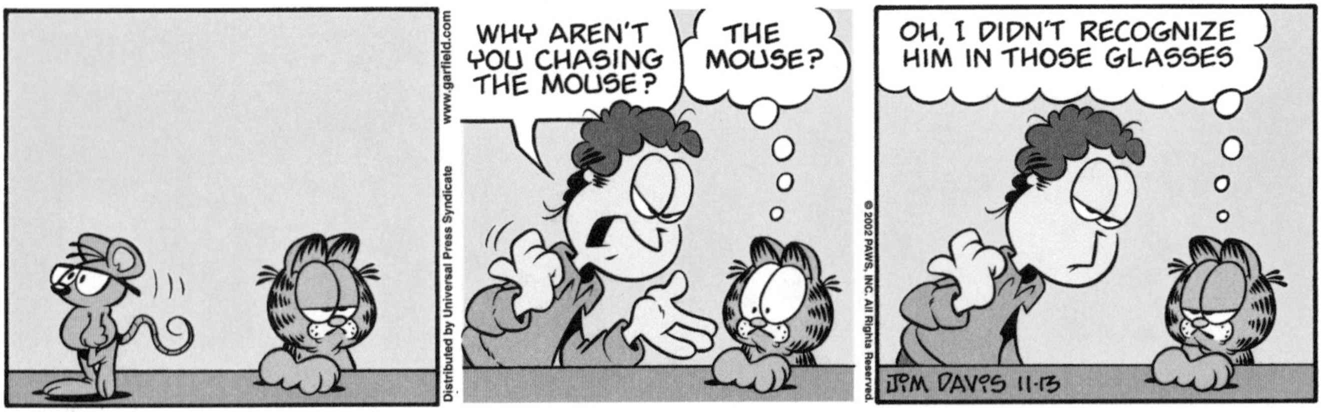
Distributed by Universal Press Syndicate www.garfield.com
WHY AREN'T YOU CHASING THE MOUSE?
THE MOUSE?
OH, I DIDN'T RECOGNIZE HIM IN THOSE GLASSES
© 2002 PAWS, INC. All Rights Reserved.
JIM DAVIS 11-13

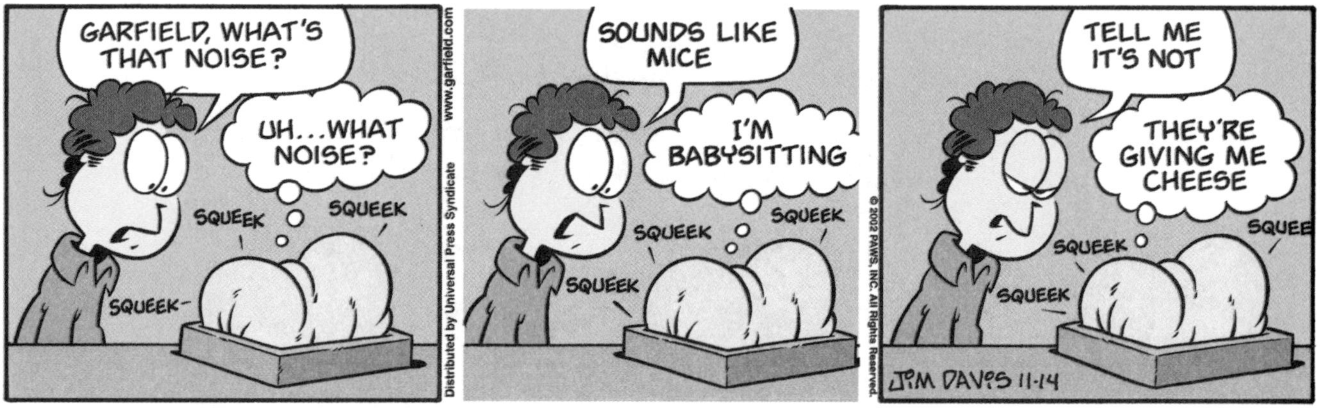
GARFIELD, WHAT'S THAT NOISE?
UH...WHAT NOISE?
SQUEEK
SQUEEK
SQUEEK
Distributed by Universal Press Syndicate www.garfield.com
SOUNDS LIKE MICE
I'M BABYSITTING
SQUEEK
SQUEEK
SQUEEK
© 2002 PAWS, INC. All Rights Reserved.
TELL ME IT'S NOT
THEY'RE GIVING ME CHEESE
SQUEEK
SQUEE
SQUEEK
JIM DAVIS 11-14

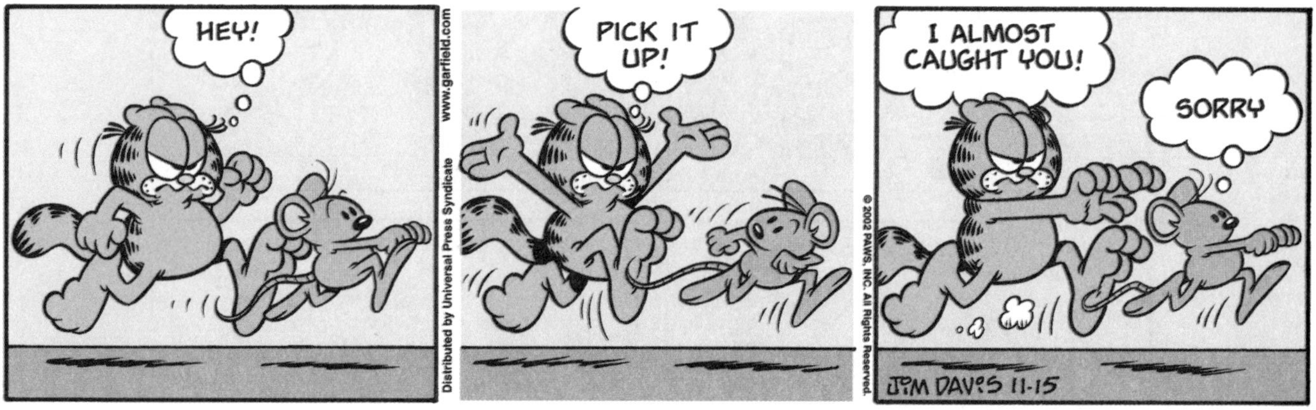
HEY!
Distributed by Universal Press Syndicate www.garfield.com
PICK IT UP!
© 2002 PAWS, INC. All Rights Reserved.
I ALMOST CAUGHT YOU!
SORRY
JIM DAVIS 11-15

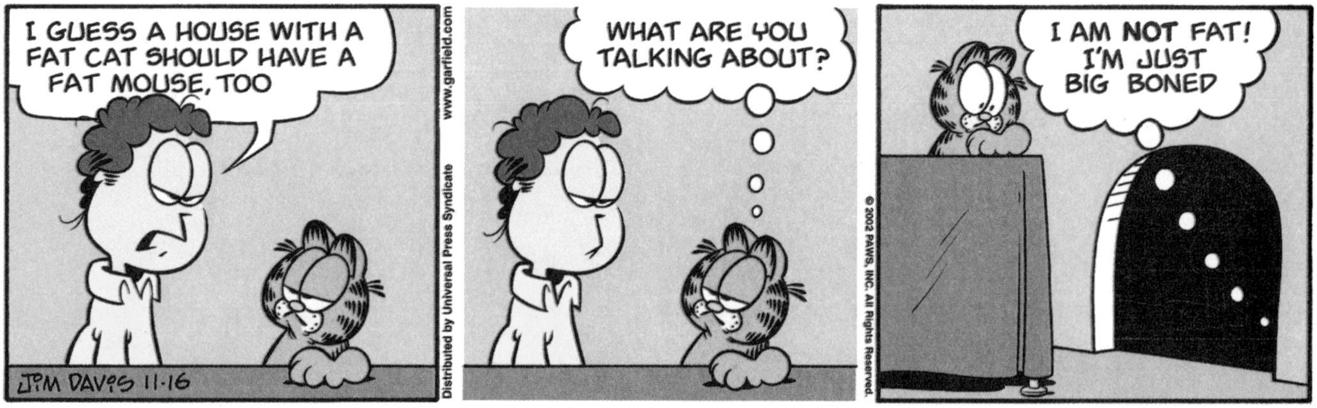
I GUESS A HOUSE WITH A FAT CAT SHOULD HAVE A FAT MOUSE, TOO
JIM DAVIS 11-16
Distributed by Universal Press Syndicate www.garfield.com
WHAT ARE YOU TALKING ABOUT?
© 2002 PAWS, INC. All Rights Reserved.
I AM NOT FAT! I'M JUST BIG BONED

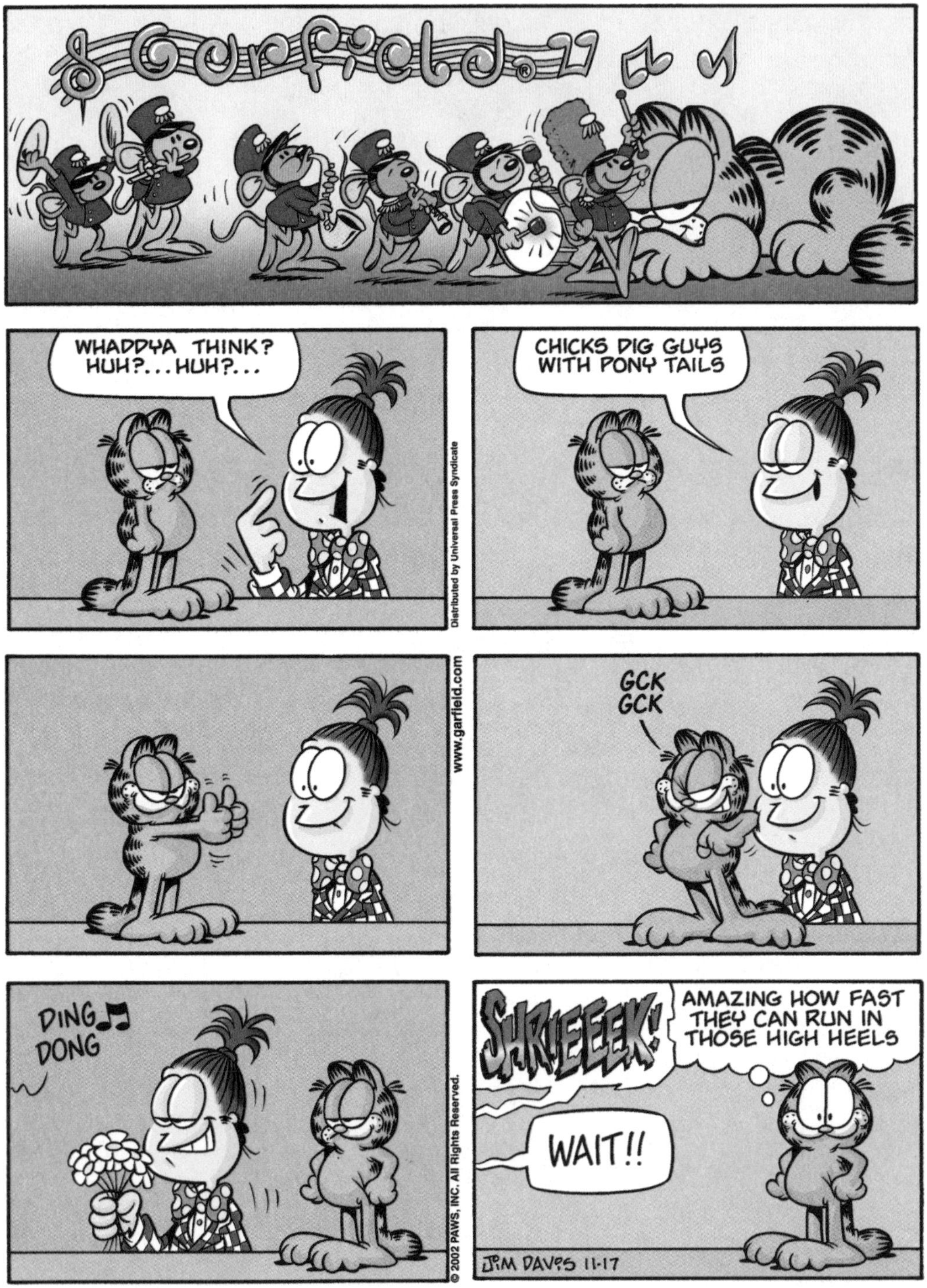
Garfield®
WHADDYA THINK? HUH?... HUH?...
CHICKS DIG GUYS WITH PONY TAILS
GCK GCK
DING DONG
SHRIEEEK!
WAIT!!
AMAZING HOW FAST THEY CAN RUN IN THOSE HIGH HEELS
JIM DAVIS 11-17
Distributed by Universal Press Syndicate
www.garfield.com
© 2002 PAWS, INC. All Rights Reserved.

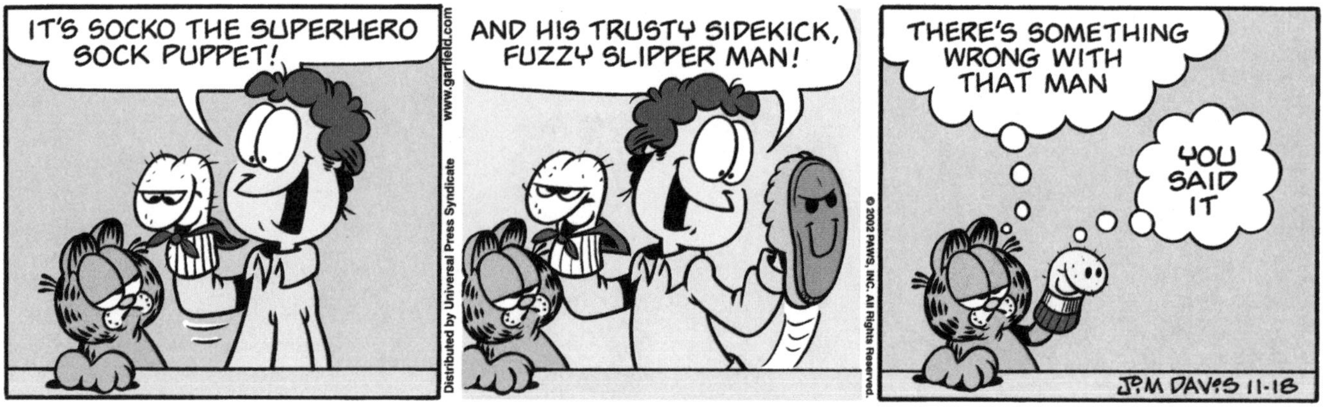
IT'S SOCKO THE SUPERHERO SOCK PUPPET!
www.garfield.com
Distributed by Universal Press Syndicate
AND HIS TRUSTY SIDEKICK, FUZZY SLIPPER MAN!
© 2002 PAWS, INC. All Rights Reserved.
THERE'S SOMETHING WRONG WITH THAT MAN
YOU SAID IT
JIM DAVIS 11-18

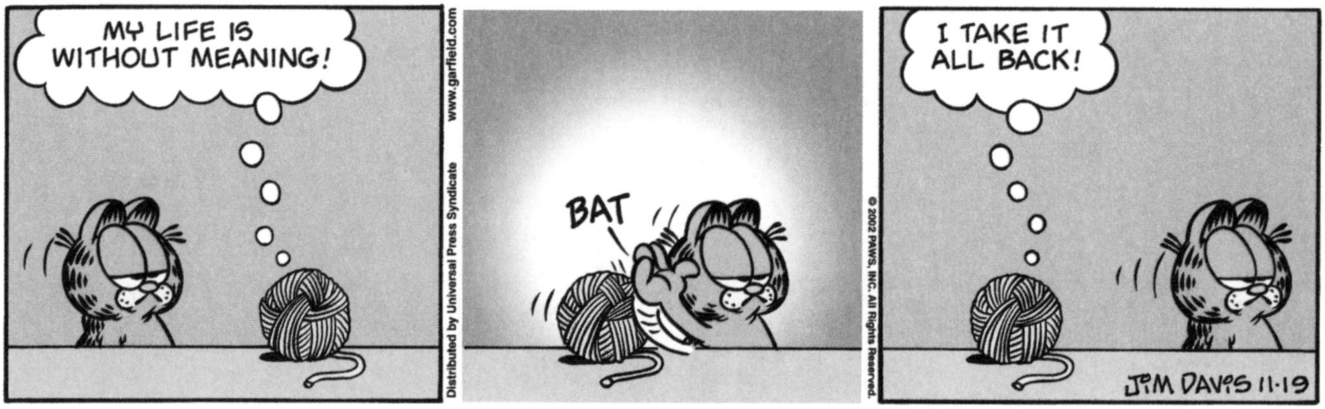
MY LIFE IS WITHOUT MEANING!
www.garfield.com
Distributed by Universal Press Syndicate
BAT
© 2002 PAWS, INC. All Rights Reserved.
I TAKE IT ALL BACK!
JIM DAVIS 11-19

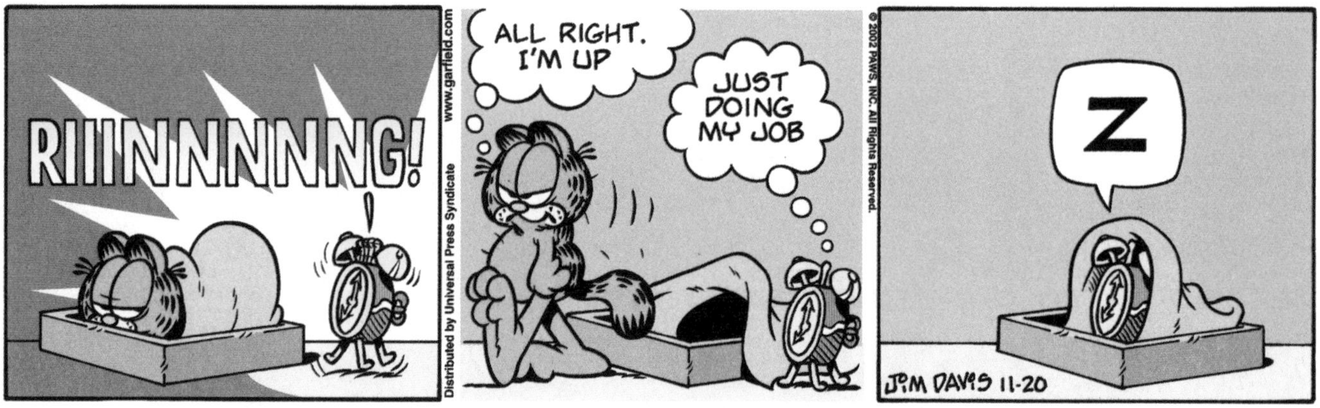
RIIINNNNNG!
!
www.garfield.com
Distributed by Universal Press Syndicate
ALL RIGHT. I'M UP
JUST DOING MY JOB
© 2002 PAWS, INC. All Rights Reserved.
Z
JIM DAVIS 11-20

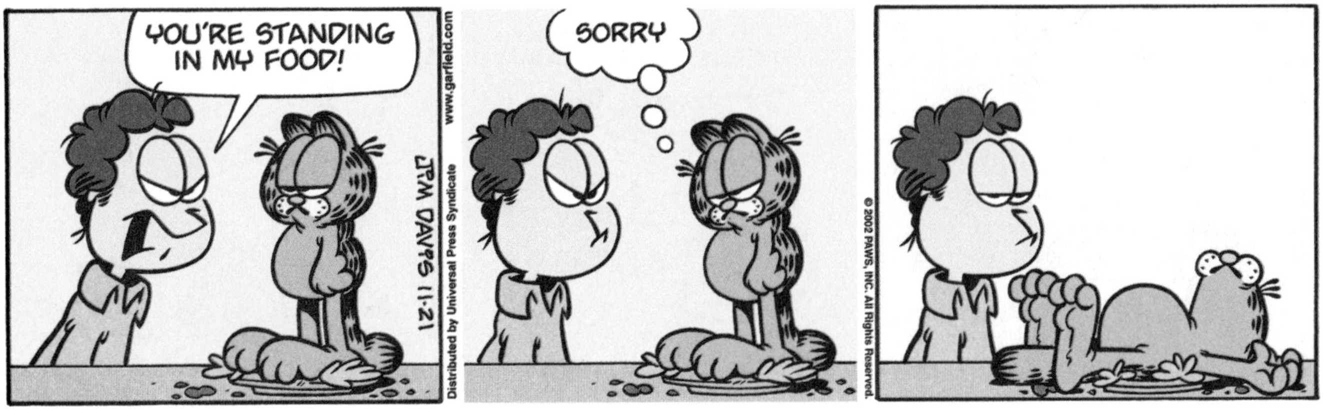
YOU'RE STANDING IN MY FOOD!
SORRY
JIM DAVIS 11-21
www.garfield.com
Distributed by Universal Press Syndicate
© 2002 PAWS, INC. All Rights Reserved.

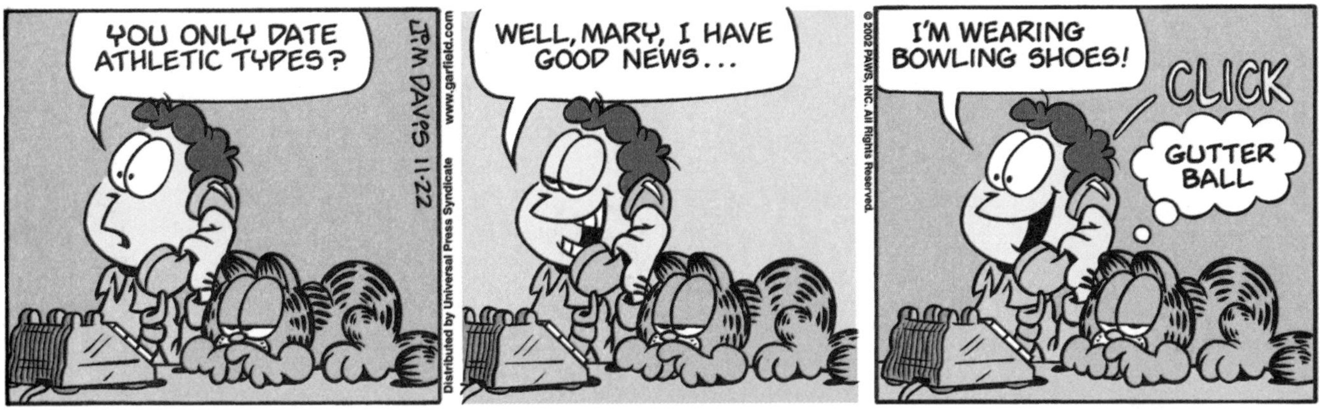
YOU ONLY DATE ATHLETIC TYPES?
WELL, MARY, I HAVE GOOD NEWS...
I'M WEARING BOWLING SHOES!
CLICK
GUTTER BALL
JIM DAVIS 11-22
www.garfield.com
Distributed by Universal Press Syndicate
© 2002 PAWS, INC. All Rights Reserved.

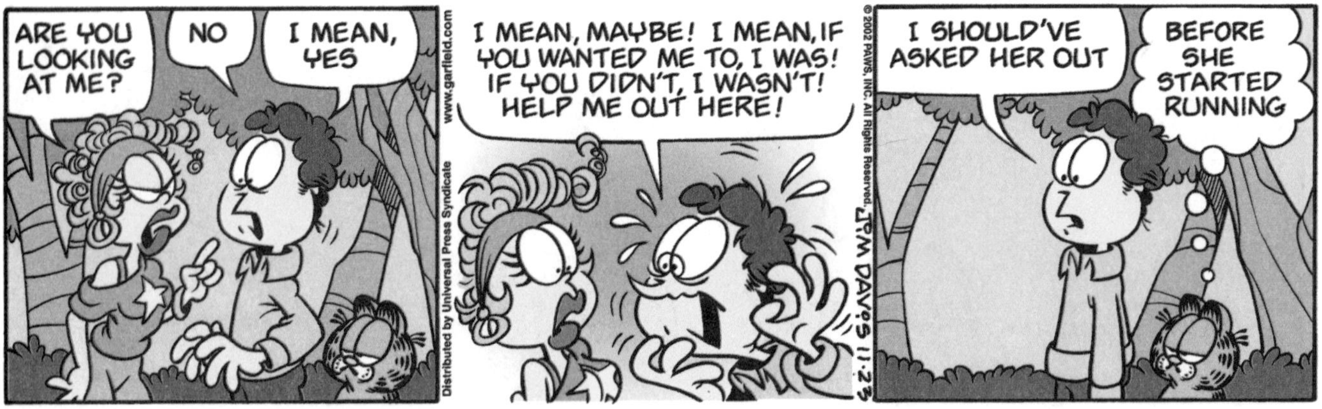
ARE YOU LOOKING AT ME?
NO
I MEAN, YES
I MEAN, MAYBE! I MEAN, IF YOU WANTED ME TO, I WAS! IF YOU DIDN'T, I WASN'T! HELP ME OUT HERE!
I SHOULD'VE ASKED HER OUT
BEFORE SHE STARTED RUNNING
JIM DAVIS 11-23
www.garfield.com
Distributed by Universal Press Syndicate
© 2002 PAWS, INC. All Rights Reserved.

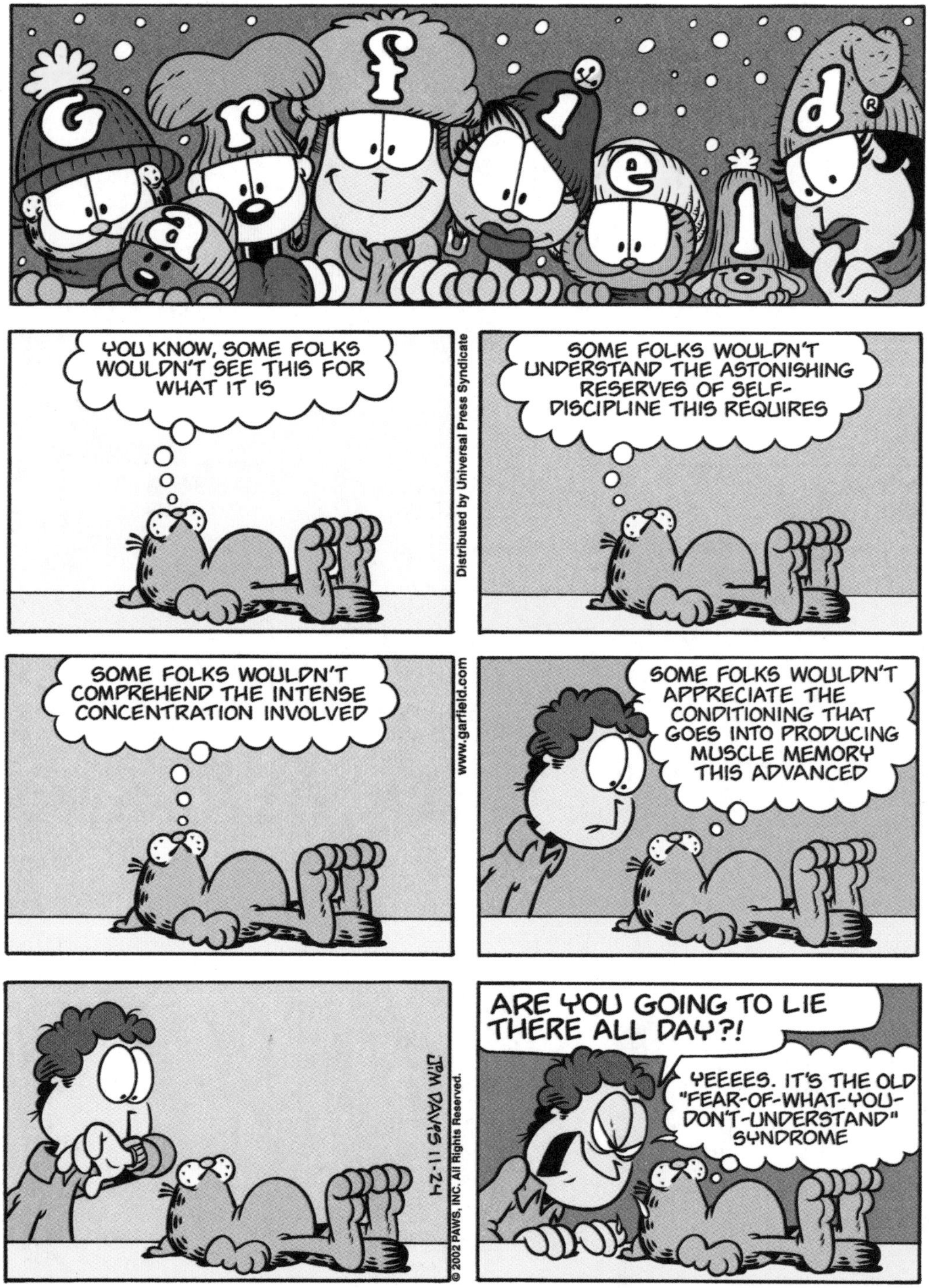
Garfield®
YOU KNOW, SOME FOLKS WOULDN'T SEE THIS FOR WHAT IT IS
SOME FOLKS WOULDN'T UNDERSTAND THE ASTONISHING RESERVES OF SELF-DISCIPLINE THIS REQUIRES
SOME FOLKS WOULDN'T COMPREHEND THE INTENSE CONCENTRATION INVOLVED
SOME FOLKS WOULDN'T APPRECIATE THE CONDITIONING THAT GOES INTO PRODUCING MUSCLE MEMORY THIS ADVANCED
ARE YOU GOING TO LIE THERE ALL DAY?!
YEEEES. IT'S THE OLD "FEAR-OF-WHAT-YOU-DON'T-UNDERSTAND" SYNDROME
Distributed by Universal Press Syndicate
www.garfield.com
JIM DAVIS 11-24
© 2002 PAWS, INC. All Rights Reserved.

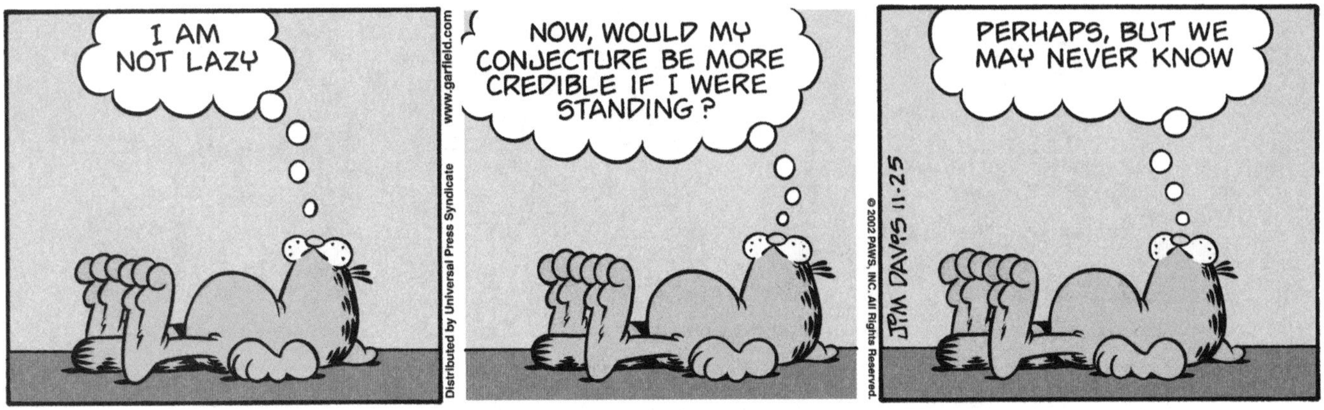
I AM NOT LAZY
Distributed by Universal Press Syndicate www.garfield.com
NOW, WOULD MY CONJECTURE BE MORE CREDIBLE IF I WERE STANDING?
© 2002 PAWS, INC. All Rights Reserved.
PERHAPS, BUT WE MAY NEVER KNOW
JIM DAVIS 11-25

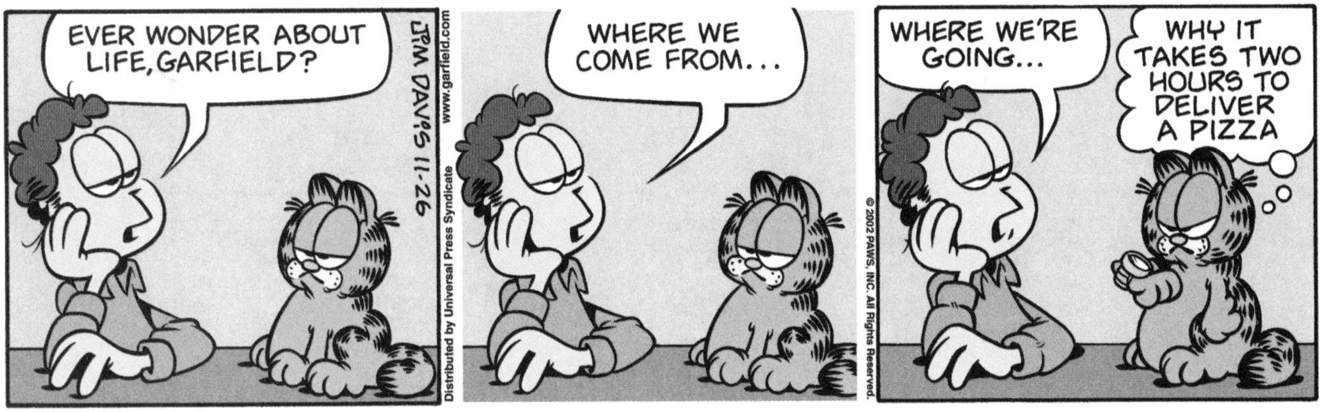
EVER WONDER ABOUT LIFE, GARFIELD?
JIM DAVIS 11-26
Distributed by Universal Press Syndicate www.garfield.com
WHERE WE COME FROM...
© 2002 PAWS, INC. All Rights Reserved.
WHERE WE'RE GOING...
WHY IT TAKES TWO HOURS TO DELIVER A PIZZA

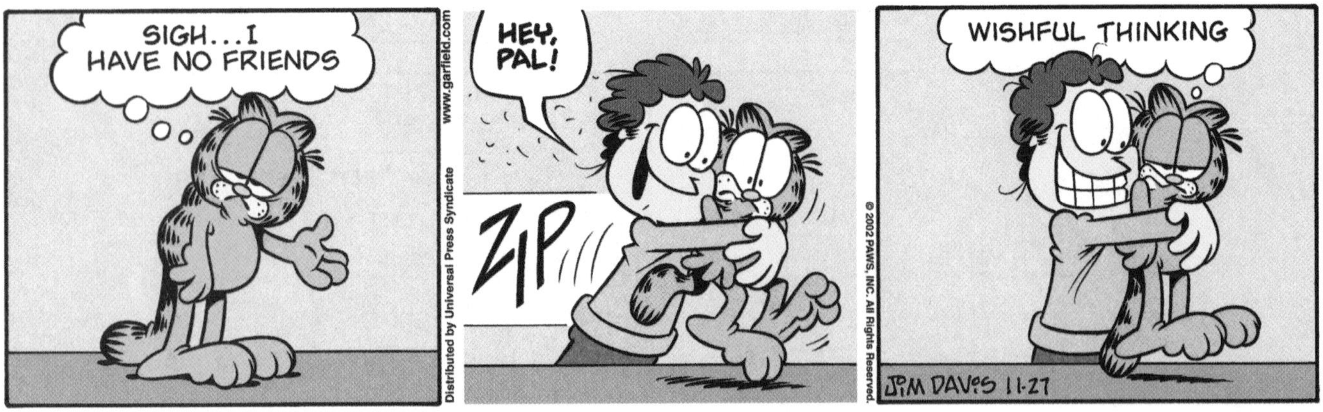
SIGH... I HAVE NO FRIENDS
Distributed by Universal Press Syndicate www.garfield.com
HEY, PAL!
ZIP
© 2002 PAWS, INC. All Rights Reserved.
WISHFUL THINKING
JIM DAVIS 11-27

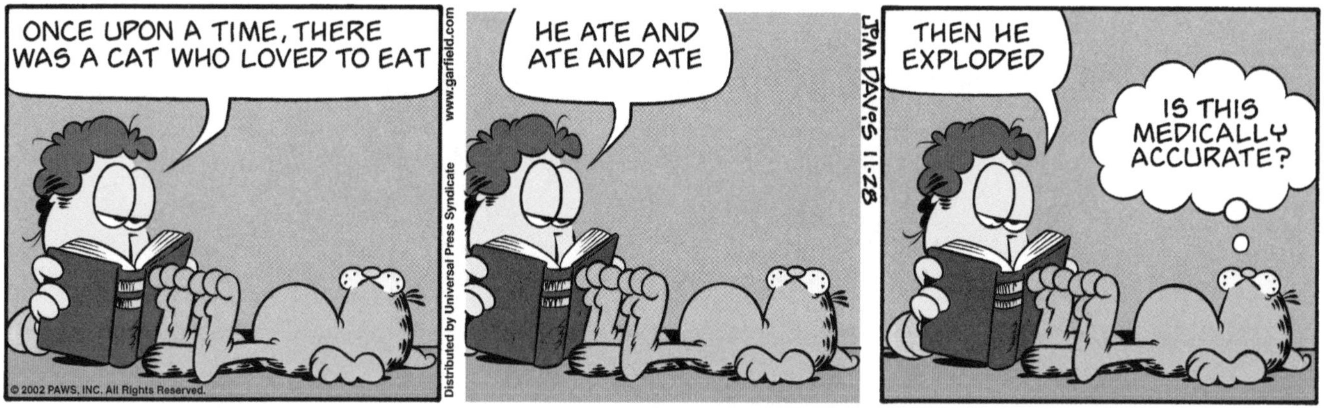
ONCE UPON A TIME, THERE WAS A CAT WHO LOVED TO EAT
HE ATE AND ATE AND ATE
THEN HE EXPLODED
IS THIS MEDICALLY ACCURATE?
JIM DAVIS 11-28
© 2002 PAWS, INC. All Rights Reserved.
Distributed by Universal Press Syndicate
www.garfield.com

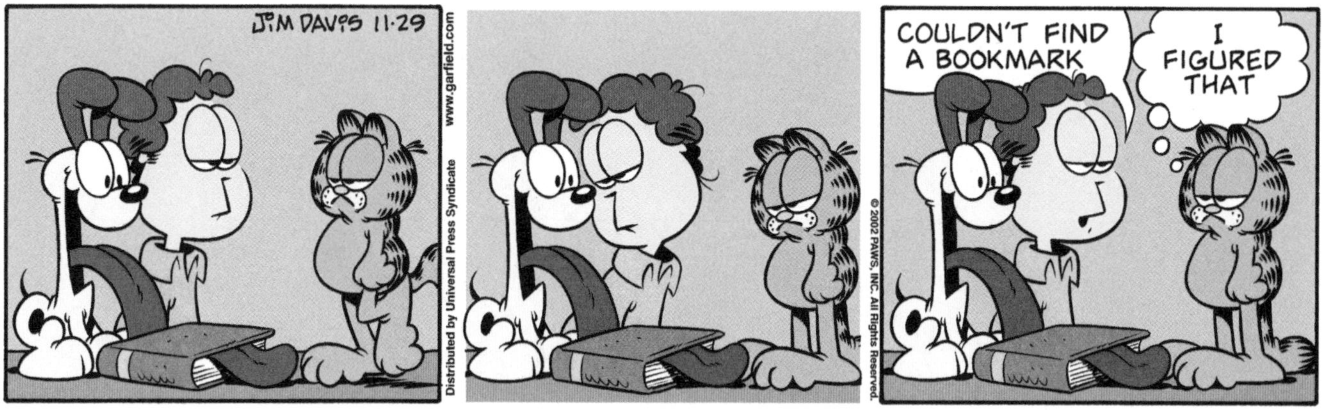
JIM DAVIS 11-29
COULDN'T FIND A BOOKMARK
I FIGURED THAT
© 2002 PAWS, INC. All Rights Reserved.
Distributed by Universal Press Syndicate
www.garfield.com

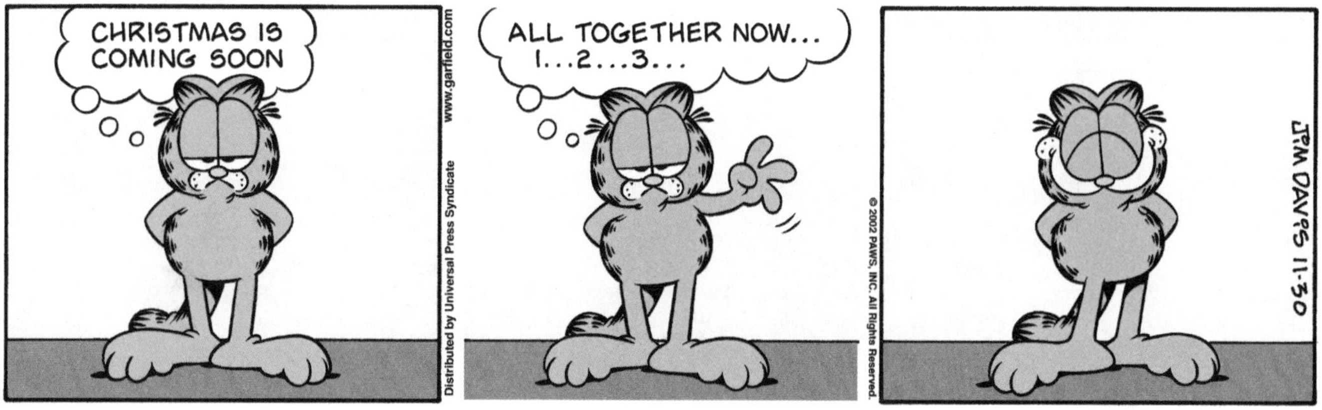
CHRISTMAS IS COMING SOON
ALL TOGETHER NOW... 1...2...3...
JIM DAVIS 11-30
© 2002 PAWS, INC. All Rights Reserved.
Distributed by Universal Press Syndicate
www.garfield.com

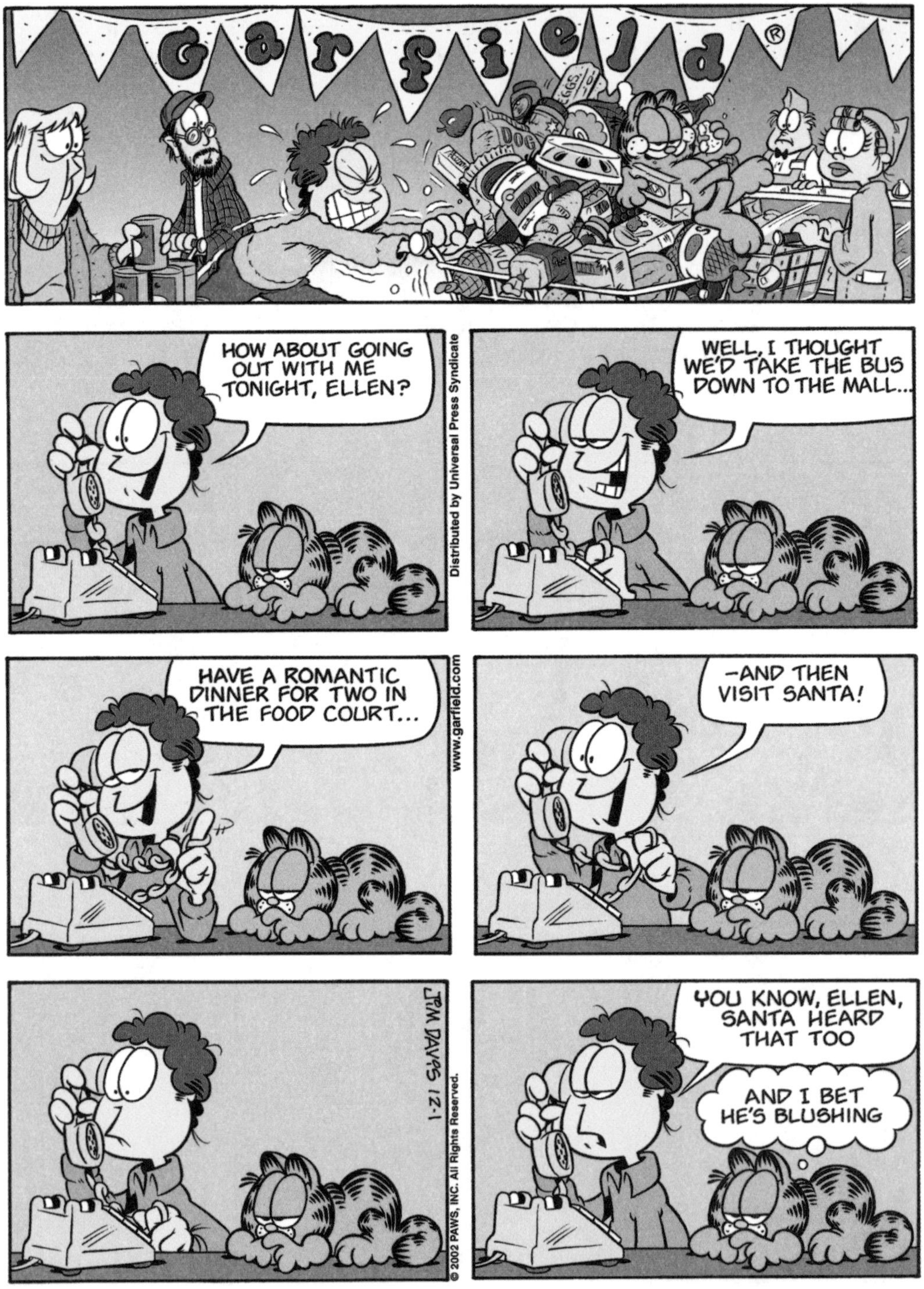
Garfield®
HOW ABOUT GOING OUT WITH ME TONIGHT, ELLEN?
WELL, I THOUGHT WE'D TAKE THE BUS DOWN TO THE MALL...
HAVE A ROMANTIC DINNER FOR TWO IN THE FOOD COURT...
–AND THEN VISIT SANTA!
YOU KNOW, ELLEN, SANTA HEARD THAT TOO
AND I BET HE'S BLUSHING
Distributed by Universal Press Syndicate
www.garfield.com
JIM DAVIS 12-1
© 2002 PAWS, INC. All Rights Reserved.

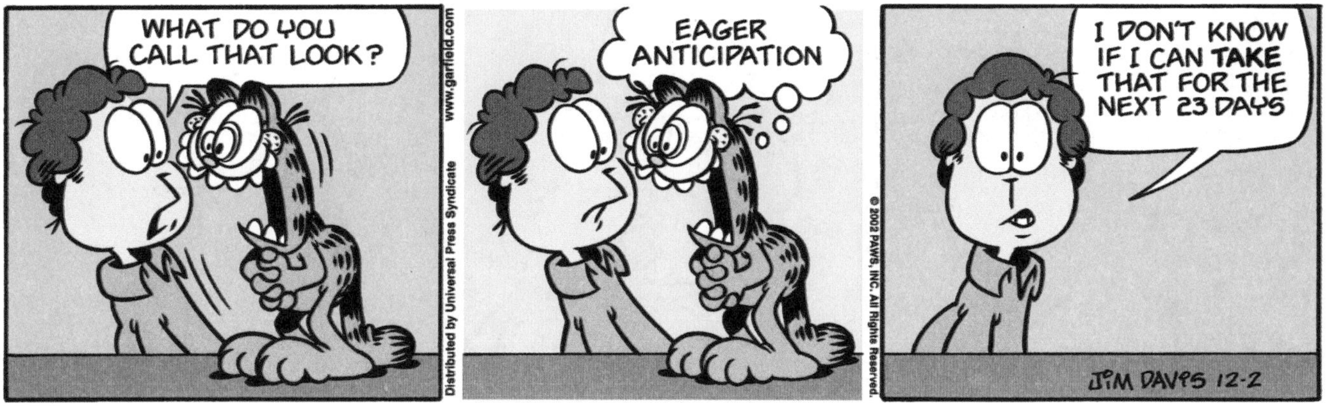
WHAT DO YOU CALL THAT LOOK?
EAGER ANTICIPATION
I DON'T KNOW IF I CAN **TAKE** THAT FOR THE NEXT 23 DAYS
JIM DAVIS 12-2
Distributed by Universal Press Syndicate www.garfield.com
© 2002 PAWS, INC. All Rights Reserved.

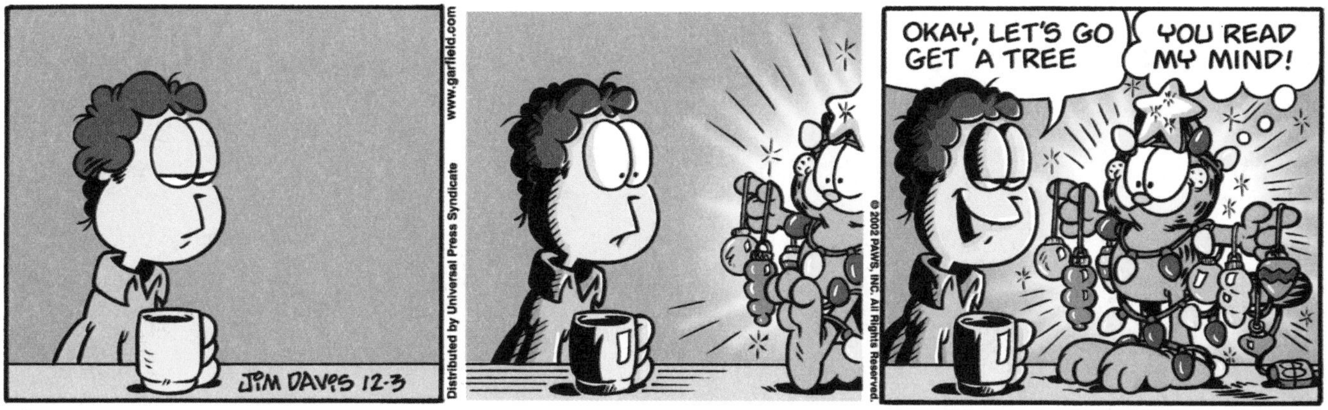
JIM DAVIS 12-3
OKAY, LET'S GO GET A TREE
YOU READ MY MIND!
Distributed by Universal Press Syndicate www.garfield.com
© 2002 PAWS, INC. All Rights Reserved.

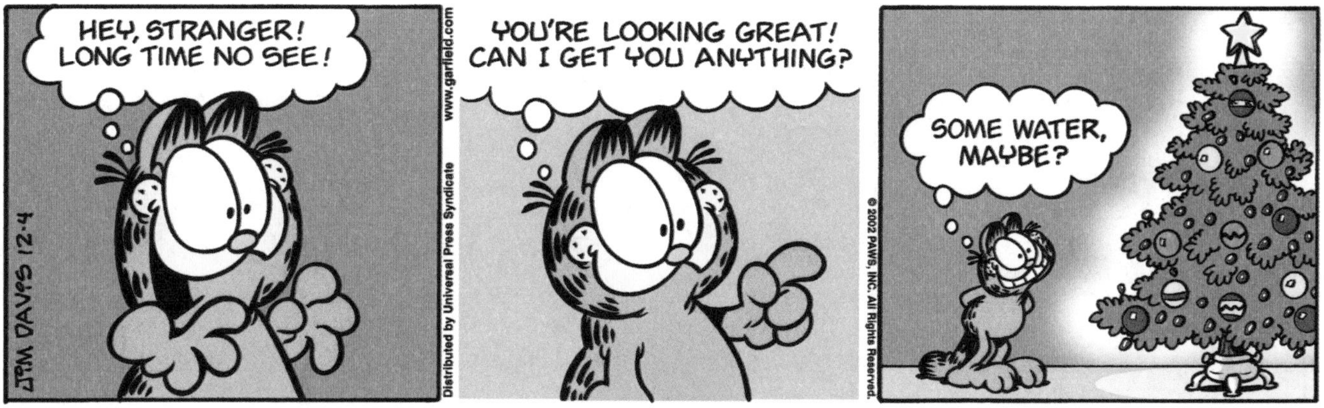
HEY, STRANGER! LONG TIME NO SEE!
JIM DAVIS 12-4
YOU'RE LOOKING GREAT! CAN I GET YOU ANYTHING?
SOME WATER, MAYBE?
Distributed by Universal Press Syndicate www.garfield.com
© 2002 PAWS, INC. All Rights Reserved.

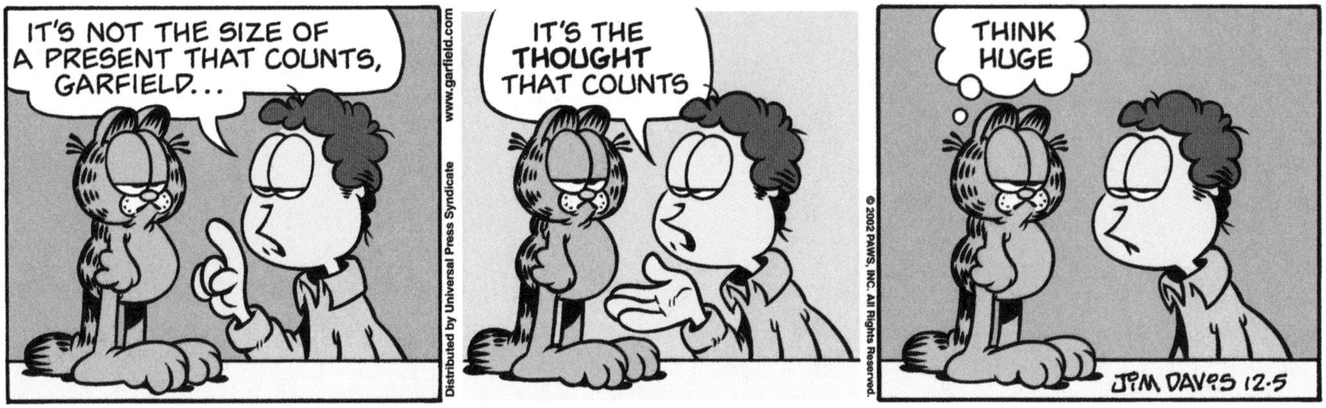
IT'S NOT THE SIZE OF A PRESENT THAT COUNTS, GARFIELD...
IT'S THE THOUGHT THAT COUNTS
THINK HUGE
JIM DAVIS 12·5
www.garfield.com
Distributed by Universal Press Syndicate
© 2002 PAWS, INC. All Rights Reserved.

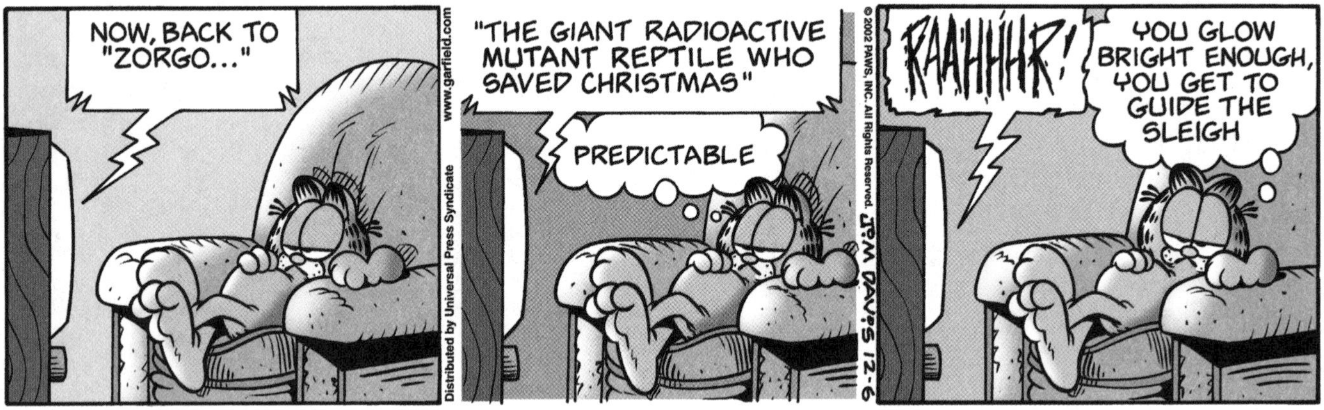
NOW, BACK TO "ZORGO..."
"THE GIANT RADIOACTIVE MUTANT REPTILE WHO SAVED CHRISTMAS"
PREDICTABLE
RAAHHHR!
YOU GLOW BRIGHT ENOUGH, YOU GET TO GUIDE THE SLEIGH
JIM DAVIS 12·6
www.garfield.com
Distributed by Universal Press Syndicate
© 2002 PAWS, INC. All Rights Reserved.

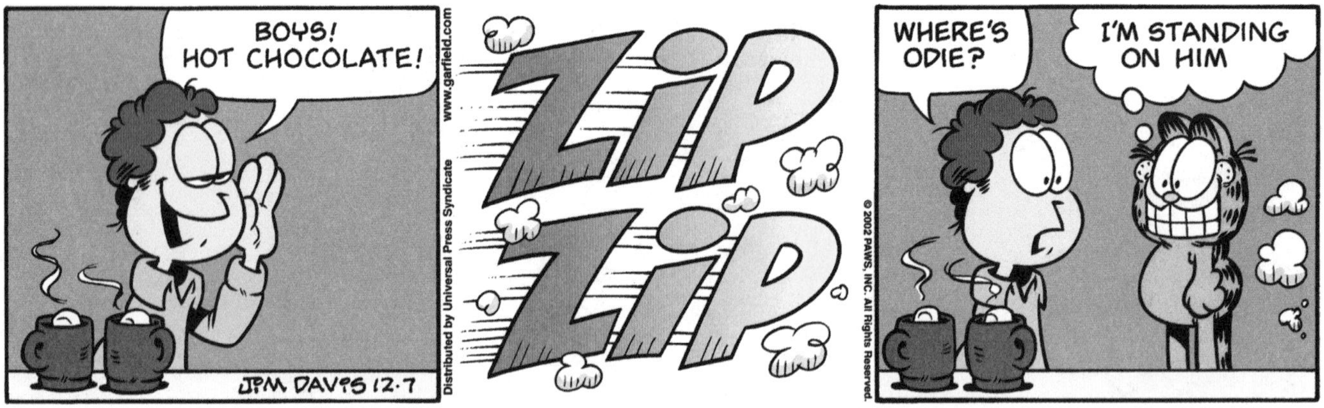
BOYS! HOT CHOCOLATE!
ZIP
ZIP
WHERE'S ODIE?
I'M STANDING ON HIM
JIM DAVIS 12·7
www.garfield.com
Distributed by Universal Press Syndicate
© 2002 PAWS, INC. All Rights Reserved.

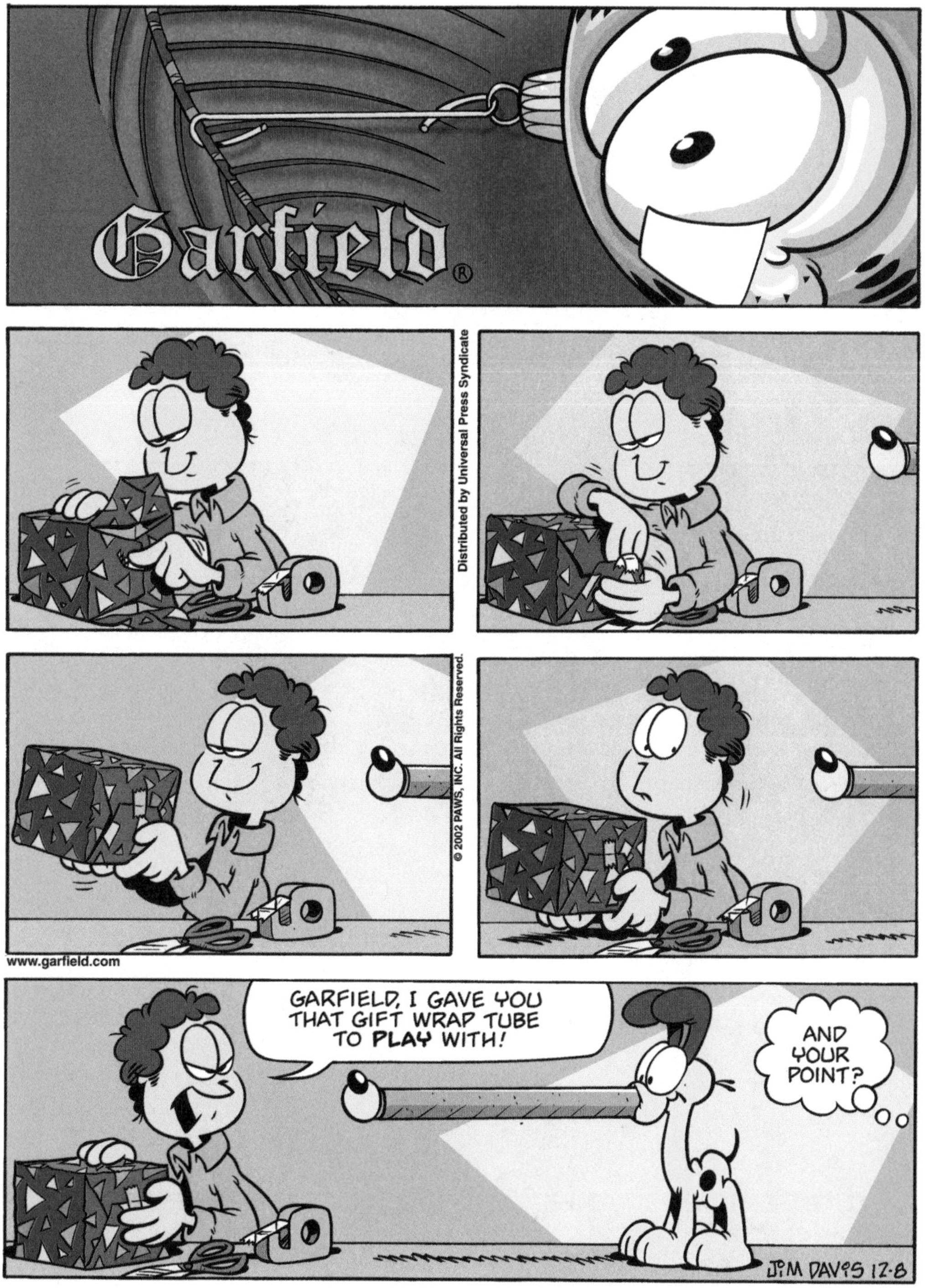
Garfield®
Distributed by Universal Press Syndicate
© 2002 PAWS, INC. All Rights Reserved.
www.garfield.com
GARFIELD, I GAVE YOU THAT GIFT WRAP TUBE TO PLAY WITH!
AND YOUR POINT?
JIM DAVIS 12-8

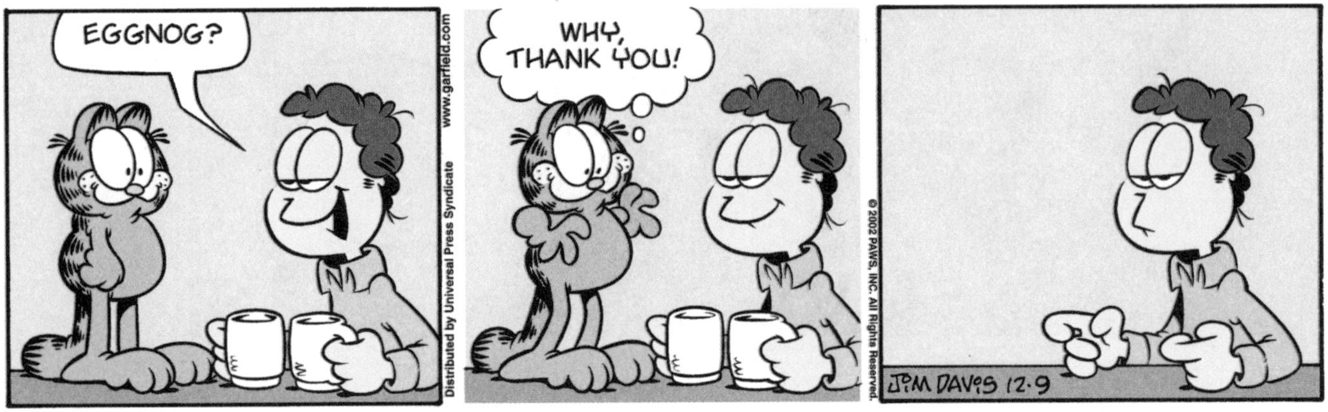
EGGNOG?
WHY, THANK YOU!
www.garfield.com
Distributed by Universal Press Syndicate
© 2002 PAWS, INC. All Rights Reserved.
JIM DAVIS 12·9

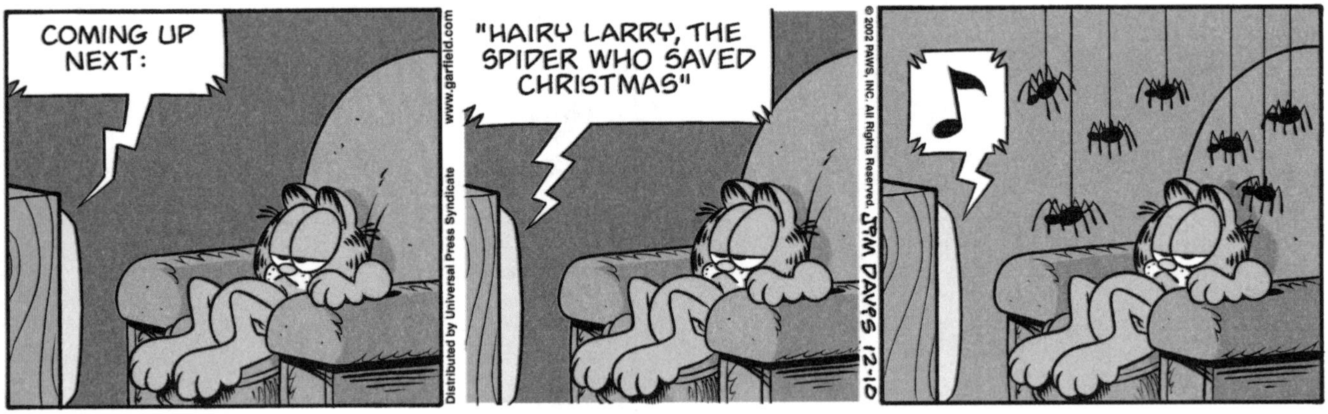
COMING UP NEXT:
"HAIRY LARRY, THE SPIDER WHO SAVED CHRISTMAS"
www.garfield.com
Distributed by Universal Press Syndicate
© 2002 PAWS, INC. All Rights Reserved.
JIM DAVIS 12-10

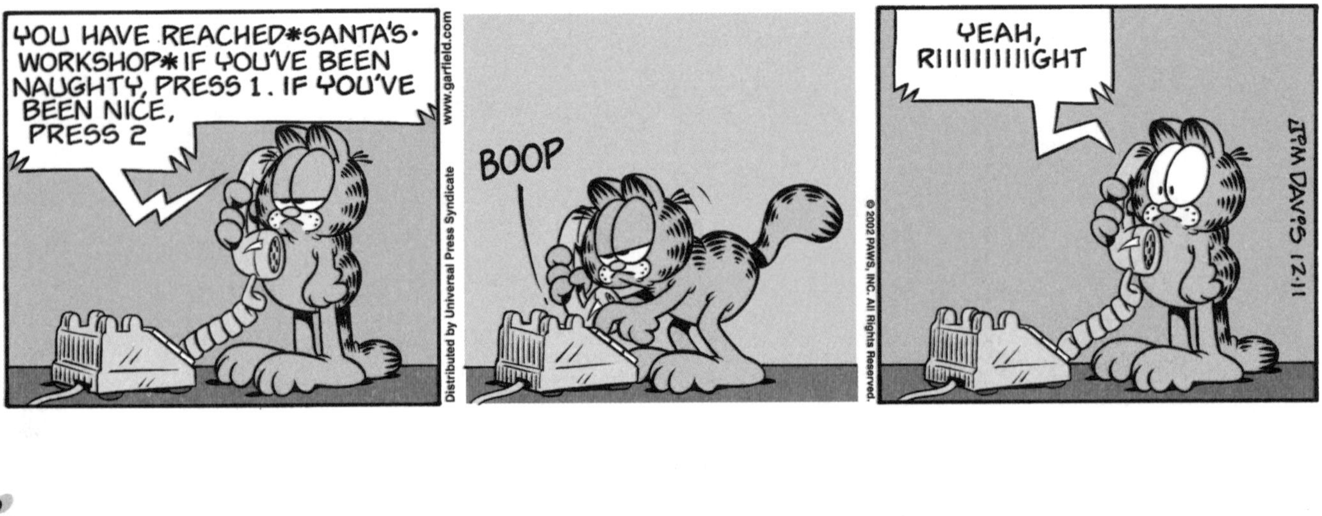
YOU HAVE REACHED*SANTA'S·WORKSHOP*IF YOU'VE BEEN NAUGHTY, PRESS 1. IF YOU'VE BEEN NICE, PRESS 2
BOOP
YEAH, RIIIIIIIIIIGHT
www.garfield.com
Distributed by Universal Press Syndicate
© 2002 PAWS, INC. All Rights Reserved.
JIM DAVIS 12·11

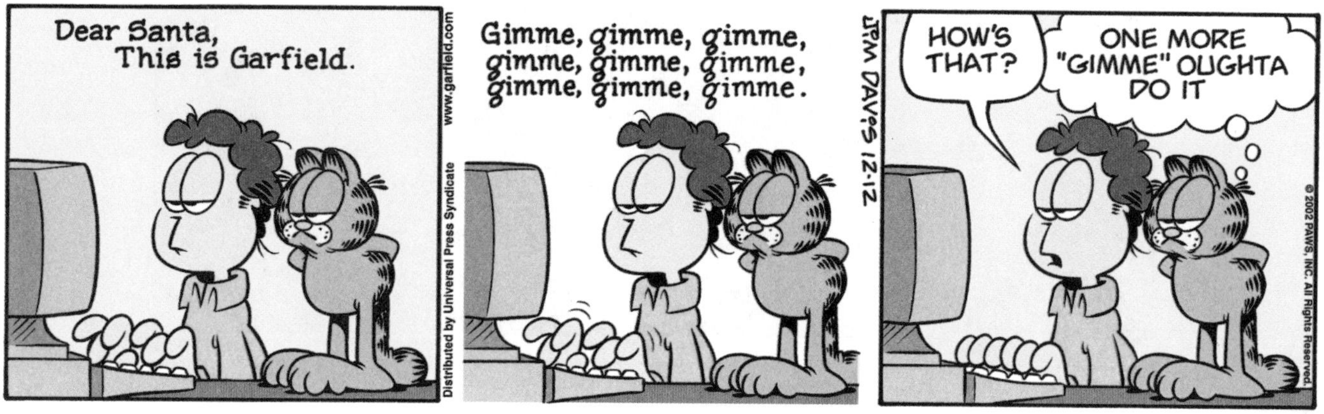
Dear Santa,
This is Garfield.
Gimme, gimme, gimme, gimme, gimme, gimme, gimme, gimme, gimme.
HOW'S THAT?
ONE MORE "GIMME" OUGHTA DO IT
JIM DAVIS 12-12
www.garfield.com
Distributed by Universal Press Syndicate
© 2002 PAWS, INC. All Rights Reserved.

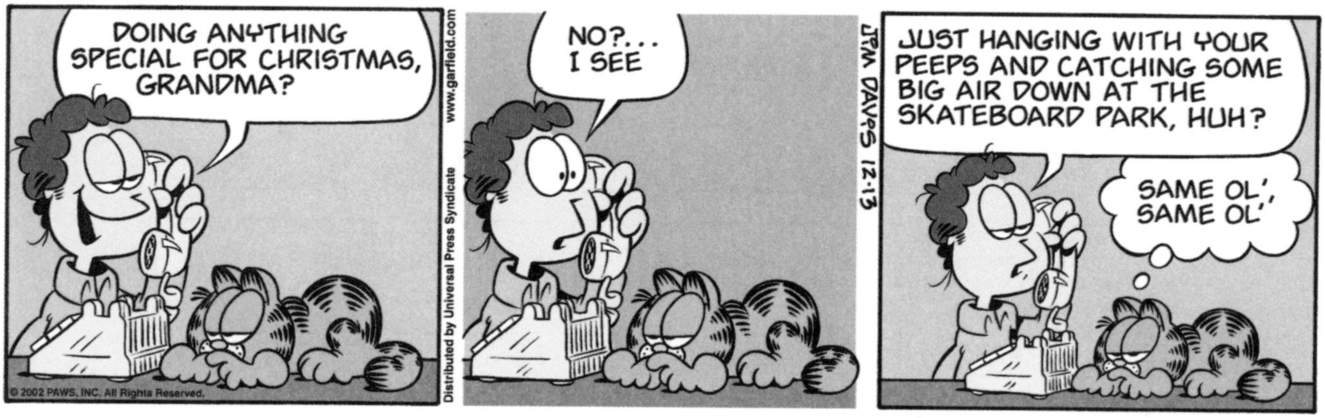
DOING ANYTHING SPECIAL FOR CHRISTMAS, GRANDMA?
NO?... I SEE
JUST HANGING WITH YOUR PEEPS AND CATCHING SOME BIG AIR DOWN AT THE SKATEBOARD PARK, HUH?
SAME OL', SAME OL'
JIM DAVIS 12-13
www.garfield.com
Distributed by Universal Press Syndicate
© 2002 PAWS, INC. All Rights Reserved.

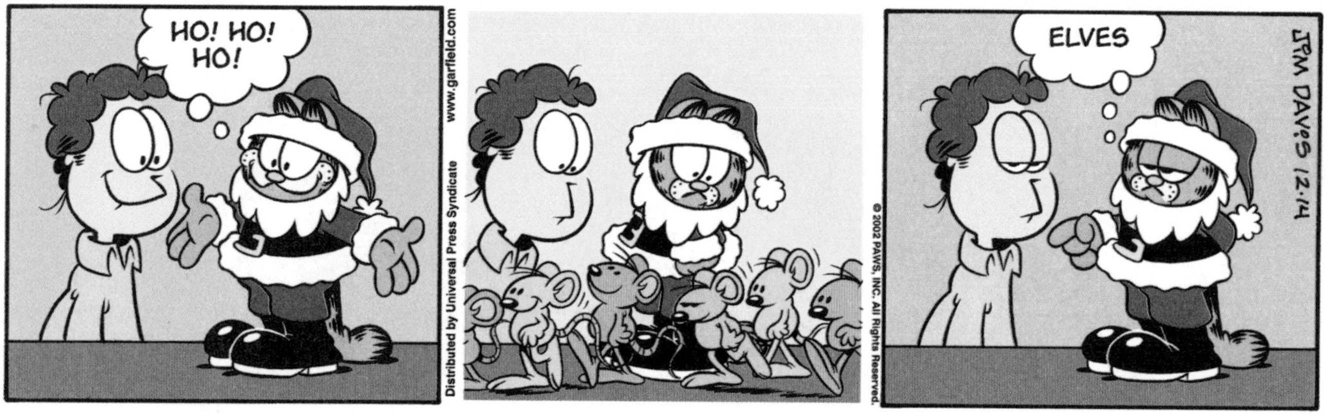
HO! HO! HO!
ELVES
JIM DAVIS 12-14
www.garfield.com
Distributed by Universal Press Syndicate
© 2002 PAWS, INC. All Rights Reserved.

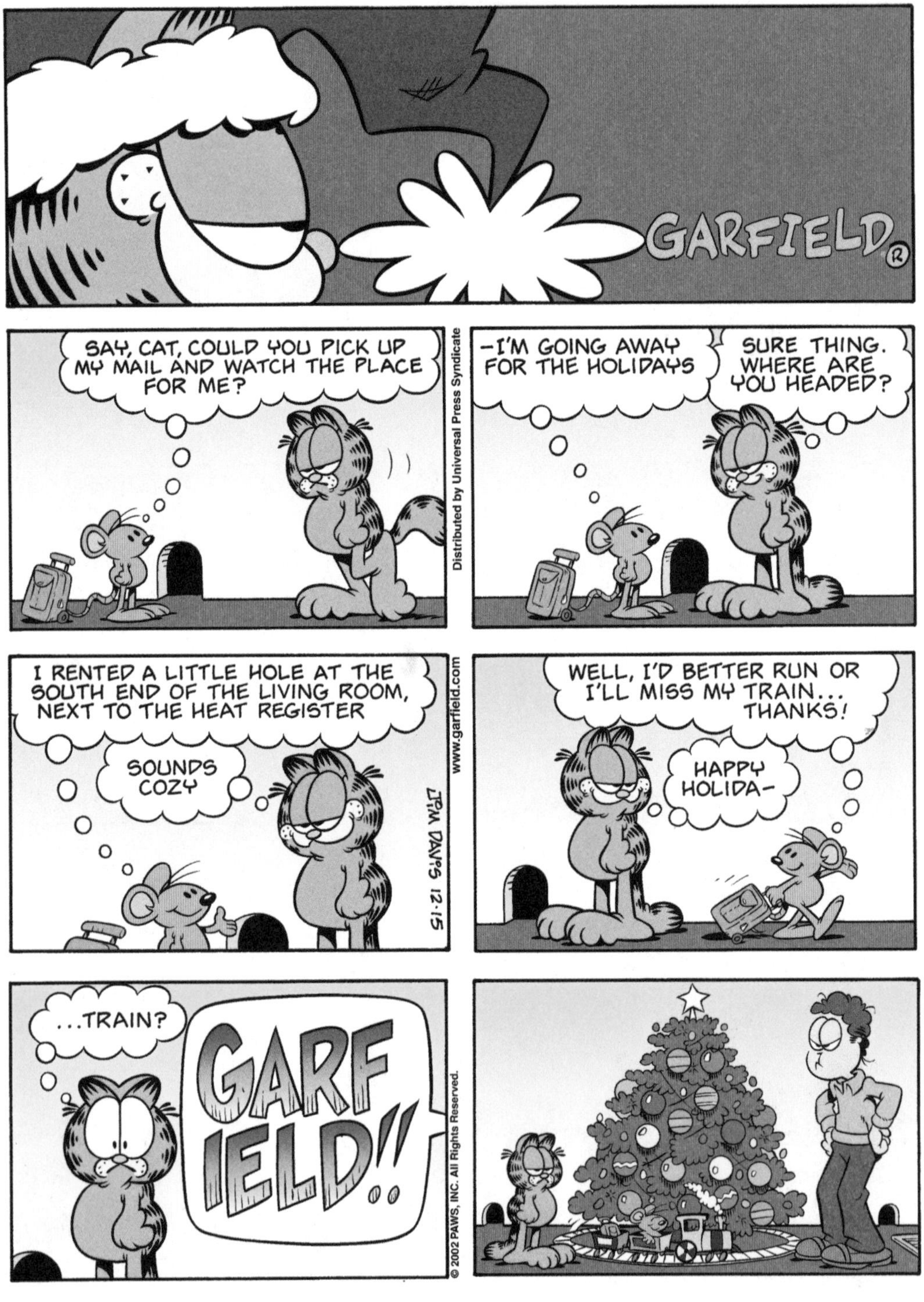
GARFIELD®
SAY, CAT, COULD YOU PICK UP MY MAIL AND WATCH THE PLACE FOR ME?
Distributed by Universal Press Syndicate
–I'M GOING AWAY FOR THE HOLIDAYS
SURE THING. WHERE ARE YOU HEADED?
I RENTED A LITTLE HOLE AT THE SOUTH END OF THE LIVING ROOM, NEXT TO THE HEAT REGISTER
SOUNDS COZY
www.garfield.com
JIM DAVIS 12-15
WELL, I'D BETTER RUN OR I'LL MISS MY TRAIN... THANKS!
HAPPY HOLIDA–
...TRAIN?
GARFIELD!!
© 2002 PAWS, INC. All Rights Reserved.

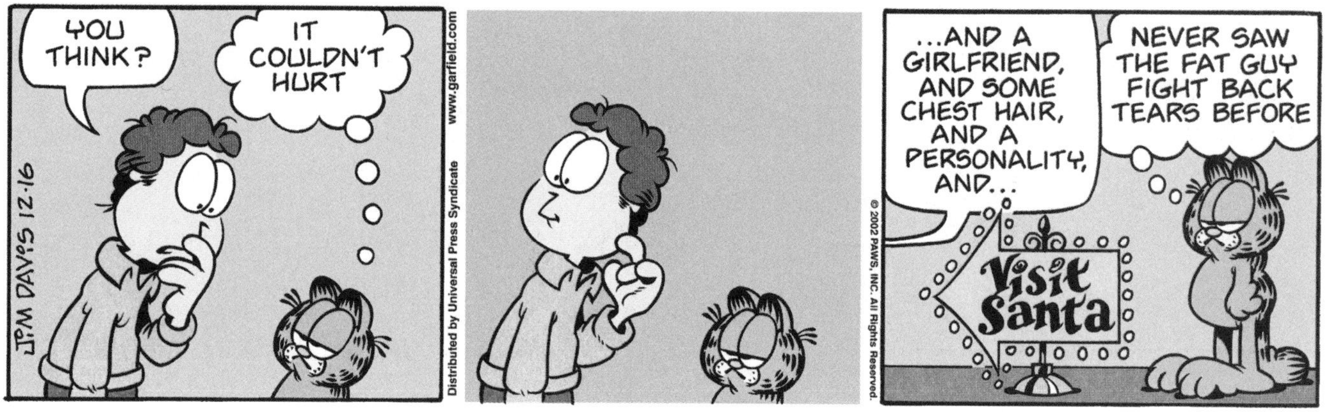
JIM DAVIS 12-16
YOU THINK?
IT COULDN'T HURT
Distributed by Universal Press Syndicate www.garfield.com
...AND A GIRLFRIEND, AND SOME CHEST HAIR, AND A PERSONALITY, AND...
Visit Santa
NEVER SAW THE FAT GUY FIGHT BACK TEARS BEFORE
© 2002 PAWS, INC. All Rights Reserved.

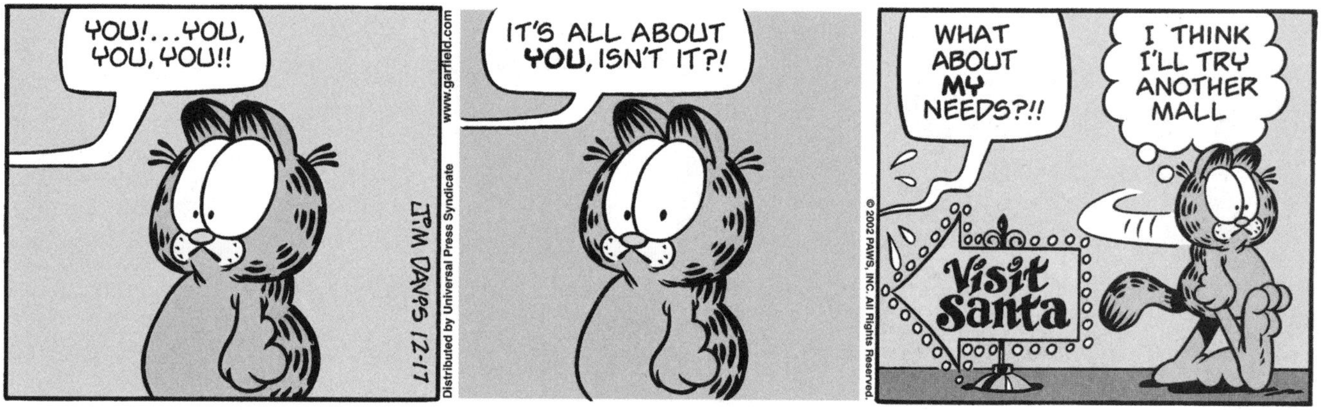
YOU!...YOU, YOU, YOU!!
JIM DAVIS 12-17
Distributed by Universal Press Syndicate www.garfield.com
IT'S ALL ABOUT YOU, ISN'T IT?!
WHAT ABOUT MY NEEDS?!!
Visit Santa
I THINK I'LL TRY ANOTHER MALL
© 2002 PAWS, INC. All Rights Reserved.

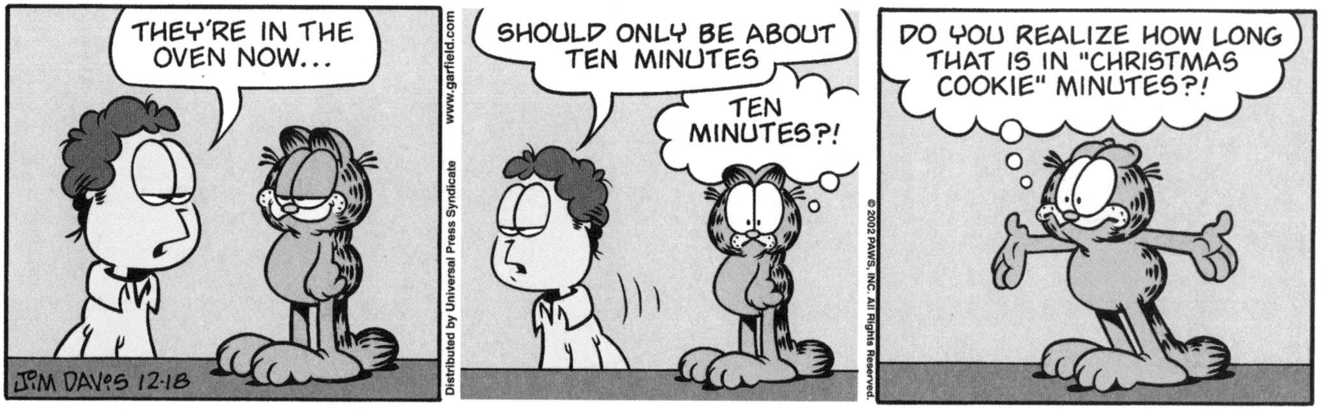
THEY'RE IN THE OVEN NOW...
JIM DAVIS 12-18
Distributed by Universal Press Syndicate www.garfield.com
SHOULD ONLY BE ABOUT TEN MINUTES
TEN MINUTES?!
© 2002 PAWS, INC. All Rights Reserved.
DO YOU REALIZE HOW LONG THAT IS IN "CHRISTMAS COOKIE" MINUTES?!

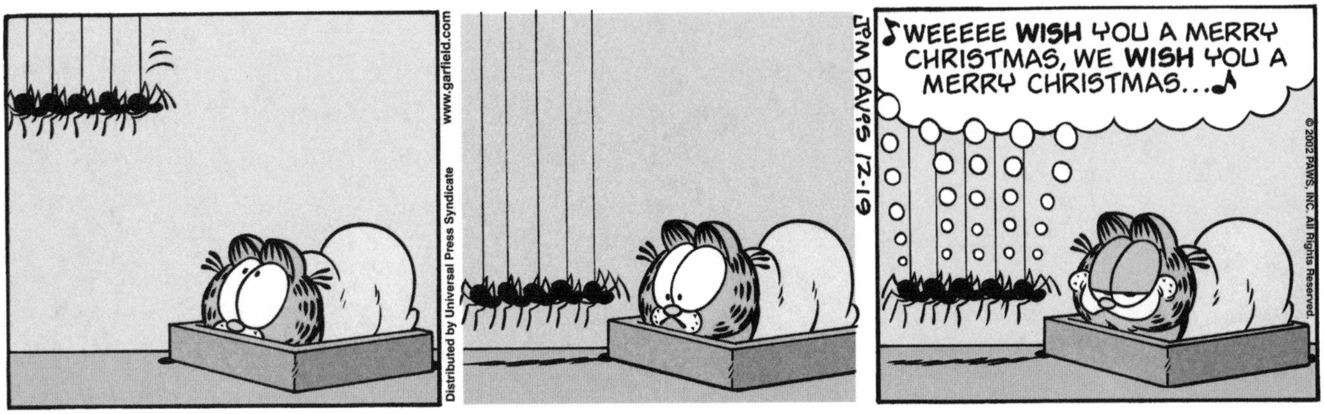
www.garfield.com
Distributed by Universal Press Syndicate
JIM DAVIS 12-19
♪ WEEEEE **WISH** YOU A MERRY CHRISTMAS, WE **WISH** YOU A MERRY CHRISTMAS...♪
© 2002 PAWS, INC. All Rights Reserved.

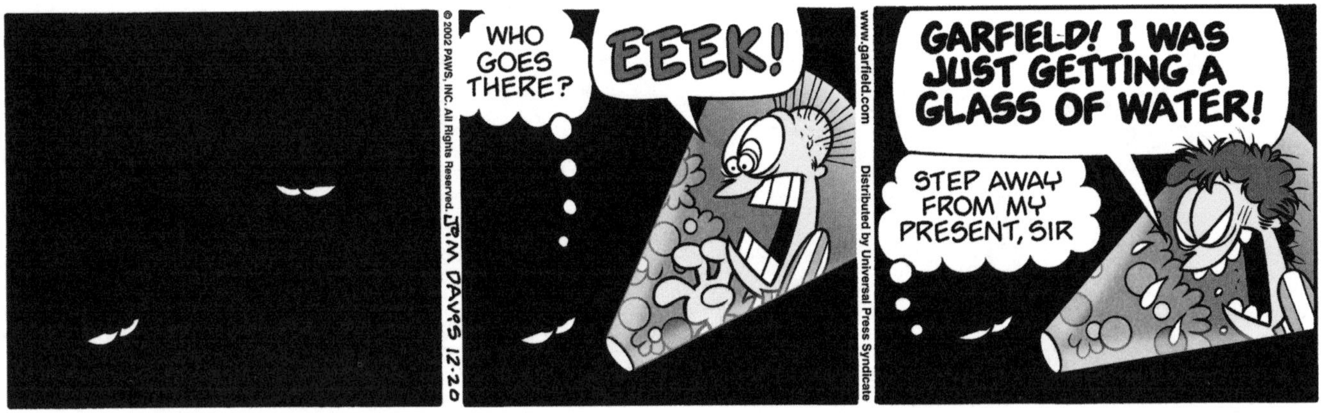
© 2002 PAWS, INC. All Rights Reserved.
JIM DAVIS 12-20
WHO GOES THERE?
EEEK!
www.garfield.com
Distributed by Universal Press Syndicate
GARFIELD! I WAS JUST GETTING A GLASS OF WATER!
STEP AWAY FROM MY PRESENT, SIR

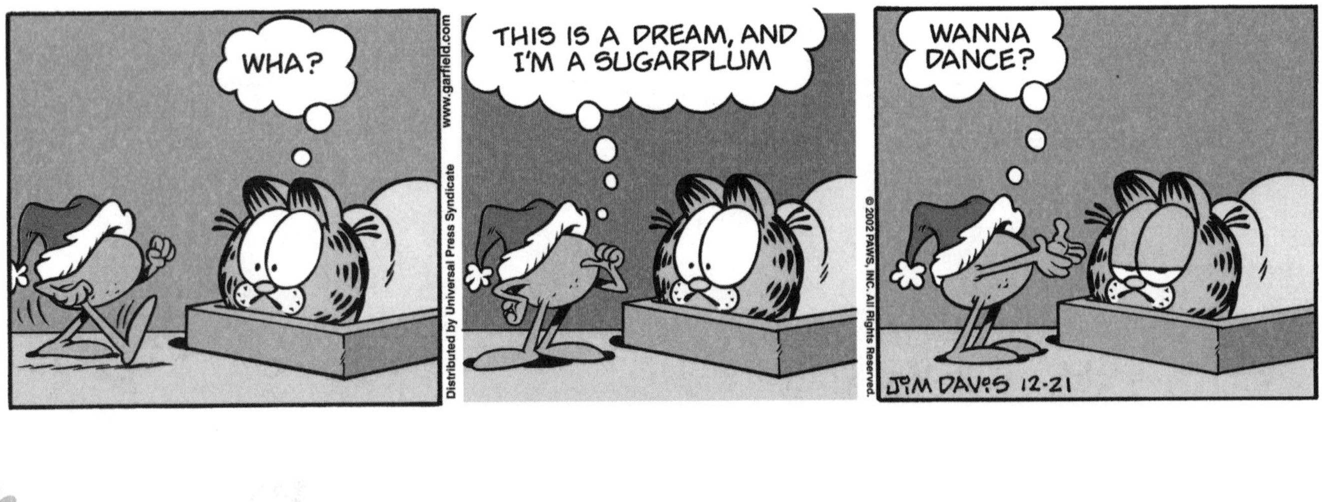
WHA?
www.garfield.com
Distributed by Universal Press Syndicate
THIS IS A DREAM, AND I'M A SUGARPLUM
© 2002 PAWS, INC. All Rights Reserved.
WANNA DANCE?
JIM DAVIS 12-21

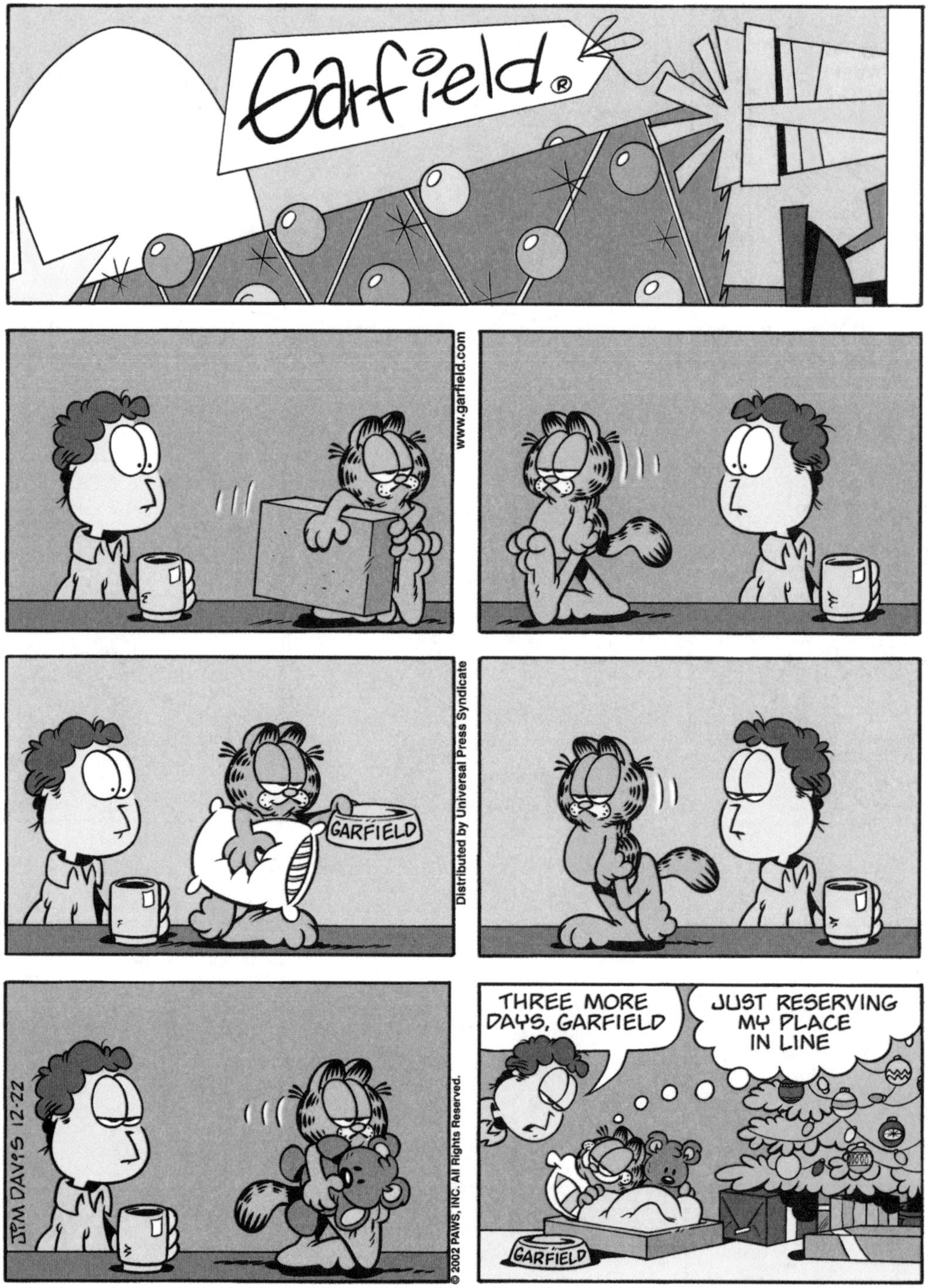
Garfield®
www.garfield.com
GARFIELD
Distributed by Universal Press Syndicate
JIM DAVIS 12-22
© 2002 PAWS, INC. All Rights Reserved.
THREE MORE DAYS, GARFIELD
JUST RESERVING MY PLACE IN LINE
GARFIELD

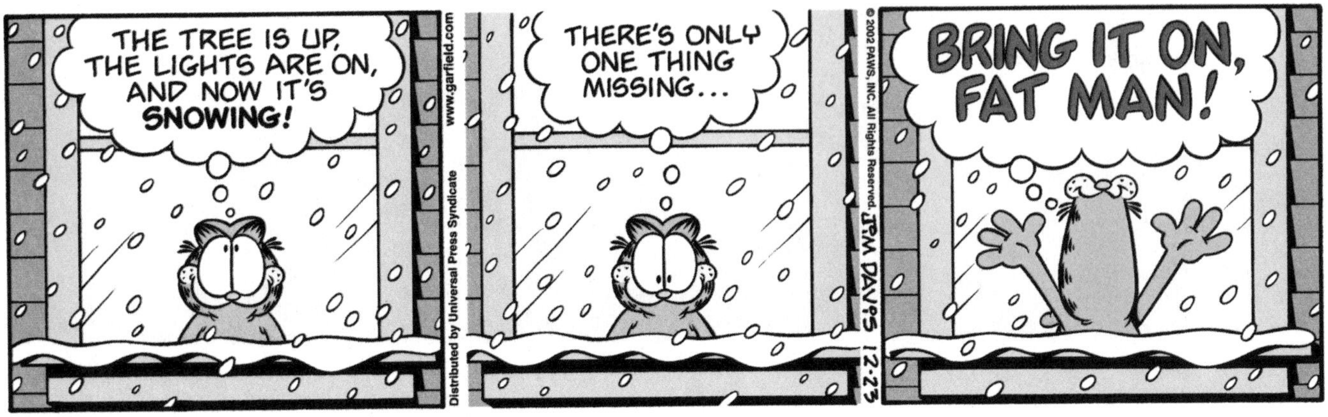
THE TREE IS UP, THE LIGHTS ARE ON, AND NOW IT'S SNOWING!
www.garfield.com
Distributed by Universal Press Syndicate
THERE'S ONLY ONE THING MISSING...
© 2002 PAWS, INC. All Rights Reserved.
JIM DAVIS 12·23
BRING IT ON, FAT MAN!

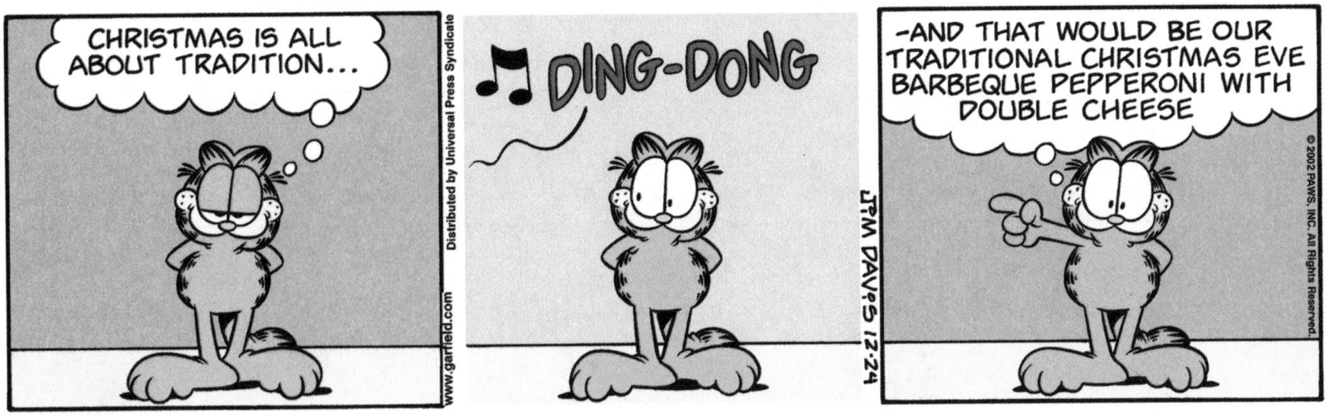
CHRISTMAS IS ALL ABOUT TRADITION...
Distributed by Universal Press Syndicate
www.garfield.com
DING-DONG
JIM DAVIS 12·24
-AND THAT WOULD BE OUR TRADITIONAL CHRISTMAS EVE BARBEQUE PEPPERONI WITH DOUBLE CHEESE
© 2002 PAWS, INC. All Rights Reserved.

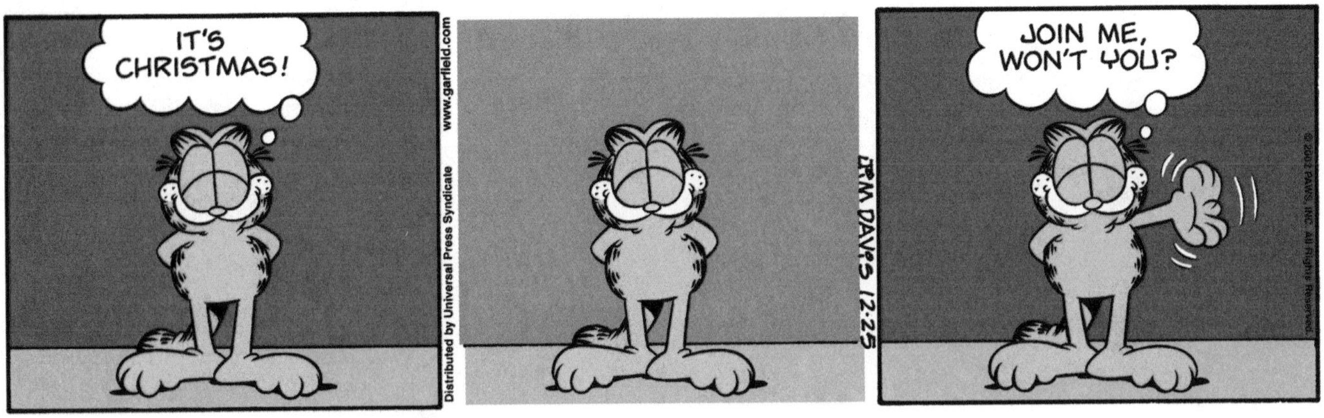
IT'S CHRISTMAS!
www.garfield.com
Distributed by Universal Press Syndicate
JIM DAVIS 12·25
JOIN ME, WON'T YOU?
© 2002 PAWS, INC. All Rights Reserved.

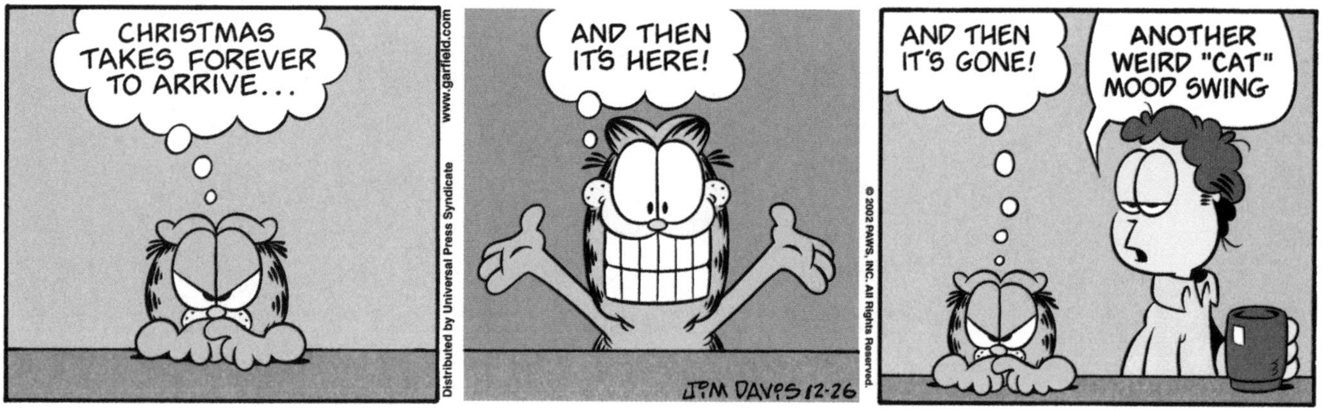
CHRISTMAS TAKES FOREVER TO ARRIVE...
AND THEN IT'S HERE!
AND THEN IT'S GONE!
ANOTHER WEIRD "CAT" MOOD SWING
JIM DAVIS 12-26
www.garfield.com
Distributed by Universal Press Syndicate
© 2002 PAWS, INC. All Rights Reserved.

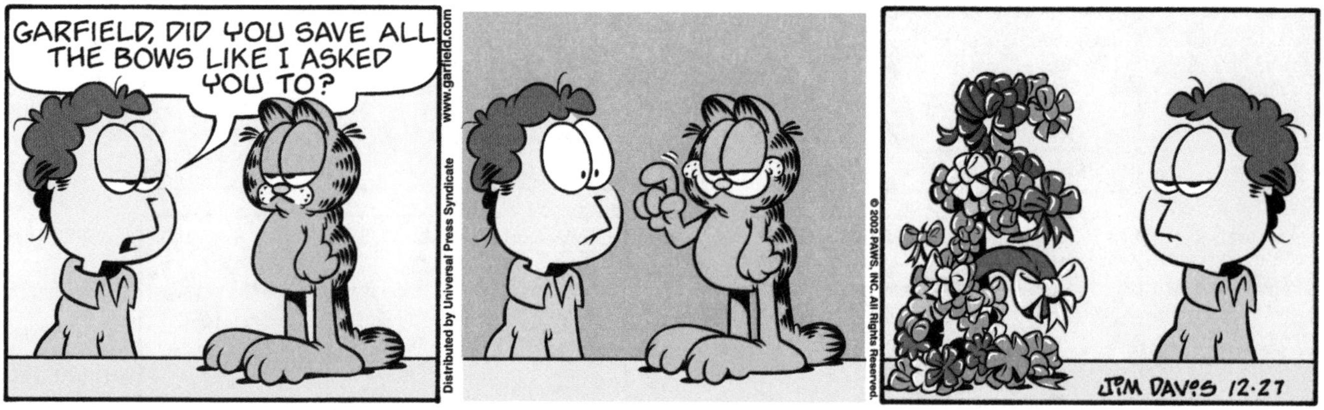
GARFIELD, DID YOU SAVE ALL THE BOWS LIKE I ASKED YOU TO?
JIM DAVIS 12-27
www.garfield.com
Distributed by Universal Press Syndicate
© 2002 PAWS, INC. All Rights Reserved.

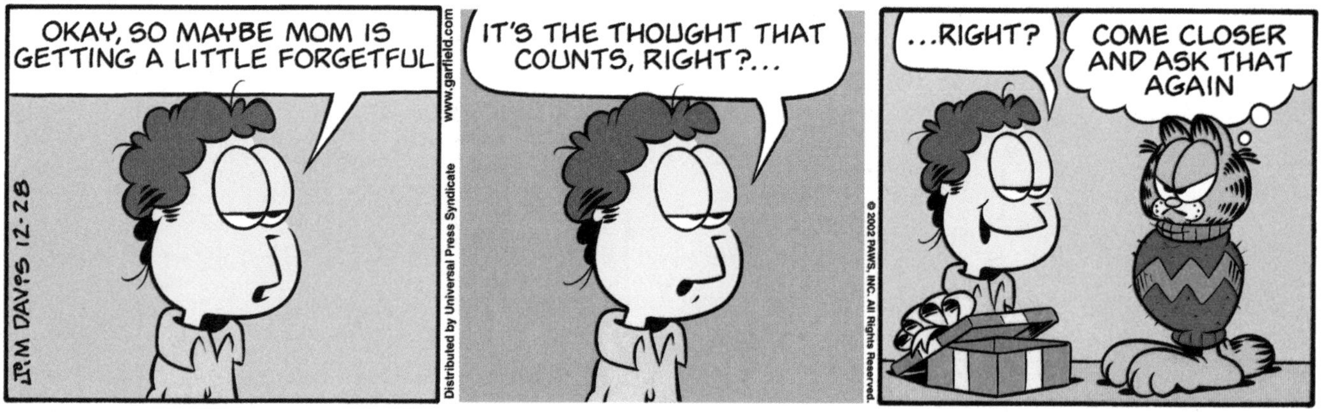
OKAY, SO MAYBE MOM IS GETTING A LITTLE FORGETFUL
IT'S THE THOUGHT THAT COUNTS, RIGHT?...
...RIGHT?
COME CLOSER AND ASK THAT AGAIN
JIM DAVIS 12-28
www.garfield.com
Distributed by Universal Press Syndicate
© 2002 PAWS, INC. All Rights Reserved.

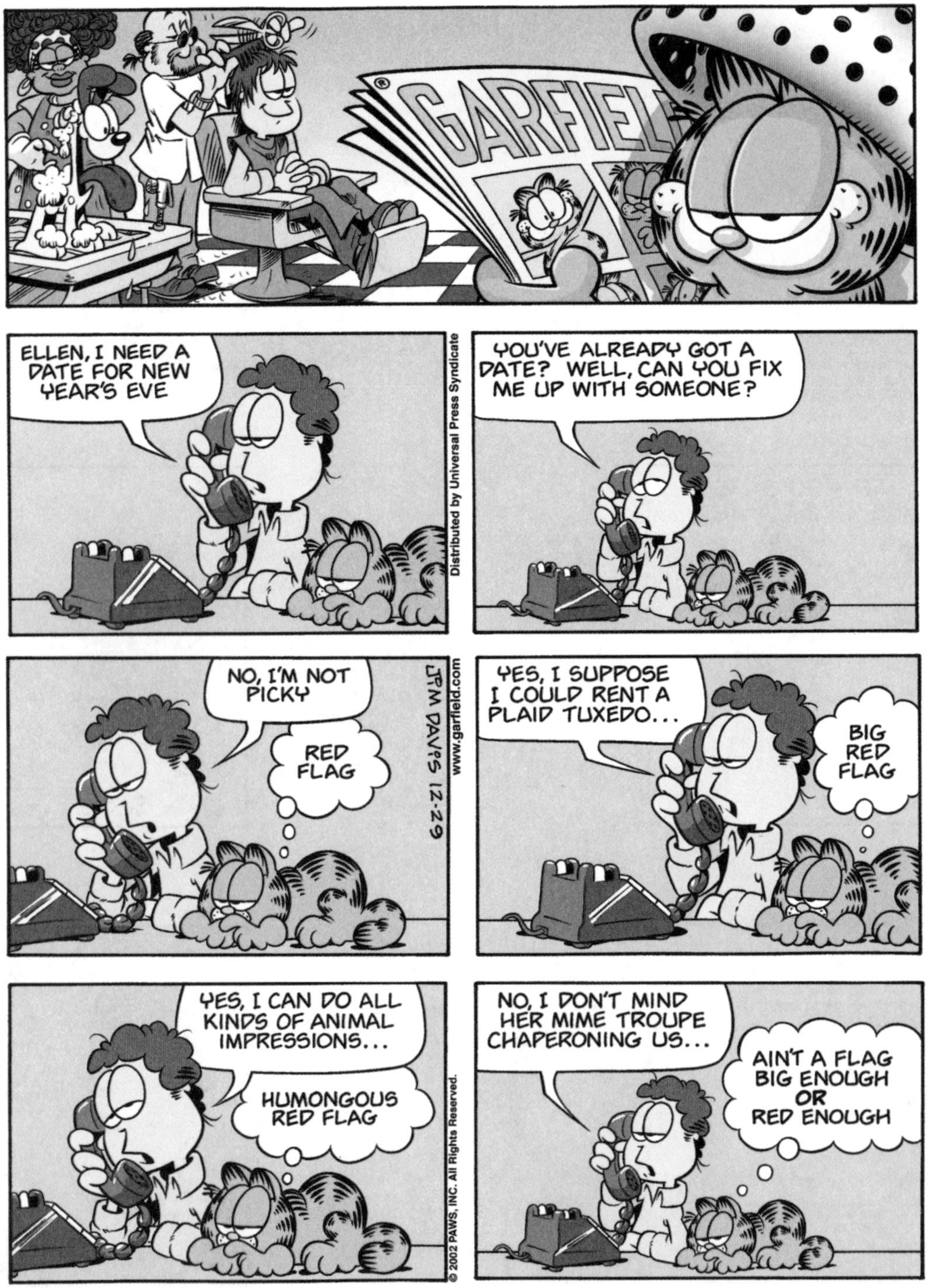
GARFIELD
ELLEN, I NEED A DATE FOR NEW YEAR'S EVE
YOU'VE ALREADY GOT A DATE? WELL, CAN YOU FIX ME UP WITH SOMEONE?
NO, I'M NOT PICKY
RED FLAG
YES, I SUPPOSE I COULD RENT A PLAID TUXEDO...
BIG RED FLAG
YES, I CAN DO ALL KINDS OF ANIMAL IMPRESSIONS...
HUMONGOUS RED FLAG
NO, I DON'T MIND HER MIME TROUPE CHAPERONING US...
AIN'T A FLAG BIG ENOUGH OR RED ENOUGH
JPM DAVIS 12-29
www.garfield.com
Distributed by Universal Press Syndicate
© 2002 PAWS, INC. All Rights Reserved.

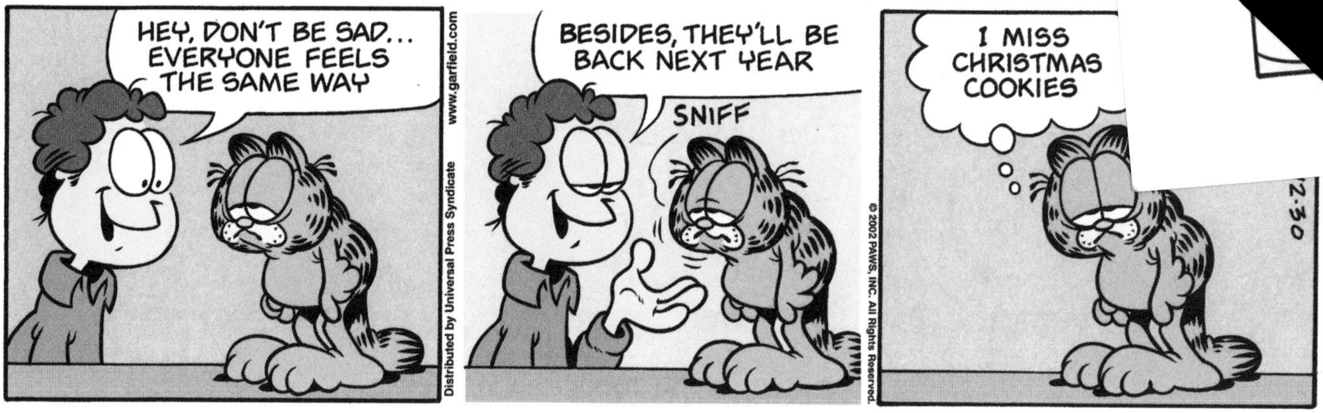
HEY, DON'T BE SAD... EVERYONE FEELS THE SAME WAY
www.garfield.com
Distributed by Universal Press Syndicate
BESIDES, THEY'LL BE BACK NEXT YEAR
SNIFF
© 2002 PAWS, INC. All Rights Reserved.
I MISS CHRISTMAS COOKIES

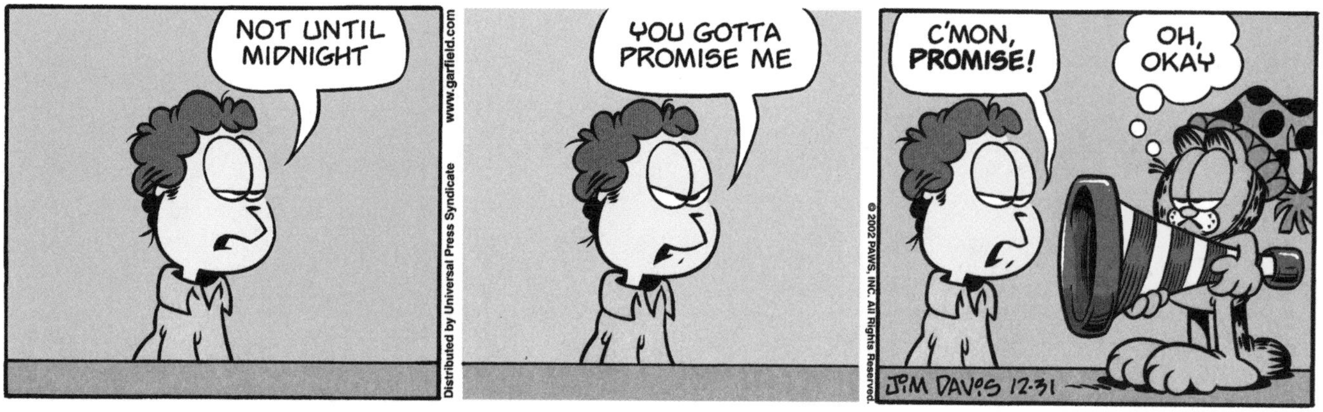
NOT UNTIL MIDNIGHT
www.garfield.com
Distributed by Universal Press Syndicate
YOU GOTTA PROMISE ME
© 2002 PAWS, INC. All Rights Reserved.
C'MON, **PROMISE**!
OH, OKAY
JIM DAVIS 12-31

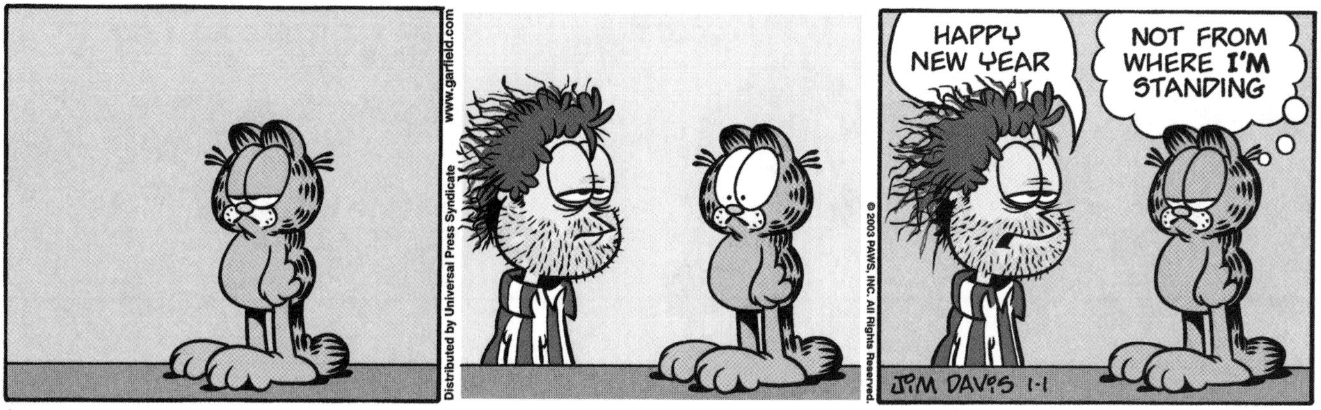
www.garfield.com
Distributed by Universal Press Syndicate
© 2003 PAWS, INC. All Rights Reserved.
HAPPY NEW YEAR
NOT FROM WHERE **I'M** STANDING
JIM DAVIS 1-1

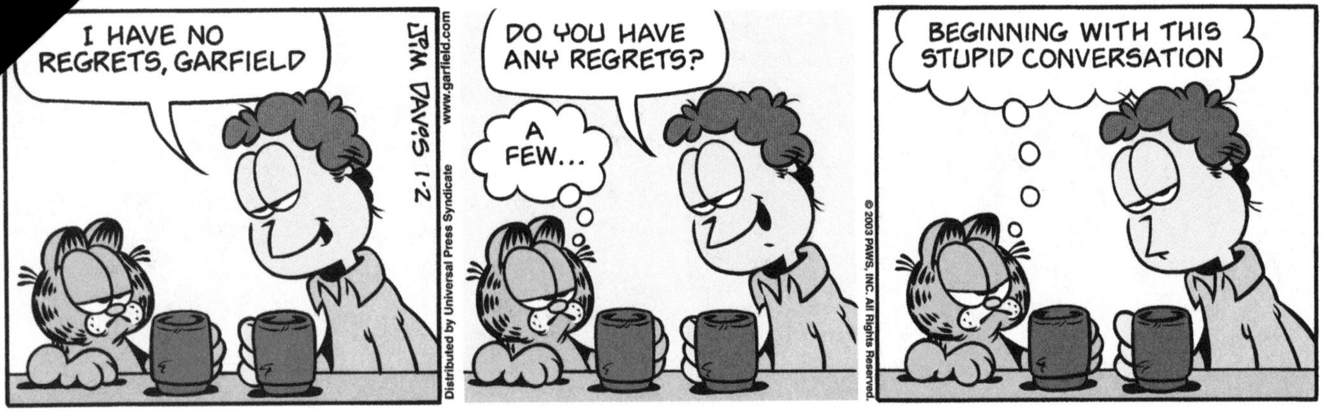
I HAVE NO REGRETS, GARFIELD
JIM DAVIS 1-2
www.garfield.com
Distributed by Universal Press Syndicate
DO YOU HAVE ANY REGRETS?
A FEW...
© 2003 PAWS, INC. All Rights Reserved.
BEGINNING WITH THIS STUPID CONVERSATION

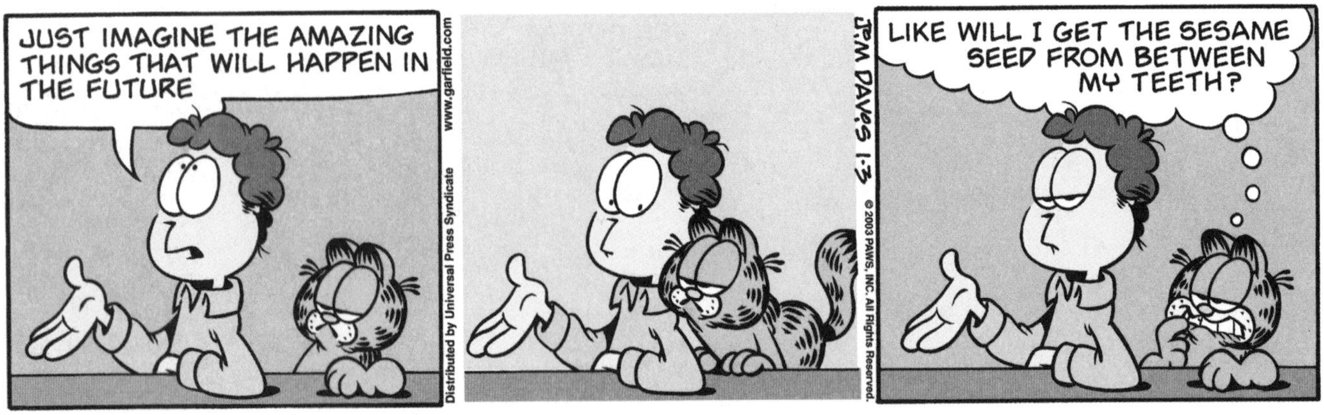
JUST IMAGINE THE AMAZING THINGS THAT WILL HAPPEN IN THE FUTURE
www.garfield.com
Distributed by Universal Press Syndicate
JIM DAVIS 1-3
© 2003 PAWS, INC. All Rights Reserved.
LIKE WILL I GET THE SESAME SEED FROM BETWEEN MY TEETH?

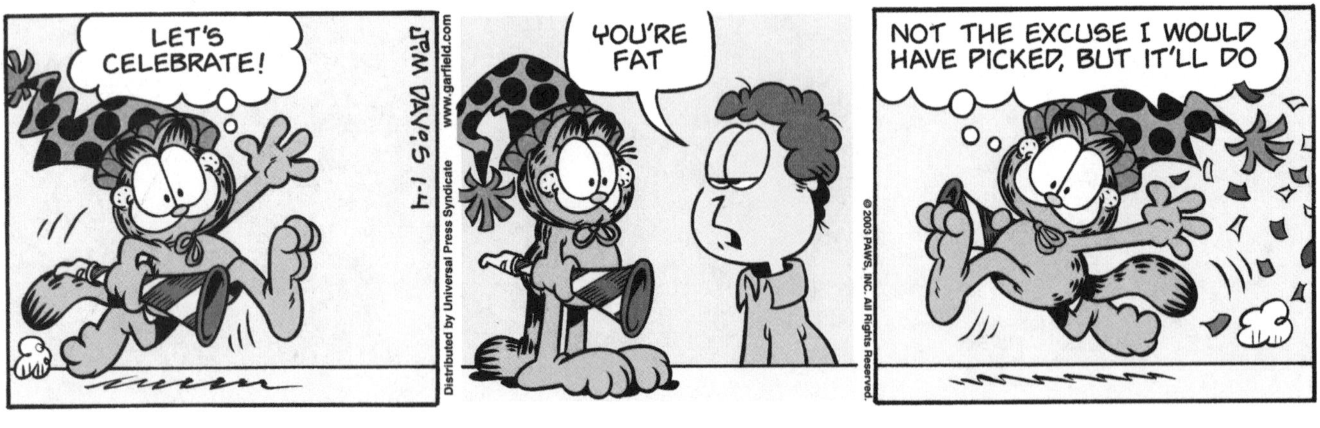
LET'S CELEBRATE!
JIM DAVIS 1-4
www.garfield.com
Distributed by Universal Press Syndicate
YOU'RE FAT
© 2003 PAWS, INC. All Rights Reserved.
NOT THE EXCUSE I WOULD HAVE PICKED, BUT IT'LL DO

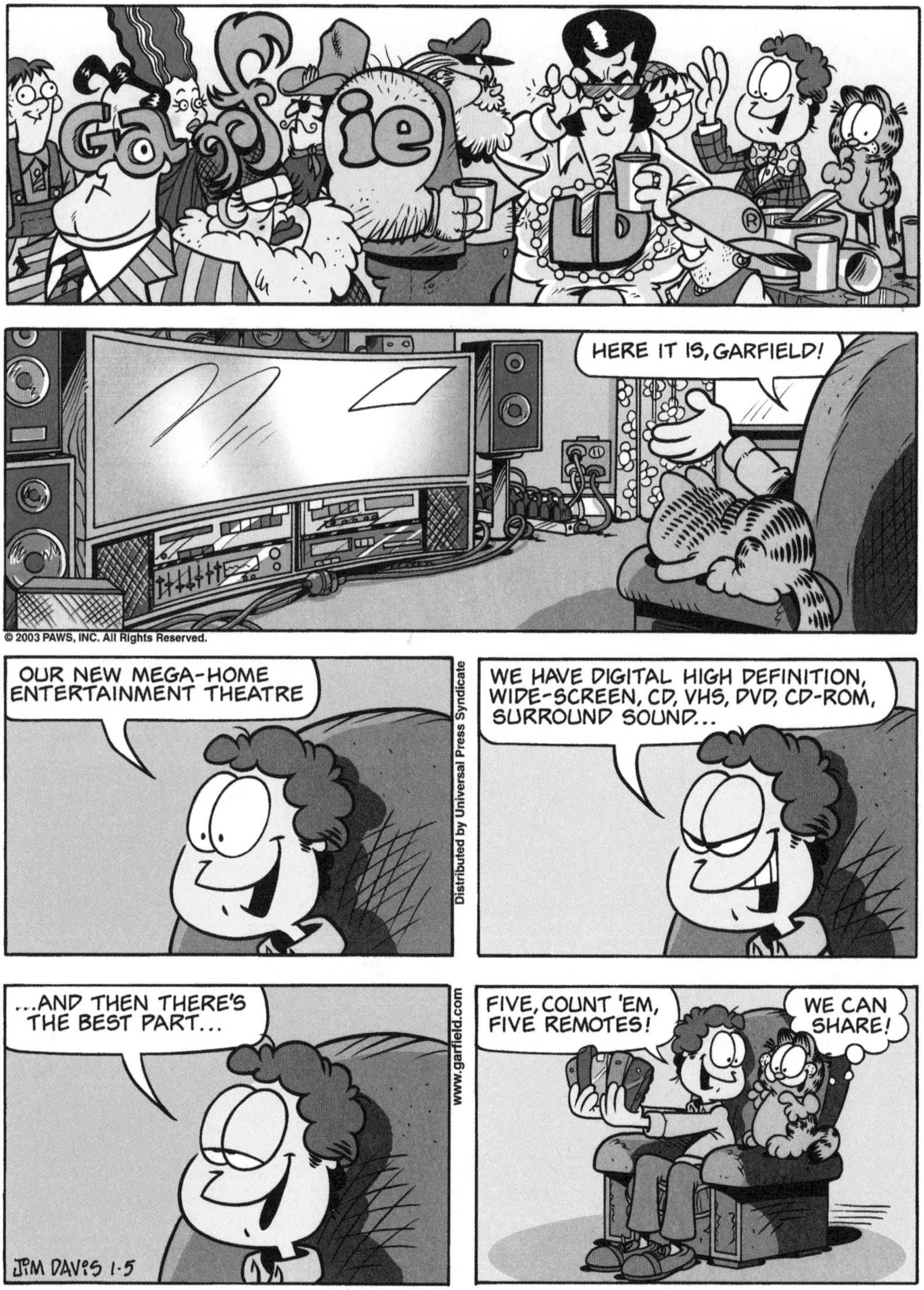
HERE IT IS, GARFIELD!
© 2003 PAWS, INC. All Rights Reserved.
OUR NEW MEGA-HOME ENTERTAINMENT THEATRE
Distributed by Universal Press Syndicate
WE HAVE DIGITAL HIGH DEFINITION, WIDE-SCREEN, CD, VHS, DVD, CD-ROM, SURROUND SOUND...
...AND THEN THERE'S THE BEST PART...
www.garfield.com
JIM DAVIS 1-5
FIVE, COUNT 'EM, FIVE REMOTES!
WE CAN SHARE!

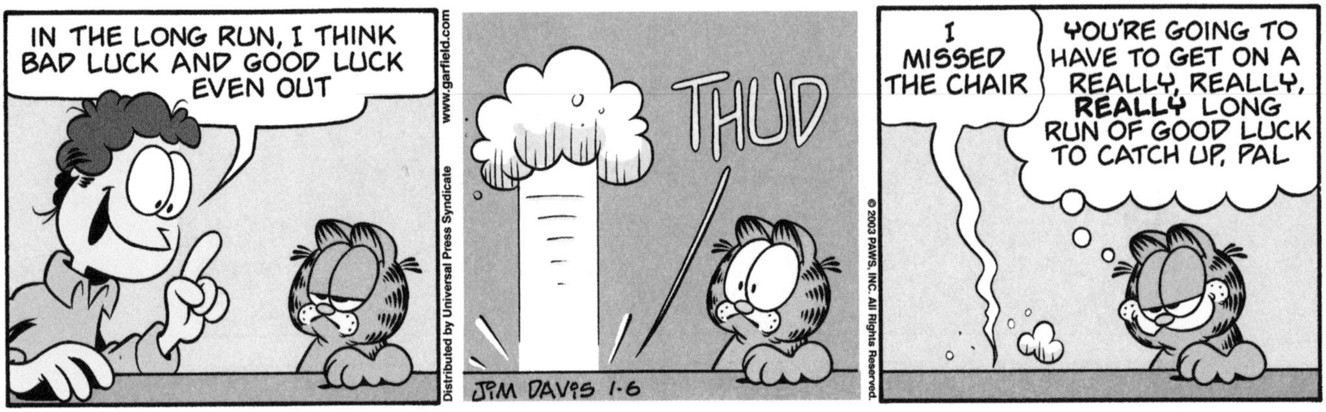
IN THE LONG RUN, I THINK BAD LUCK AND GOOD LUCK EVEN OUT
www.garfield.com
Distributed by Universal Press Syndicate
THUD
JIM DAVIS 1-6
I MISSED THE CHAIR
YOU'RE GOING TO HAVE TO GET ON A REALLY, REALLY, **REALLY** LONG RUN OF GOOD LUCK TO CATCH UP, PAL
© 2003 PAWS, INC. All Rights Reserved.

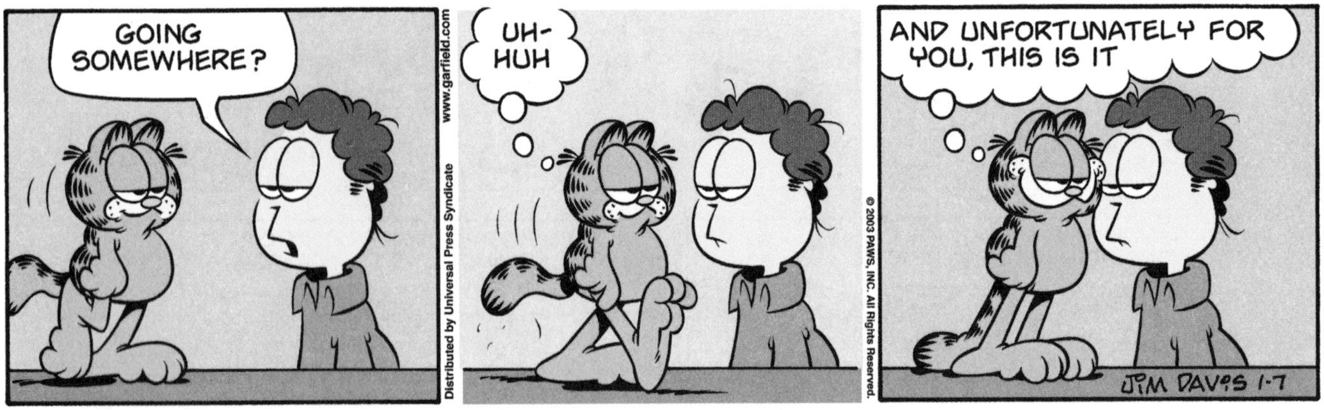
GOING SOMEWHERE?
www.garfield.com
Distributed by Universal Press Syndicate
UH-HUH
AND UNFORTUNATELY FOR YOU, THIS IS IT
© 2003 PAWS, INC. All Rights Reserved.
JIM DAVIS 1-7

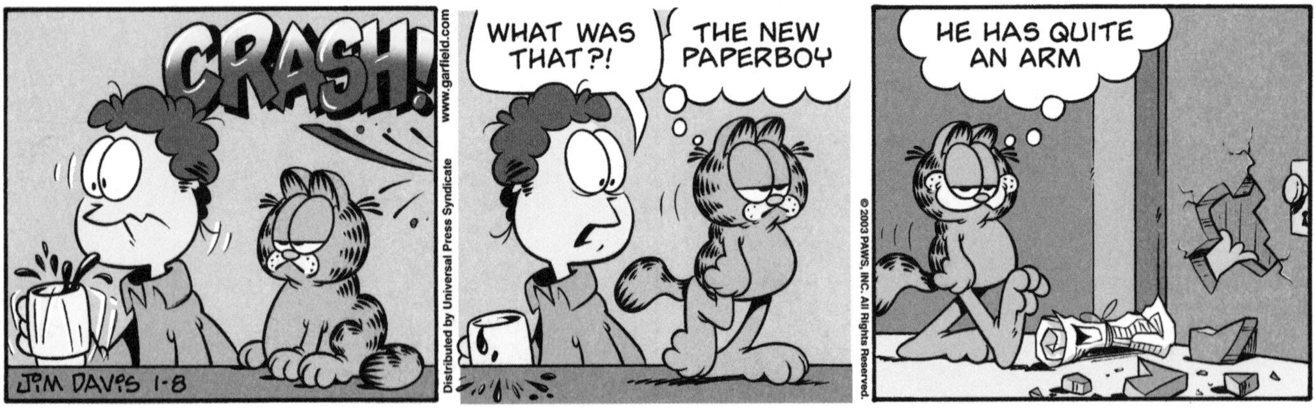
CRASH!
JIM DAVIS 1-8
www.garfield.com
Distributed by Universal Press Syndicate
WHAT WAS THAT?!
THE NEW PAPERBOY
HE HAS QUITE AN ARM
© 2003 PAWS, INC. All Rights Reserved.

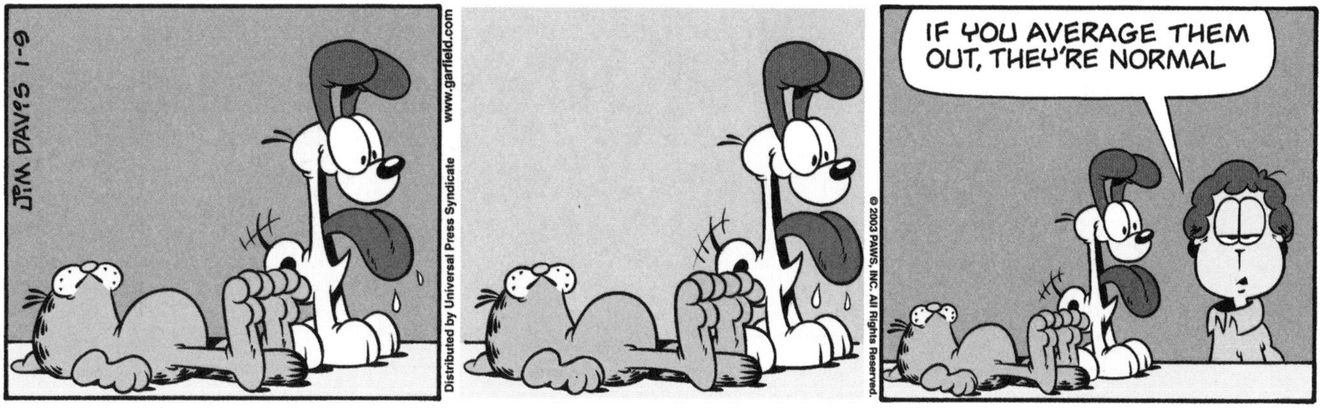
JIM DAVIS 1-9
Distributed by Universal Press Syndicate www.garfield.com
© 2003 PAWS, INC. All Rights Reserved.
IF YOU AVERAGE THEM OUT, THEY'RE NORMAL

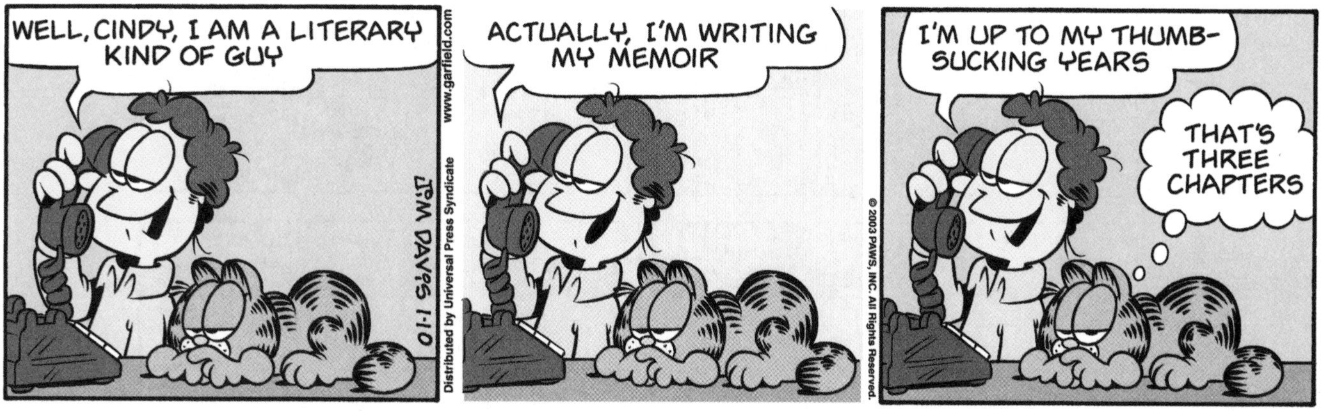
WELL, CINDY, I AM A LITERARY KIND OF GUY
JIM DAVIS 1-10
Distributed by Universal Press Syndicate www.garfield.com
ACTUALLY, I'M WRITING MY MEMOIR
© 2003 PAWS, INC. All Rights Reserved.
I'M UP TO MY THUMB-SUCKING YEARS
THAT'S THREE CHAPTERS

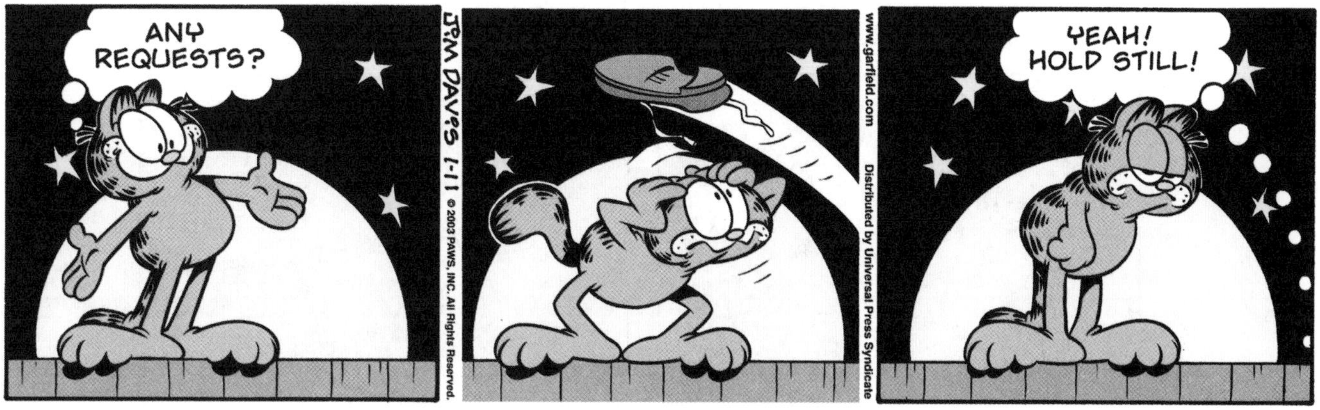
ANY REQUESTS?
JIM DAVIS 1-11 © 2003 PAWS, INC. All Rights Reserved.
www.garfield.com Distributed by Universal Press Syndicate
YEAH! HOLD STILL!

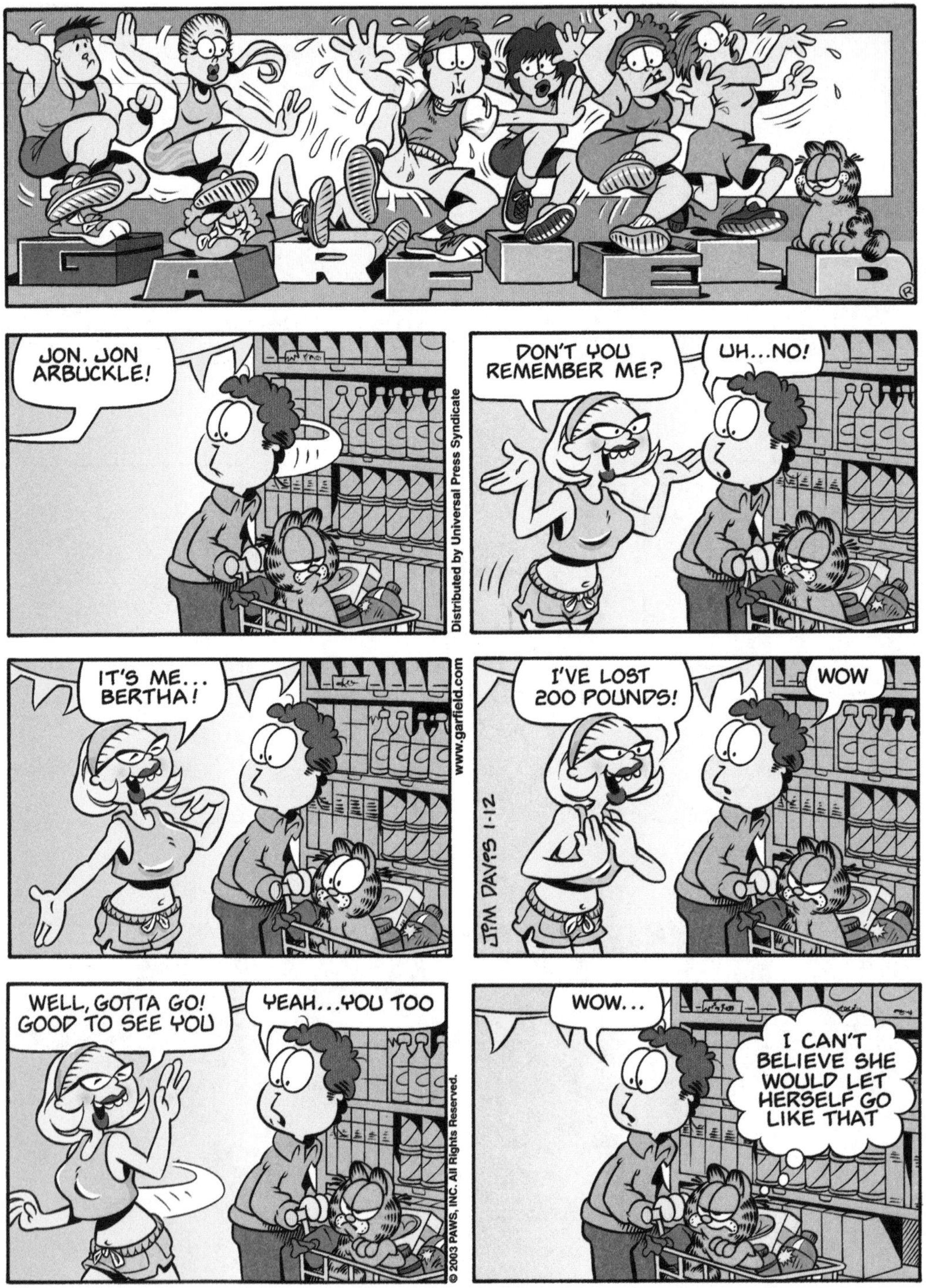
GARFIELD
JON. JON ARBUCKLE!
DON'T YOU REMEMBER ME?
UH...NO!
IT'S ME... BERTHA!
I'VE LOST 200 POUNDS!
WOW
WELL, GOTTA GO! GOOD TO SEE YOU
YEAH...YOU TOO
WOW...
I CAN'T BELIEVE SHE WOULD LET HERSELF GO LIKE THAT
Distributed by Universal Press Syndicate
www.garfield.com
JIM DAVIS 1-12
© 2003 PAWS, INC. All Rights Reserved.

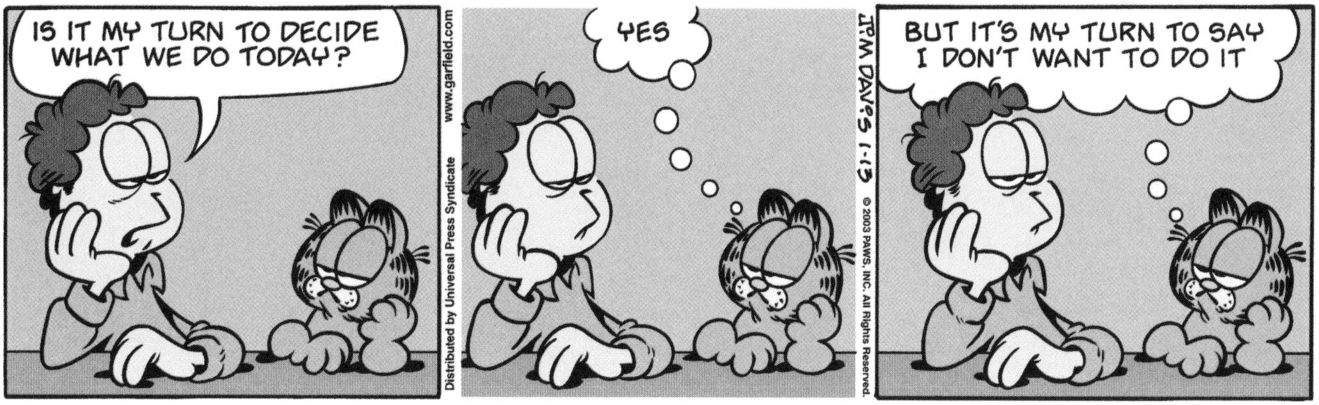
IS IT MY TURN TO DECIDE WHAT WE DO TODAY?
YES
BUT IT'S MY TURN TO SAY I DON'T WANT TO DO IT
JPM DAVPS 1-13
Distributed by Universal Press Syndicate www.garfield.com
© 2003 PAWS, INC. All Rights Reserved.

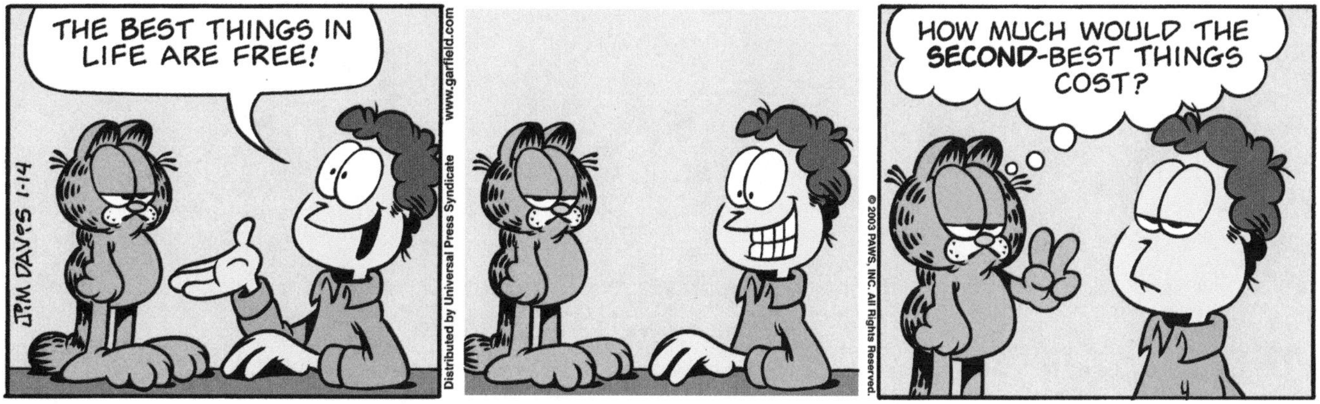
THE BEST THINGS IN LIFE ARE FREE!
HOW MUCH WOULD THE **SECOND**-BEST THINGS COST?
JPM DAVPS 1-14
Distributed by Universal Press Syndicate www.garfield.com
© 2003 PAWS, INC. All Rights Reserved.

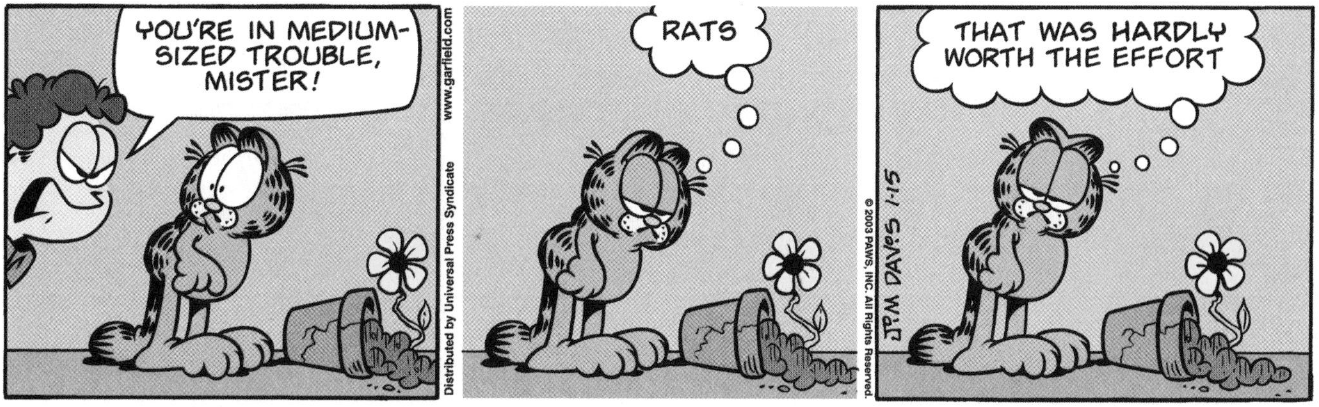
YOU'RE IN MEDIUM-SIZED TROUBLE, MISTER!
RATS
THAT WAS HARDLY WORTH THE EFFORT
JPM DAVPS 1-15
Distributed by Universal Press Syndicate www.garfield.com
© 2003 PAWS, INC. All Rights Reserved.

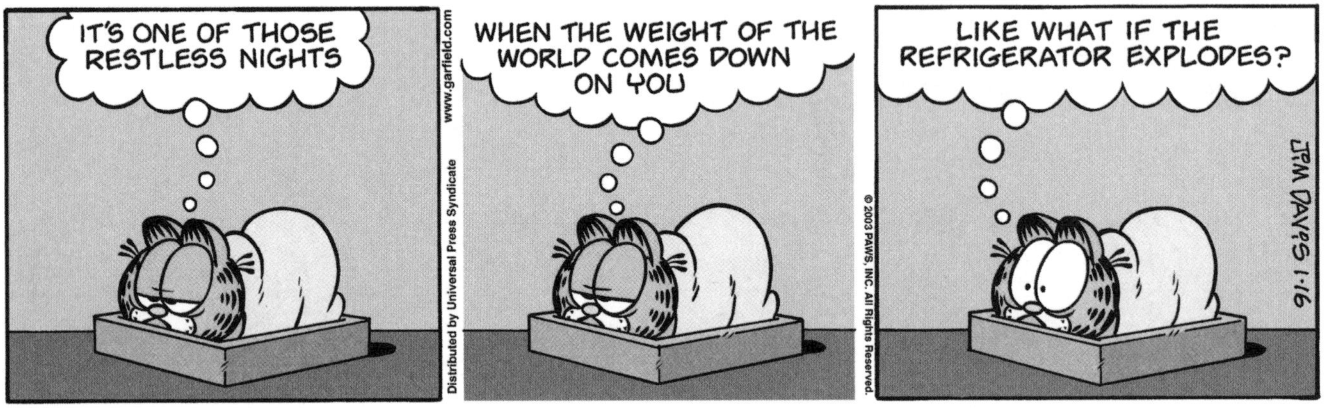
IT'S ONE OF THOSE RESTLESS NIGHTS
www.garfield.com
Distributed by Universal Press Syndicate
WHEN THE WEIGHT OF THE WORLD COMES DOWN ON YOU
© 2003 PAWS, INC. All Rights Reserved.
LIKE WHAT IF THE REFRIGERATOR EXPLODES?
JIM DAVIS 1-16

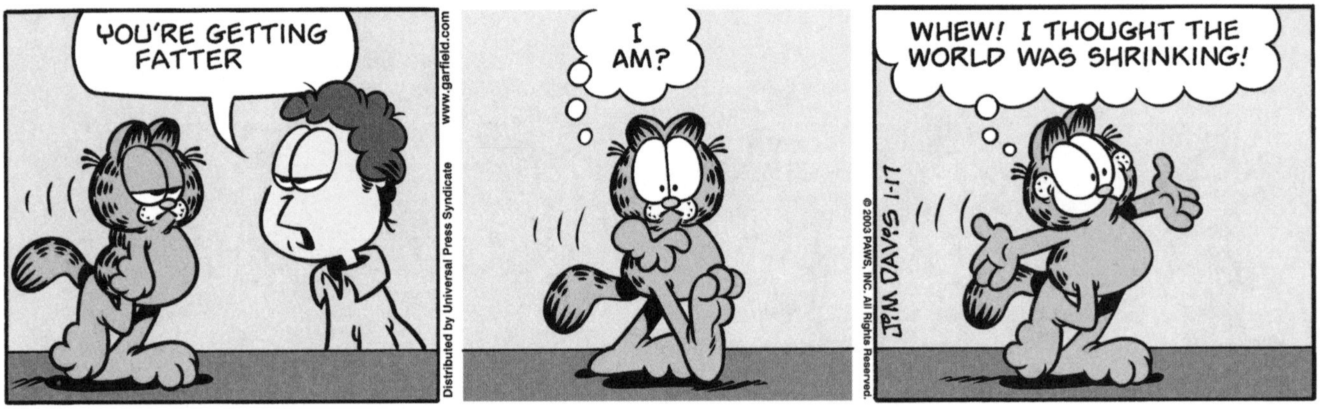
YOU'RE GETTING FATTER
www.garfield.com
Distributed by Universal Press Syndicate
I AM?
© 2003 PAWS, INC. All Rights Reserved.
JIM DAVIS 1-17
WHEW! I THOUGHT THE WORLD WAS SHRINKING!

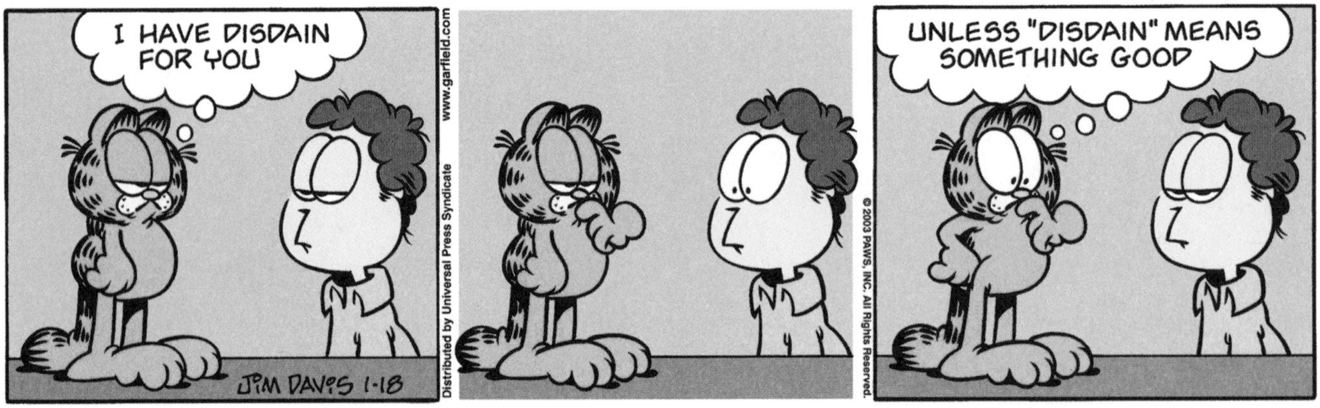
I HAVE DISDAIN FOR YOU
JIM DAVIS 1-18
www.garfield.com
Distributed by Universal Press Syndicate
© 2003 PAWS, INC. All Rights Reserved.
UNLESS "DISDAIN" MEANS SOMETHING GOOD

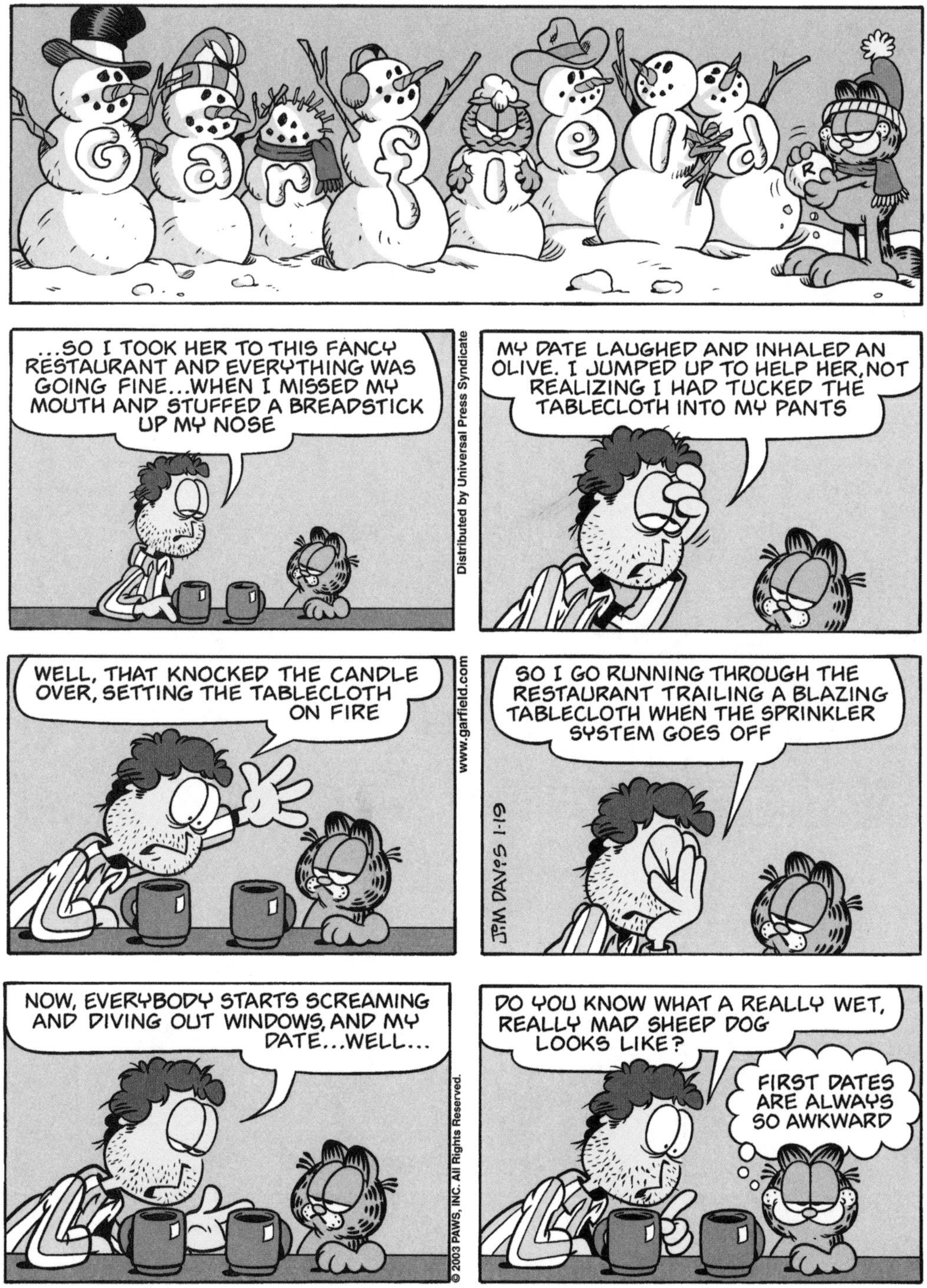
Garfield
...SO I TOOK HER TO THIS FANCY RESTAURANT AND EVERYTHING WAS GOING FINE...WHEN I MISSED MY MOUTH AND STUFFED A BREADSTICK UP MY NOSE
Distributed by Universal Press Syndicate
MY DATE LAUGHED AND INHALED AN OLIVE. I JUMPED UP TO HELP HER, NOT REALIZING I HAD TUCKED THE TABLECLOTH INTO MY PANTS
WELL, THAT KNOCKED THE CANDLE OVER, SETTING THE TABLECLOTH ON FIRE
www.garfield.com
SO I GO RUNNING THROUGH THE RESTAURANT TRAILING A BLAZING TABLECLOTH WHEN THE SPRINKLER SYSTEM GOES OFF
JPM DAVIS 1-19
NOW, EVERYBODY STARTS SCREAMING AND DIVING OUT WINDOWS, AND MY DATE...WELL...
© 2003 PAWS, INC. All Rights Reserved.
DO YOU KNOW WHAT A REALLY WET, REALLY MAD SHEEP DOG LOOKS LIKE?
FIRST DATES ARE ALWAYS SO AWKWARD

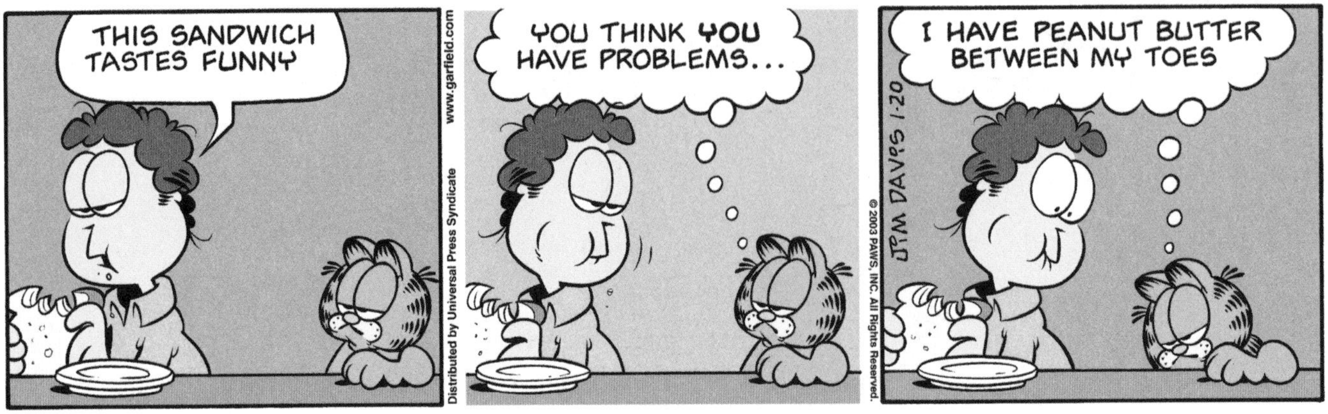
THIS SANDWICH TASTES FUNNY
YOU THINK YOU HAVE PROBLEMS...
I HAVE PEANUT BUTTER BETWEEN MY TOES
www.garfield.com
Distributed by Universal Press Syndicate
© 2003 PAWS, INC. All Rights Reserved.
JIM DAVIS 1-20

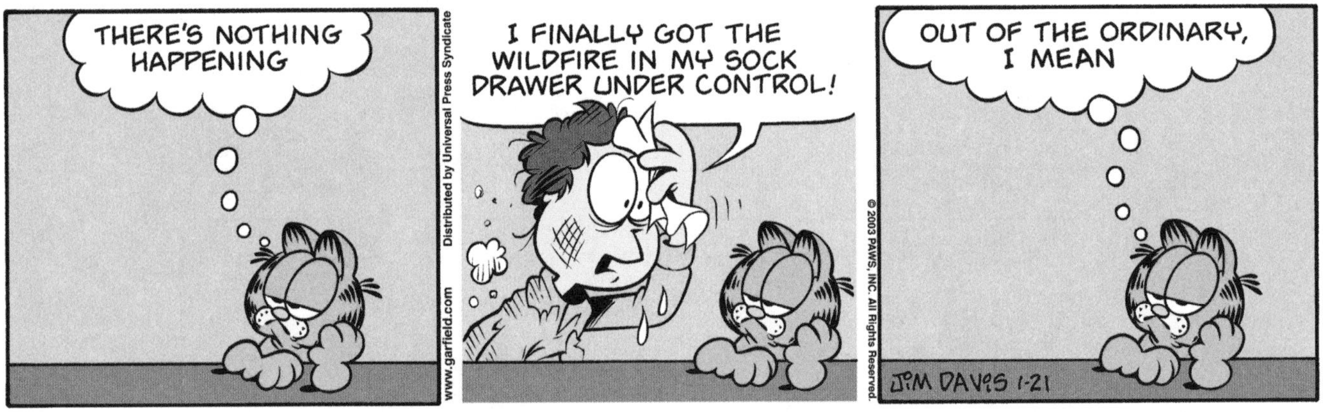
THERE'S NOTHING HAPPENING
I FINALLY GOT THE WILDFIRE IN MY SOCK DRAWER UNDER CONTROL!
OUT OF THE ORDINARY, I MEAN
www.garfield.com
Distributed by Universal Press Syndicate
© 2003 PAWS, INC. All Rights Reserved.
JIM DAVIS 1-21

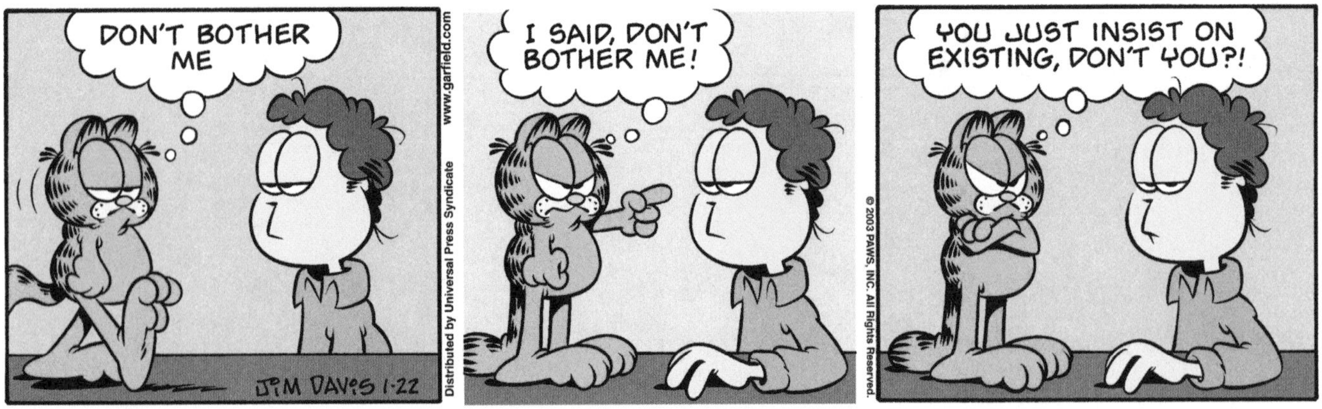
DON'T BOTHER ME
I SAID, DON'T BOTHER ME!
YOU JUST INSIST ON EXISTING, DON'T YOU?!
www.garfield.com
Distributed by Universal Press Syndicate
© 2003 PAWS, INC. All Rights Reserved.
JIM DAVIS 1-22

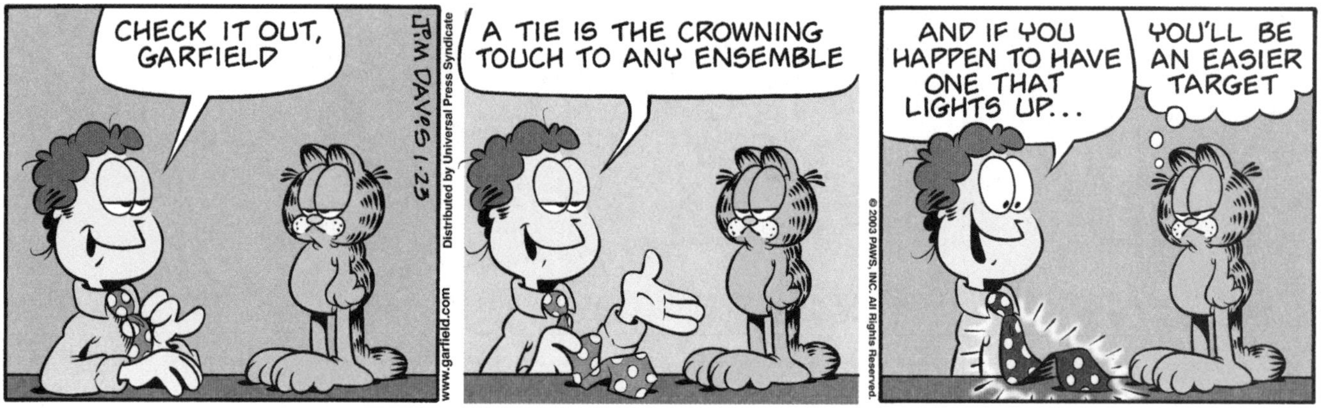
CHECK IT OUT, GARFIELD
JIM DAVIS 1-23
www.garfield.com
Distributed by Universal Press Syndicate
A TIE IS THE CROWNING TOUCH TO ANY ENSEMBLE
© 2003 PAWS, INC. All Rights Reserved.
AND IF YOU HAPPEN TO HAVE ONE THAT LIGHTS UP...
YOU'LL BE AN EASIER TARGET

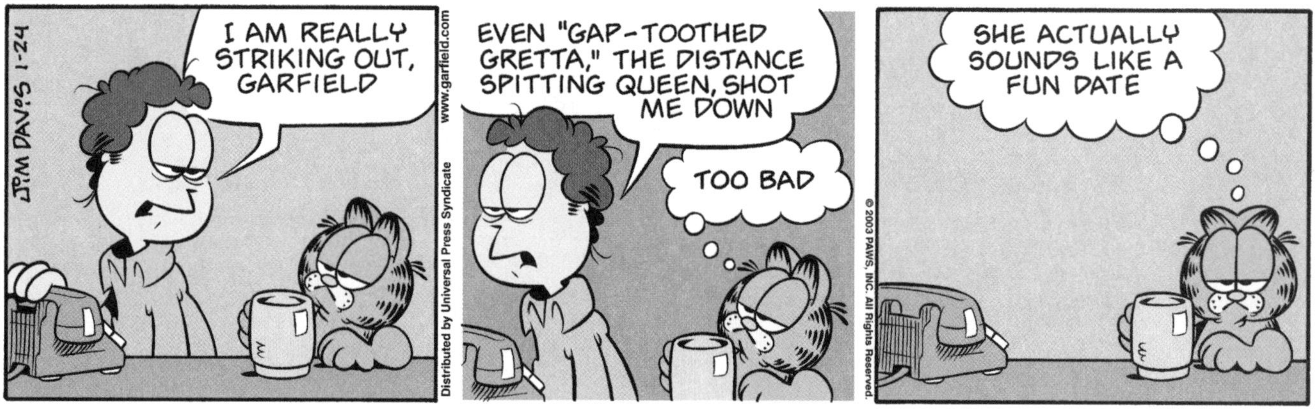
JIM DAVIS 1-24
I AM REALLY STRIKING OUT, GARFIELD
www.garfield.com
Distributed by Universal Press Syndicate
EVEN "GAP-TOOTHED GRETTA," THE DISTANCE SPITTING QUEEN, SHOT ME DOWN
TOO BAD
© 2003 PAWS, INC. All Rights Reserved.
SHE ACTUALLY SOUNDS LIKE A FUN DATE

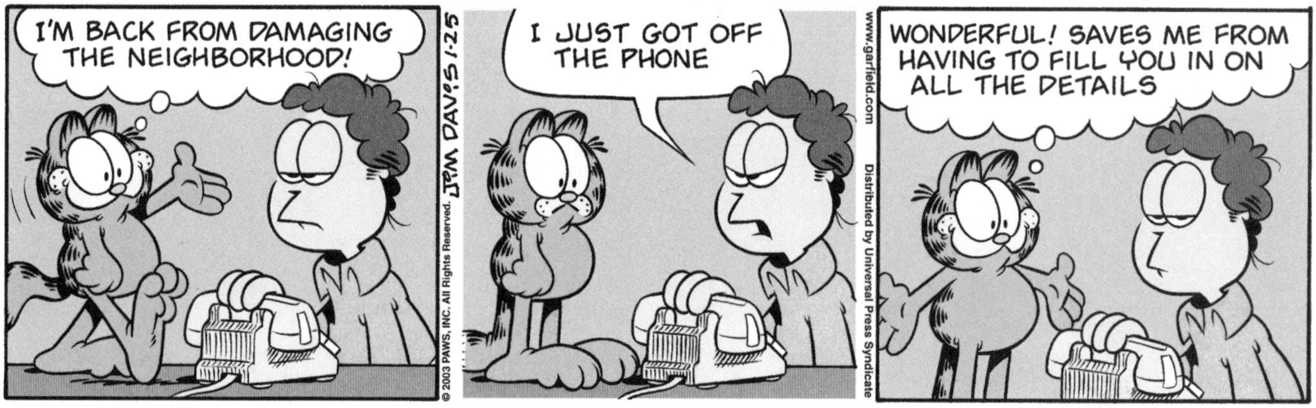
I'M BACK FROM DAMAGING THE NEIGHBORHOOD!
JIM DAVIS 1-25
© 2003 PAWS, INC. All Rights Reserved.
I JUST GOT OFF THE PHONE
www.garfield.com
Distributed by Universal Press Syndicate
WONDERFUL! SAVES ME FROM HAVING TO FILL YOU IN ON ALL THE DETAILS

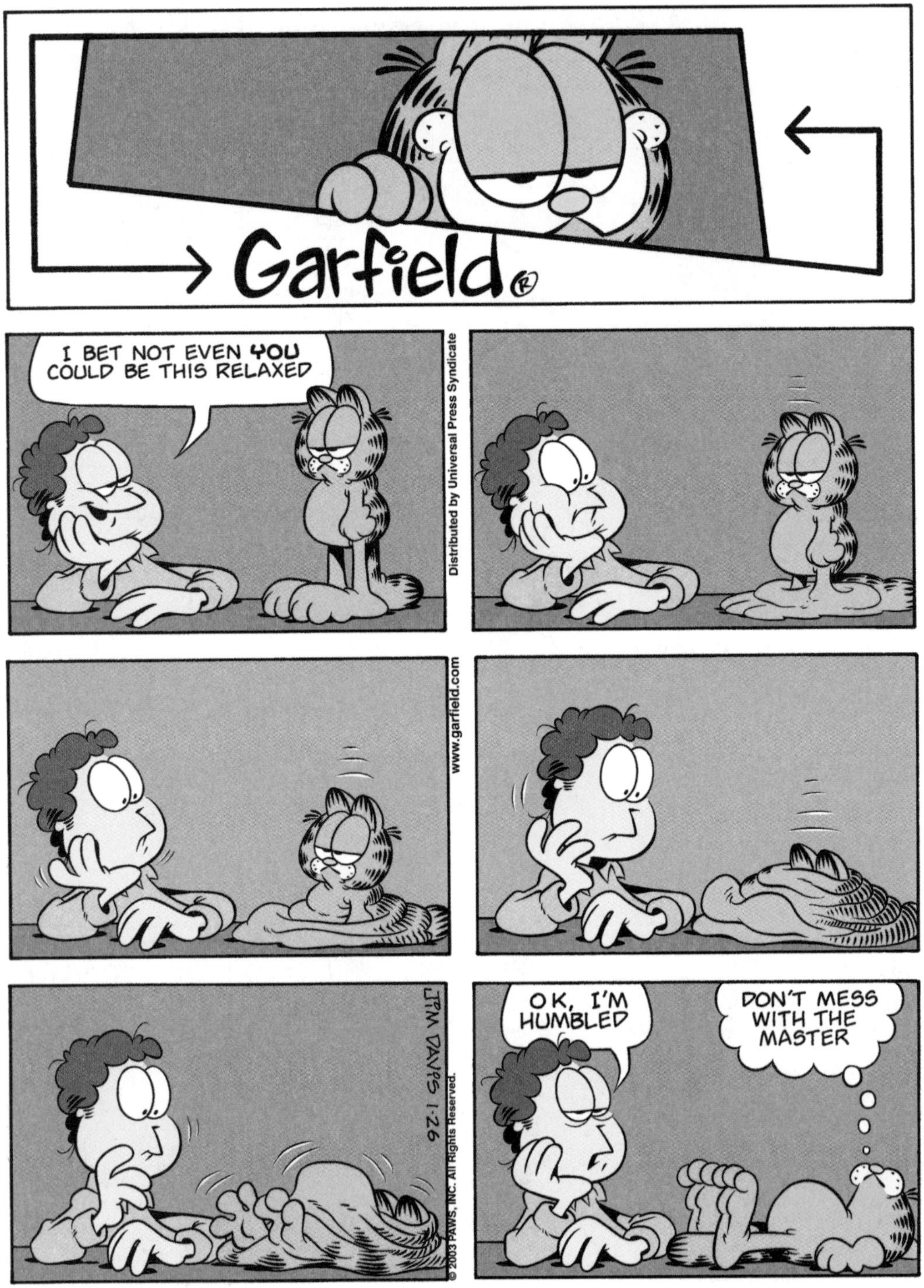
Garfield®
I BET NOT EVEN YOU COULD BE THIS RELAXED
OK, I'M HUMBLED
DON'T MESS WITH THE MASTER
JIM DAVIS 1-26
Distributed by Universal Press Syndicate
www.garfield.com
© 2003 PAWS, INC. All Rights Reserved.

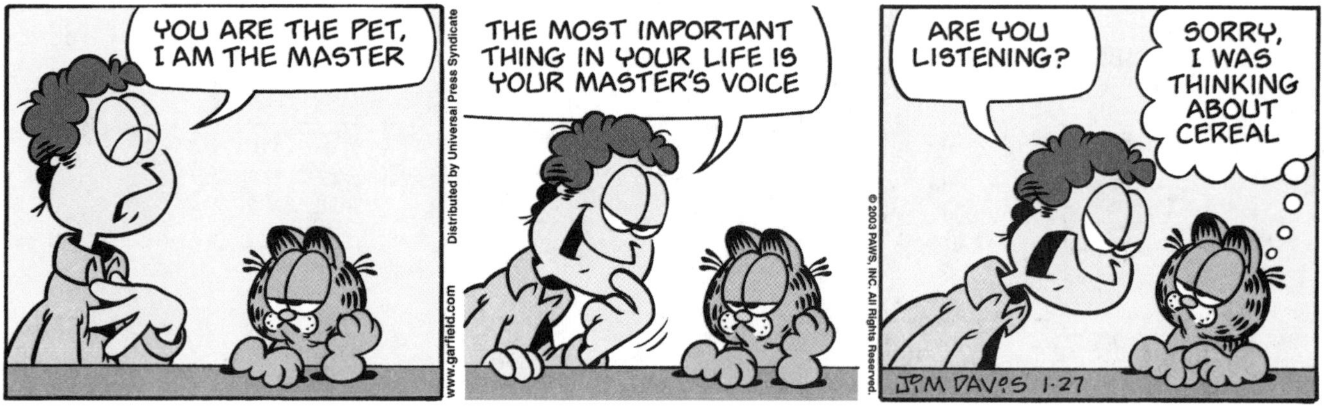
YOU ARE THE PET, I AM THE MASTER
THE MOST IMPORTANT THING IN YOUR LIFE IS YOUR MASTER'S VOICE
ARE YOU LISTENING?
SORRY, I WAS THINKING ABOUT CEREAL
JIM DAVIS 1·27
www.garfield.com
Distributed by Universal Press Syndicate
© 2003 PAWS, INC. All Rights Reserved.

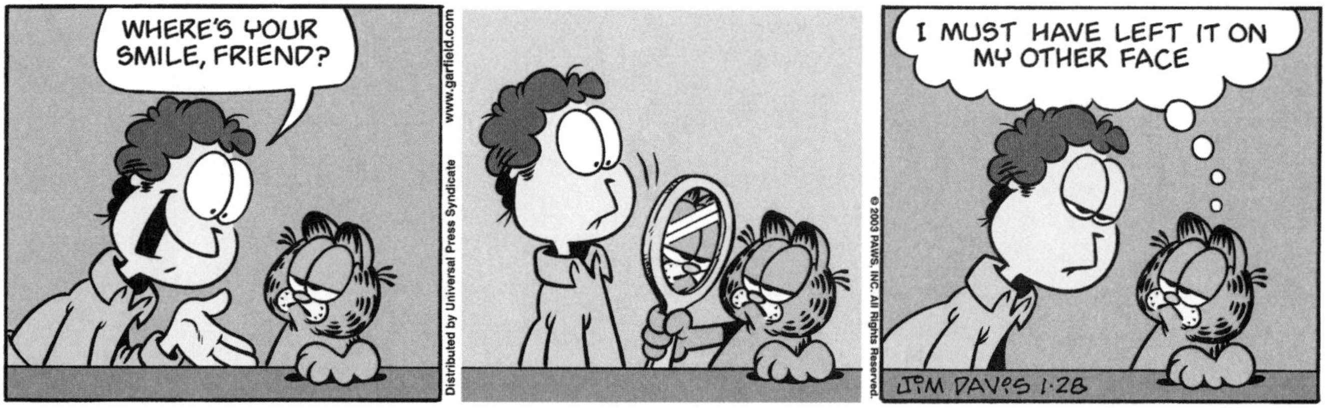
WHERE'S YOUR SMILE, FRIEND?
I MUST HAVE LEFT IT ON MY OTHER FACE
JIM DAVIS 1·28
www.garfield.com
Distributed by Universal Press Syndicate
© 2003 PAWS, INC. All Rights Reserved.

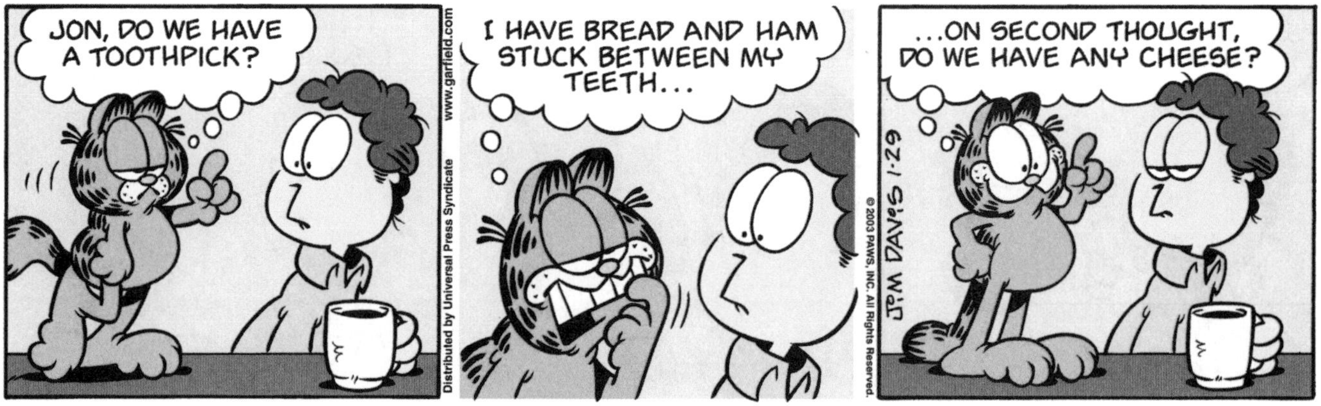
JON, DO WE HAVE A TOOTHPICK?
I HAVE BREAD AND HAM STUCK BETWEEN MY TEETH...
...ON SECOND THOUGHT, DO WE HAVE ANY CHEESE?
JIM DAVIS 1·29
www.garfield.com
Distributed by Universal Press Syndicate
© 2003 PAWS, INC. All Rights Reserved.

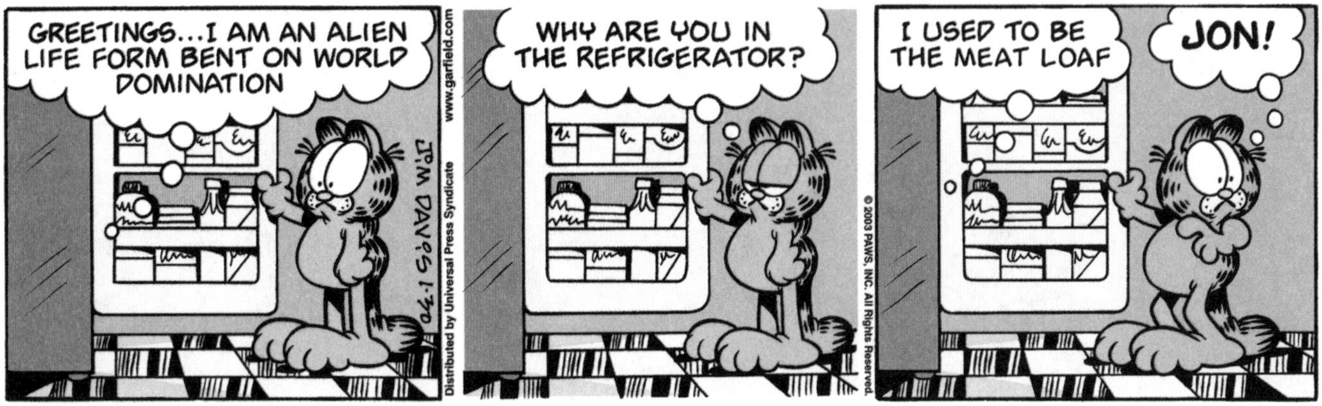
GREETINGS...I AM AN ALIEN LIFE FORM BENT ON WORLD DOMINATION
WHY ARE YOU IN THE REFRIGERATOR?
I USED TO BE THE MEAT LOAF
JON!

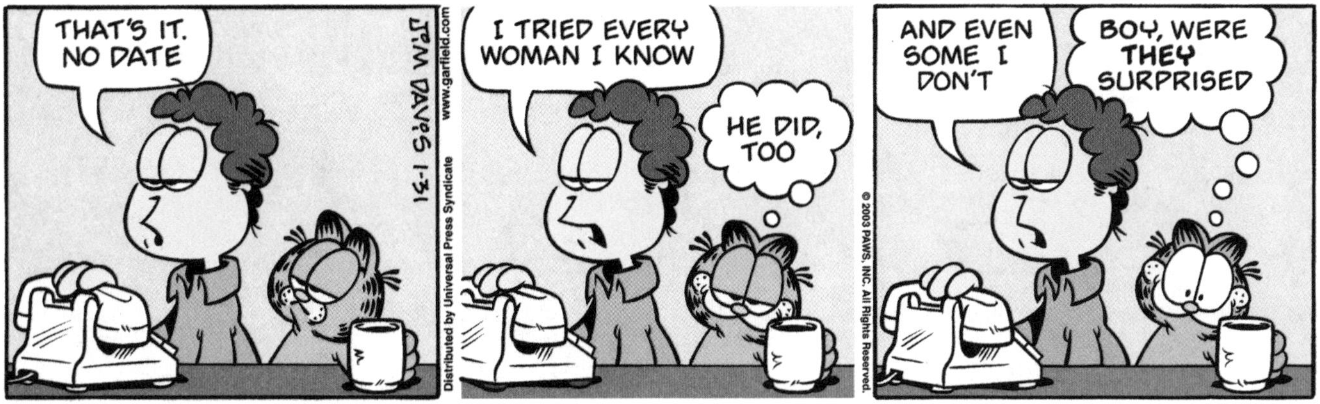
THAT'S IT. NO DATE
I TRIED EVERY WOMAN I KNOW
HE DID, TOO
AND EVEN SOME I DON'T
BOY, WERE **THEY** SURPRISED

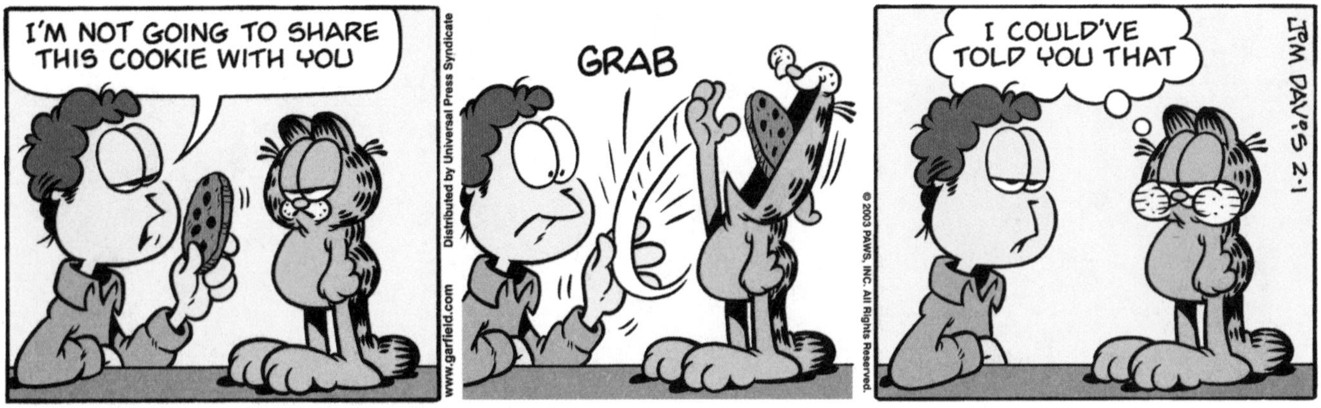
I'M NOT GOING TO SHARE THIS COOKIE WITH YOU
GRAB
I COULD'VE TOLD YOU THAT

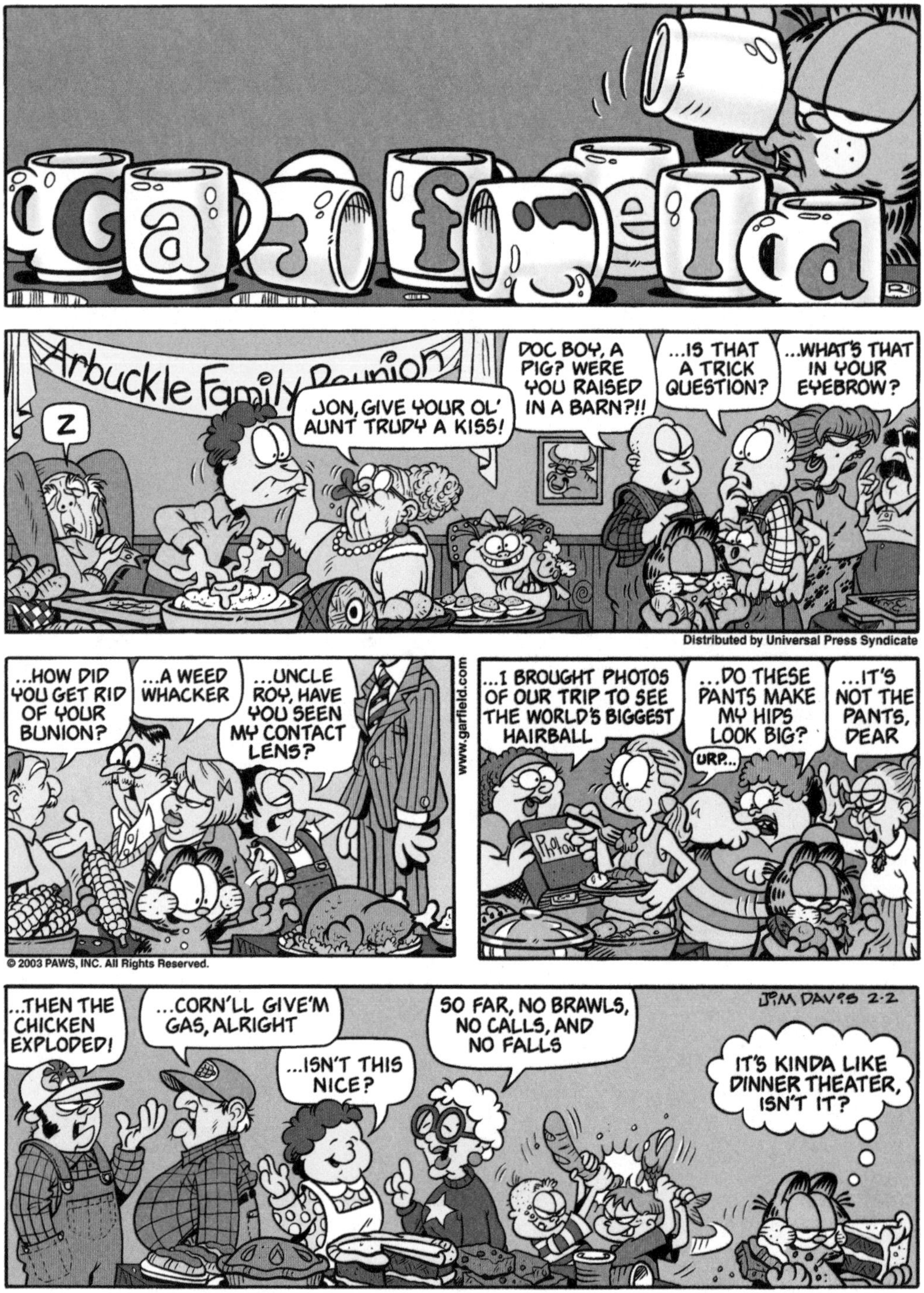
Garfield
Arbuckle Family Reunion
Z
JON, GIVE YOUR OL' AUNT TRUDY A KISS!
DOC BOY, A PIG? WERE YOU RAISED IN A BARN?!!
...IS THAT A TRICK QUESTION?
...WHAT'S THAT IN YOUR EYEBROW?
Distributed by Universal Press Syndicate
...HOW DID YOU GET RID OF YOUR BUNION?
...A WEED WHACKER
...UNCLE ROY, HAVE YOU SEEN MY CONTACT LENS?
www.garfield.com
© 2003 PAWS, INC. All Rights Reserved.
...I BROUGHT PHOTOS OF OUR TRIP TO SEE THE WORLD'S BIGGEST HAIRBALL
PHOTOS
URP...
...DO THESE PANTS MAKE MY HIPS LOOK BIG?
...IT'S NOT THE PANTS, DEAR
JIM DAVIS 2-2
...THEN THE CHICKEN EXPLODED!
...CORN'LL GIVE'M GAS, ALRIGHT
...ISN'T THIS NICE?
SO FAR, NO BRAWLS, NO CALLS, AND NO FALLS
IT'S KINDA LIKE DINNER THEATER, ISN'T IT?

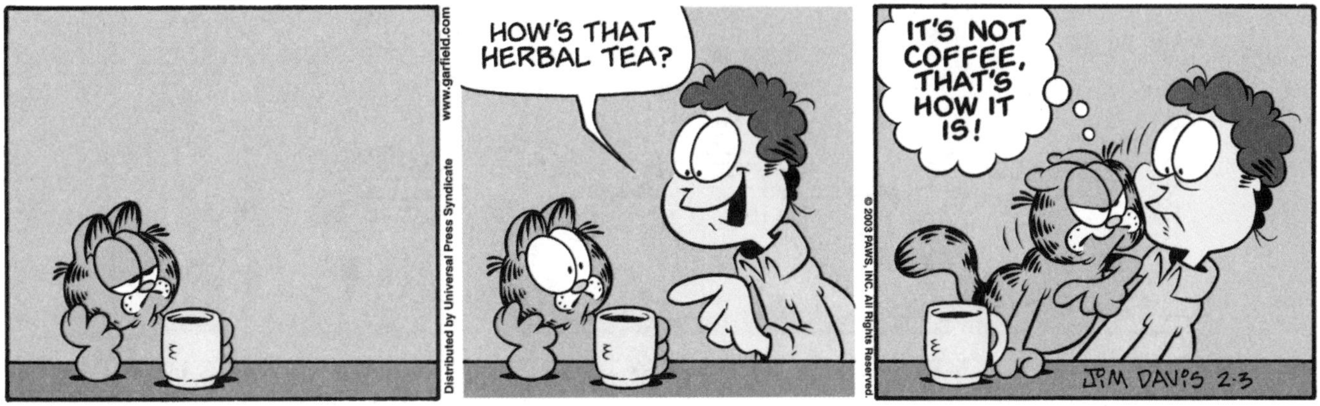
Distributed by Universal Press Syndicate www.garfield.com
HOW'S THAT HERBAL TEA?
© 2003 PAWS, INC. All Rights Reserved.
IT'S NOT COFFEE, THAT'S HOW IT IS!
JIM DAVIS 2-3

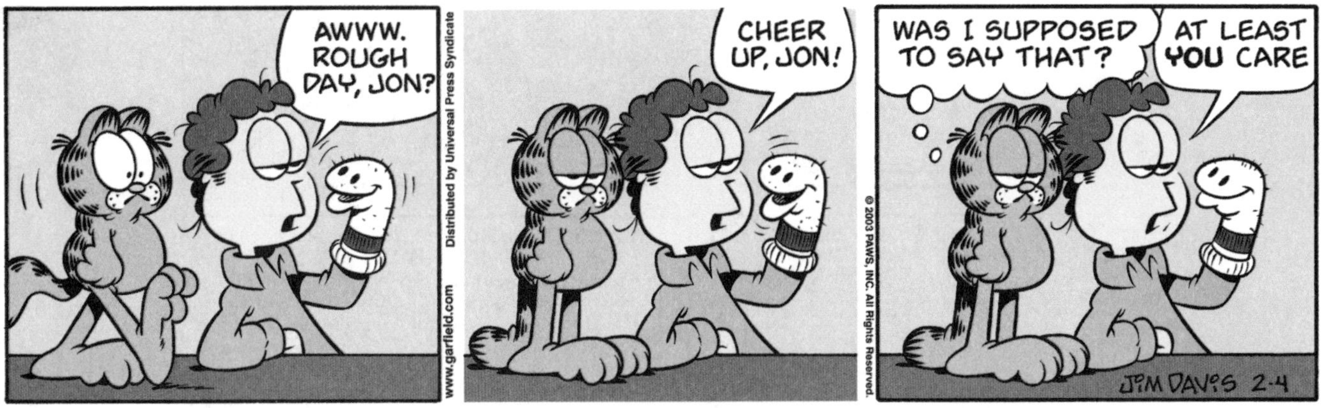
AWWW. ROUGH DAY, JON?
Distributed by Universal Press Syndicate www.garfield.com
CHEER UP, JON!
© 2003 PAWS, INC. All Rights Reserved.
WAS I SUPPOSED TO SAY THAT?
AT LEAST **YOU** CARE
JIM DAVIS 2-4

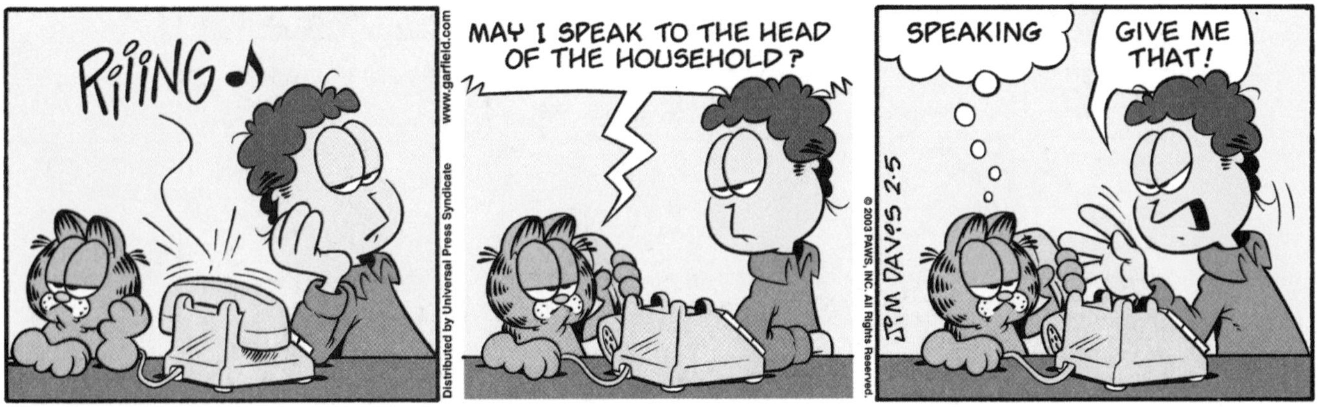
RIIING
Distributed by Universal Press Syndicate www.garfield.com
MAY I SPEAK TO THE HEAD OF THE HOUSEHOLD?
© 2003 PAWS, INC. All Rights Reserved.
JIM DAVIS 2-5
SPEAKING
GIVE ME THAT!

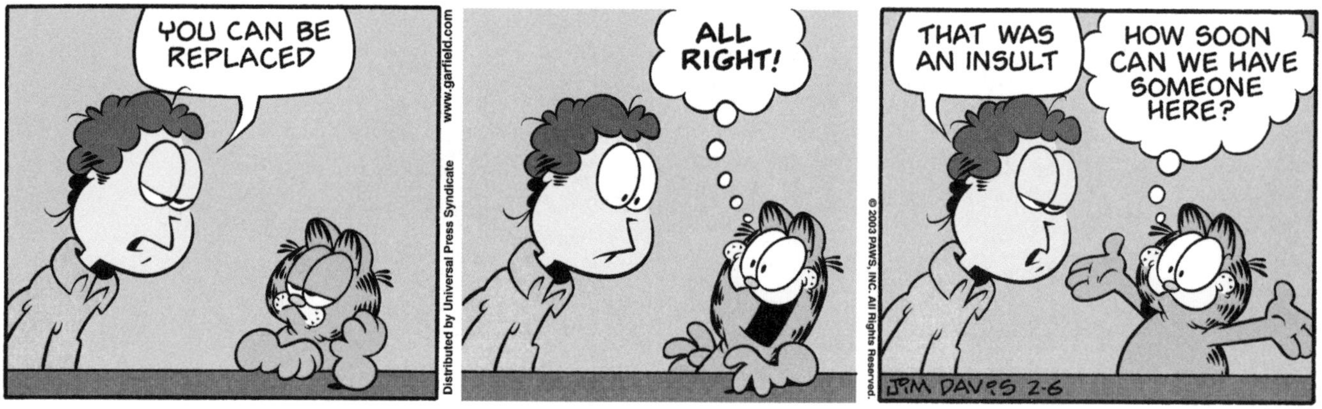
YOU CAN BE REPLACED
Distributed by Universal Press Syndicate www.garfield.com
ALL RIGHT!
© 2003 PAWS, INC. All Rights Reserved.
THAT WAS AN INSULT
HOW SOON CAN WE HAVE SOMEONE HERE?
JIM DAVIS 2-6

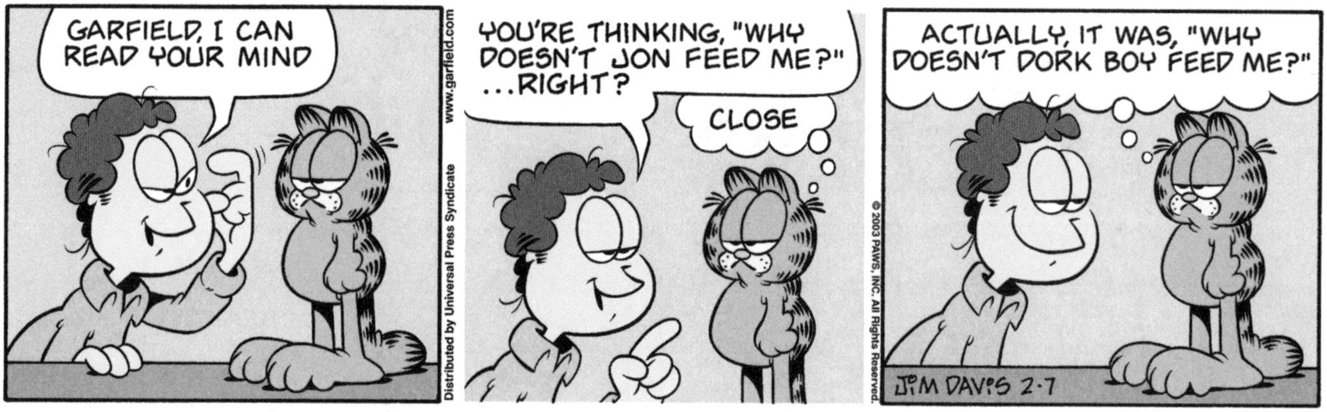
GARFIELD, I CAN READ YOUR MIND
Distributed by Universal Press Syndicate www.garfield.com
YOU'RE THINKING, "WHY DOESN'T JON FEED ME?" ...RIGHT?
CLOSE
© 2003 PAWS, INC. All Rights Reserved.
ACTUALLY, IT WAS, "WHY DOESN'T DORK BOY FEED ME?"
JIM DAVIS 2-7

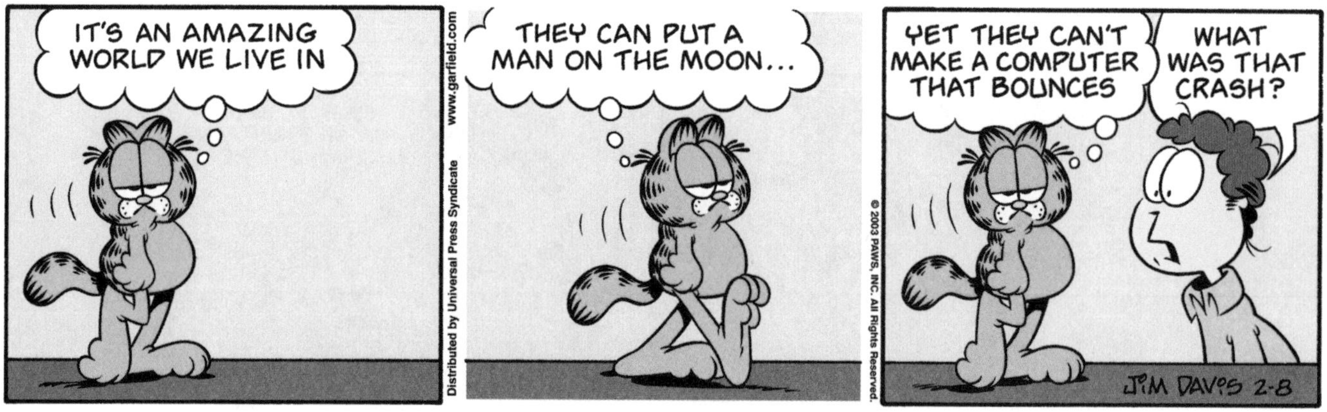
IT'S AN AMAZING WORLD WE LIVE IN
Distributed by Universal Press Syndicate www.garfield.com
THEY CAN PUT A MAN ON THE MOON...
© 2003 PAWS, INC. All Rights Reserved.
YET THEY CAN'T MAKE A COMPUTER THAT BOUNCES
WHAT WAS THAT CRASH?
JIM DAVIS 2-8

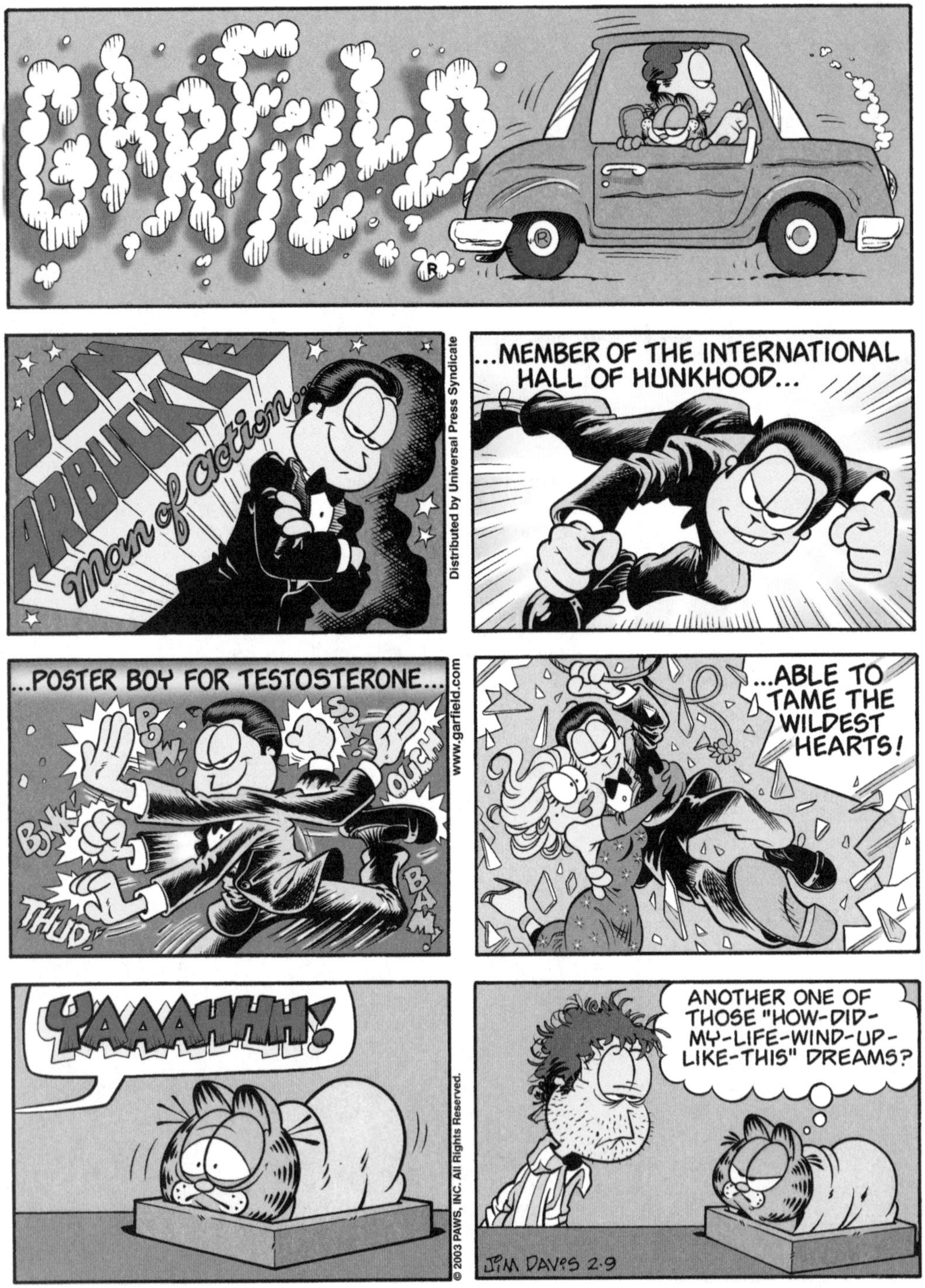
GARFIELD
JON ARBUCKLE
Man of action...
Distributed by Universal Press Syndicate
...MEMBER OF THE INTERNATIONAL HALL OF HUNKHOOD...
...POSTER BOY FOR TESTOSTERONE...
POW!
BONK!
THUD!
OUCH
BAM!
www.garfield.com
...ABLE TO TAME THE WILDEST HEARTS!
YAAAHHH!
© 2003 PAWS, INC. All Rights Reserved.
ANOTHER ONE OF THOSE "HOW-DID-MY-LIFE-WIND-UP-LIKE-THIS" DREAMS?
JIM DAVIS 2-9

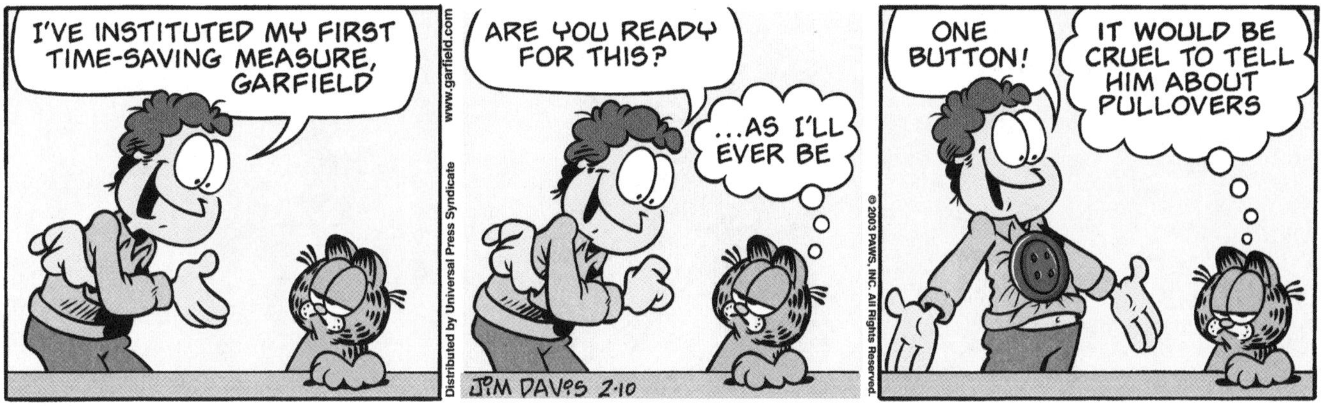
I'VE INSTITUTED MY FIRST TIME-SAVING MEASURE, GARFIELD
ARE YOU READY FOR THIS?
...AS I'LL EVER BE
JIM DAVIS 2·10
ONE BUTTON!
IT WOULD BE CRUEL TO TELL HIM ABOUT PULLOVERS

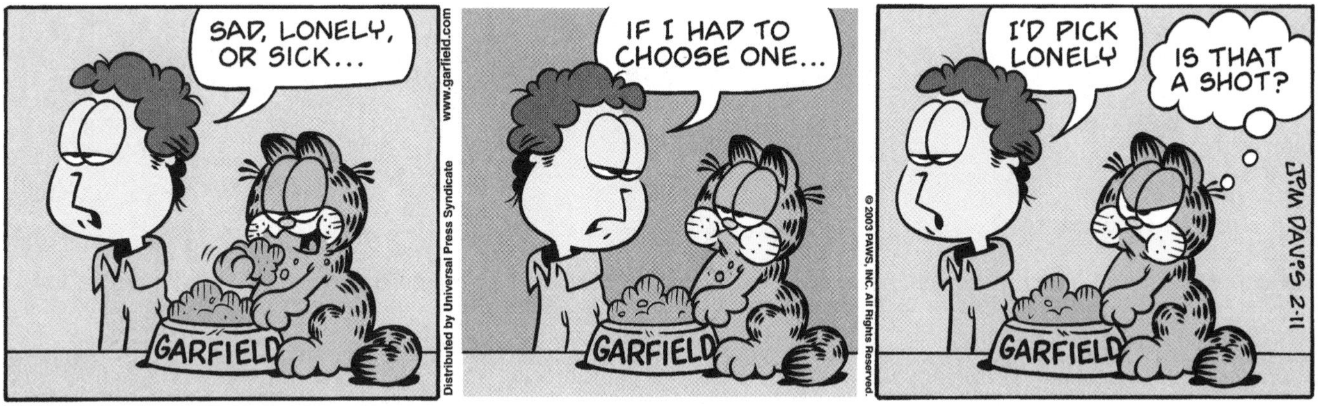
SAD, LONELY, OR SICK...
GARFIELD
IF I HAD TO CHOOSE ONE...
GARFIELD
I'D PICK LONELY
IS THAT A SHOT?
GARFIELD
JIM DAVIS 2·11

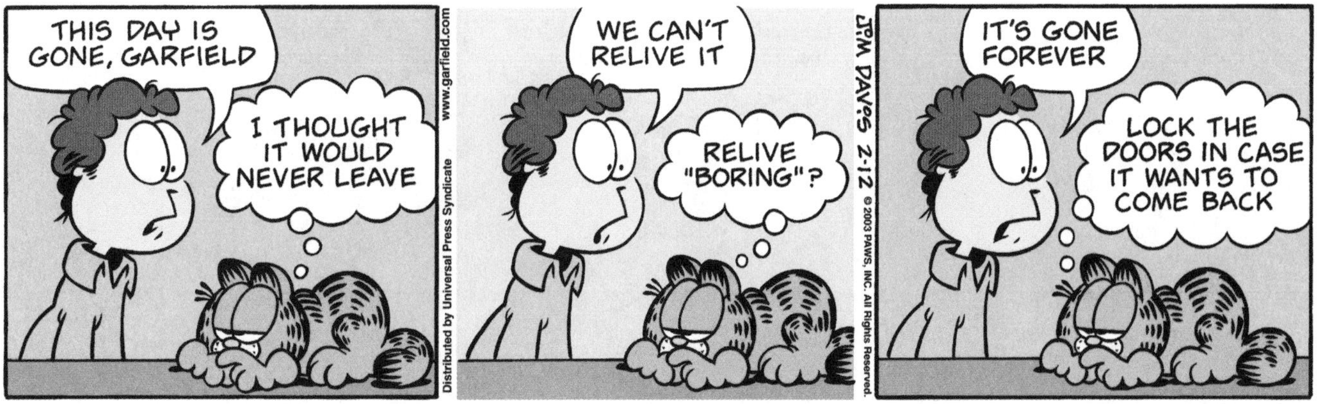
THIS DAY IS GONE, GARFIELD
I THOUGHT IT WOULD NEVER LEAVE
WE CAN'T RELIVE IT
RELIVE "BORING"?
JIM DAVIS 2·12
IT'S GONE FOREVER
LOCK THE DOORS IN CASE IT WANTS TO COME BACK

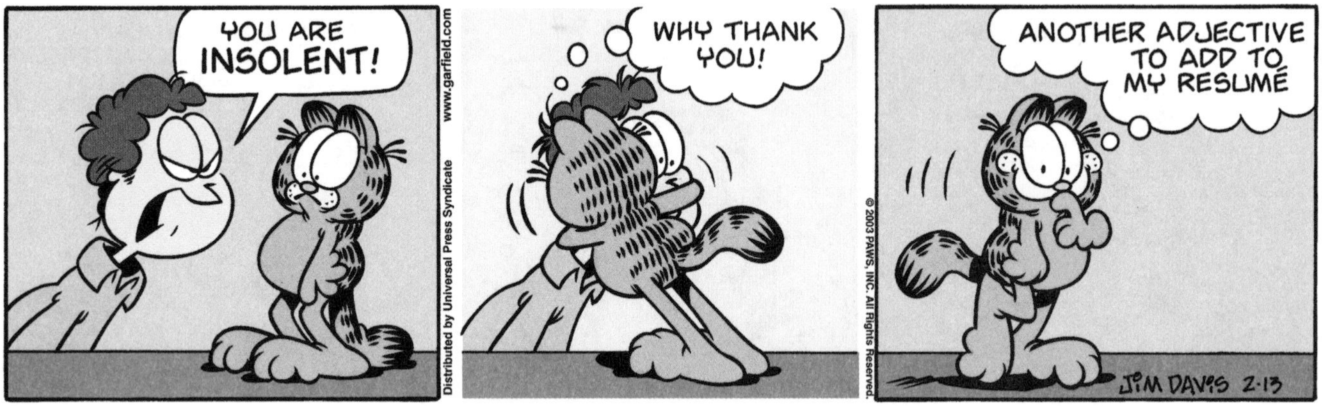
YOU ARE INSOLENT!
www.garfield.com
Distributed by Universal Press Syndicate
WHY THANK YOU!
© 2003 PAWS, INC. All Rights Reserved.
ANOTHER ADJECTIVE TO ADD TO MY RESUMÉ
JIM DAVIS 2-13

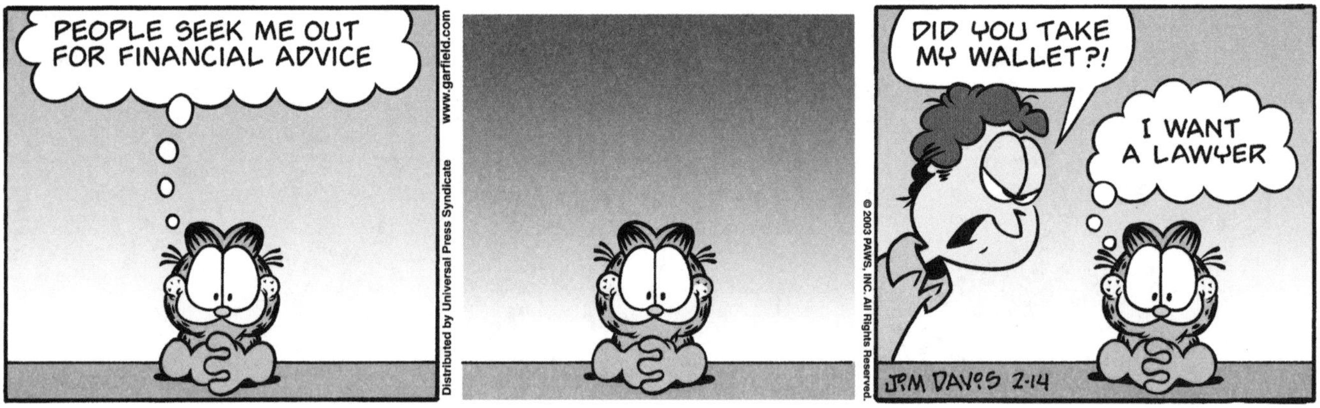
PEOPLE SEEK ME OUT FOR FINANCIAL ADVICE
www.garfield.com
Distributed by Universal Press Syndicate
© 2003 PAWS, INC. All Rights Reserved.
DID YOU TAKE MY WALLET?!
I WANT A LAWYER
JIM DAVIS 2-14

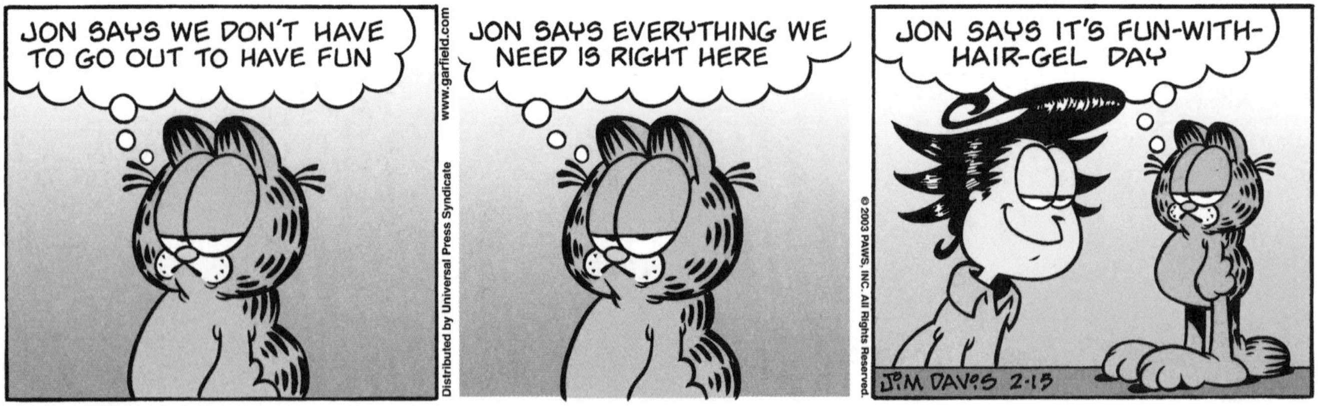
JON SAYS WE DON'T HAVE TO GO OUT TO HAVE FUN
www.garfield.com
Distributed by Universal Press Syndicate
JON SAYS EVERYTHING WE NEED IS RIGHT HERE
© 2003 PAWS, INC. All Rights Reserved.
JON SAYS IT'S FUN-WITH-HAIR-GEL DAY
JIM DAVIS 2-15

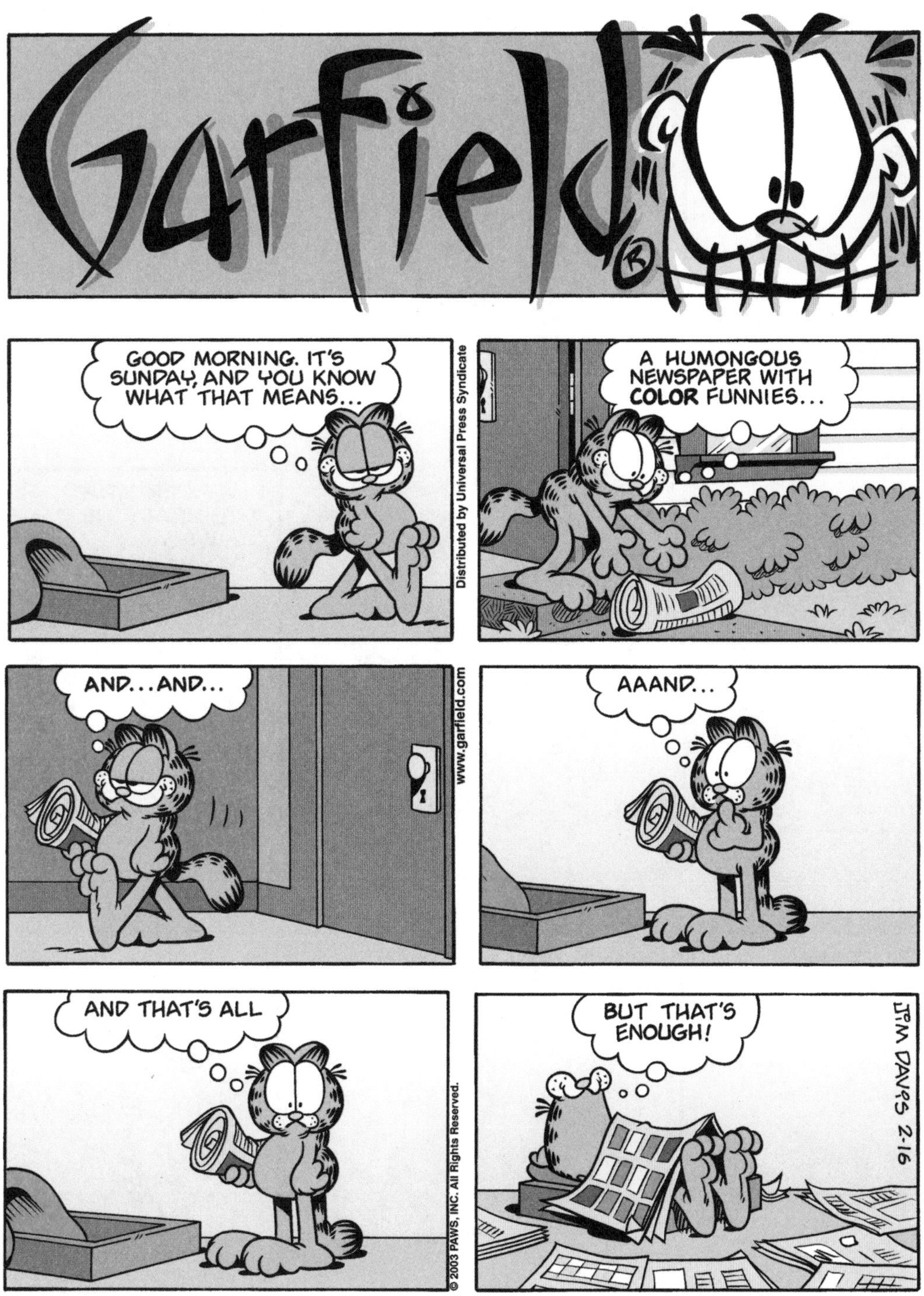
Garfield®
GOOD MORNING. IT'S SUNDAY, AND YOU KNOW WHAT THAT MEANS...
A HUMONGOUS NEWSPAPER WITH COLOR FUNNIES...
Distributed by Universal Press Syndicate
AND...AND...
AAAND...
www.garfield.com
AND THAT'S ALL
BUT THAT'S ENOUGH!
© 2003 PAWS, INC. All Rights Reserved.
JIM DAVIS 2-16

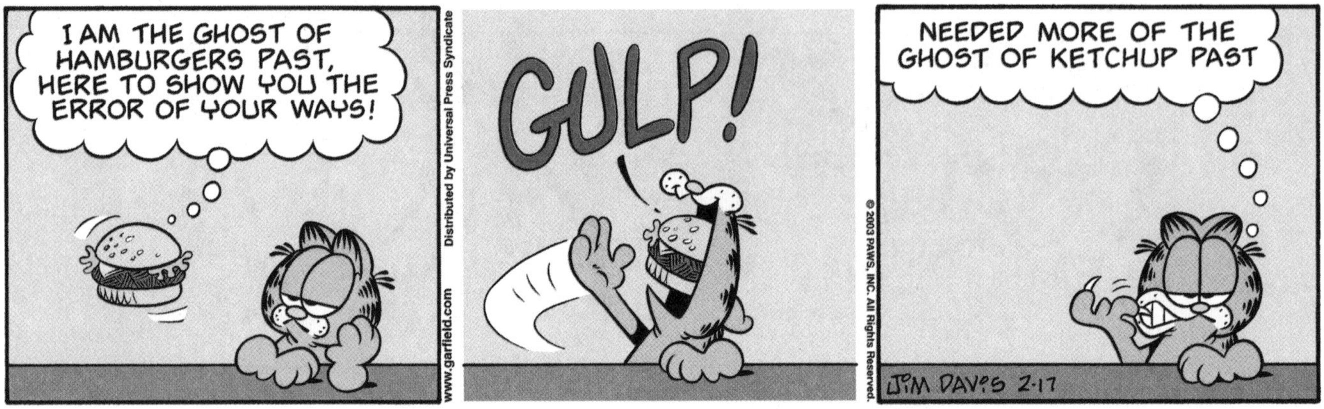
I AM THE GHOST OF HAMBURGERS PAST, HERE TO SHOW YOU THE ERROR OF YOUR WAYS!
GULP!
NEEDED MORE OF THE GHOST OF KETCHUP PAST
JIM DAVIS 2-17
www.garfield.com Distributed by Universal Press Syndicate
© 2003 PAWS, INC. All Rights Reserved.

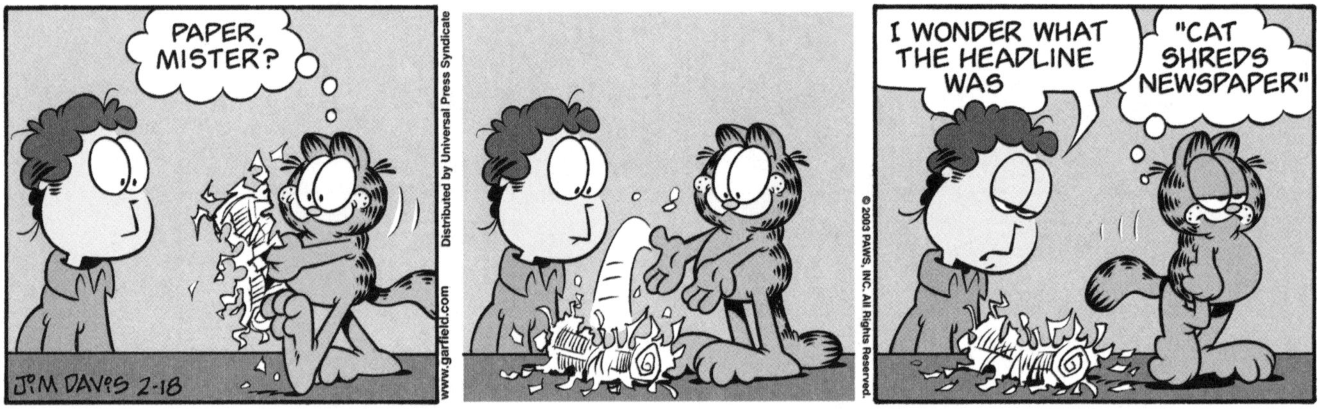
PAPER, MISTER?
I WONDER WHAT THE HEADLINE WAS
"CAT SHREDS NEWSPAPER"
JIM DAVIS 2-18
www.garfield.com Distributed by Universal Press Syndicate
© 2003 PAWS, INC. All Rights Reserved.

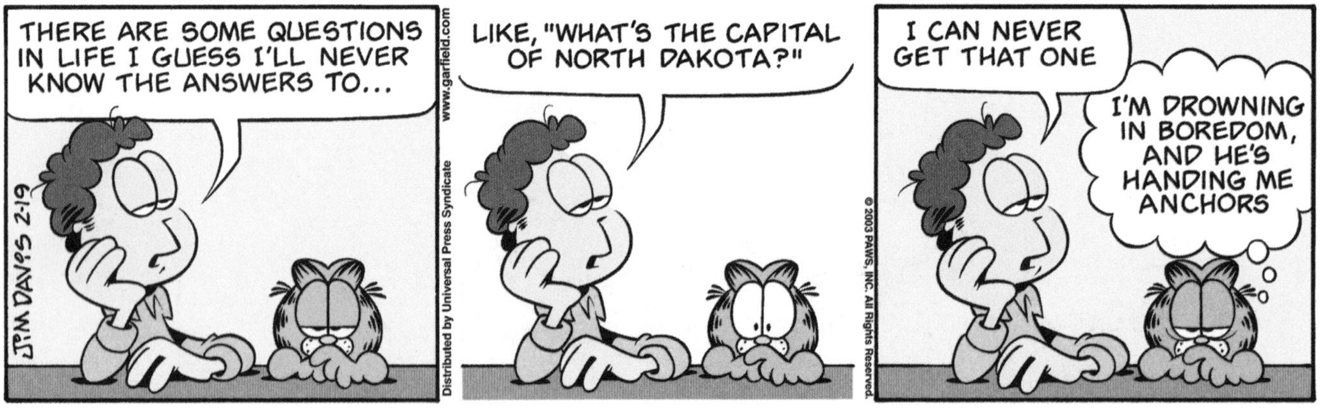
THERE ARE SOME QUESTIONS IN LIFE I GUESS I'LL NEVER KNOW THE ANSWERS TO...
LIKE, "WHAT'S THE CAPITAL OF NORTH DAKOTA?"
I CAN NEVER GET THAT ONE
I'M DROWNING IN BOREDOM, AND HE'S HANDING ME ANCHORS
JIM DAVIS 2-19
www.garfield.com Distributed by Universal Press Syndicate
© 2003 PAWS, INC. All Rights Reserved.

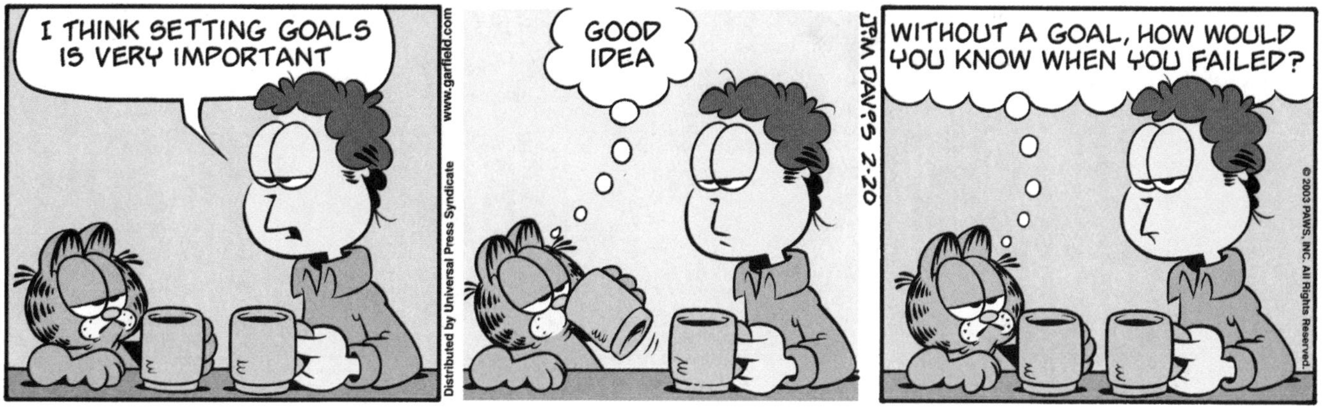
I THINK SETTING GOALS IS VERY IMPORTANT
www.garfield.com
Distributed by Universal Press Syndicate
GOOD IDEA
JIM DAVIS 2-20
WITHOUT A GOAL, HOW WOULD YOU KNOW WHEN YOU FAILED?
© 2003 PAWS, INC. All Rights Reserved.

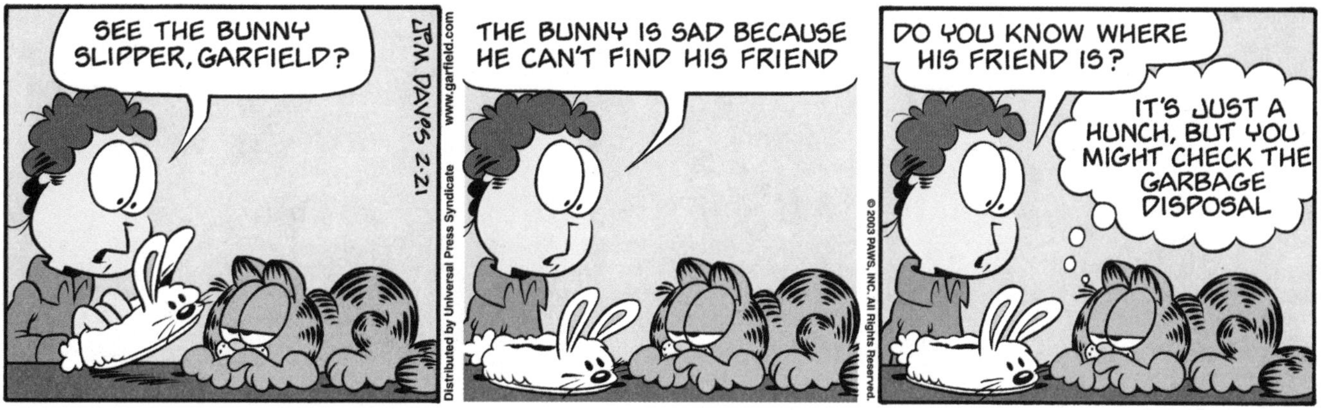
SEE THE BUNNY SLIPPER, GARFIELD?
JIM DAVIS 2-21
www.garfield.com
Distributed by Universal Press Syndicate
THE BUNNY IS SAD BECAUSE HE CAN'T FIND HIS FRIEND
© 2003 PAWS, INC. All Rights Reserved.
DO YOU KNOW WHERE HIS FRIEND IS?
IT'S JUST A HUNCH, BUT YOU MIGHT CHECK THE GARBAGE DISPOSAL

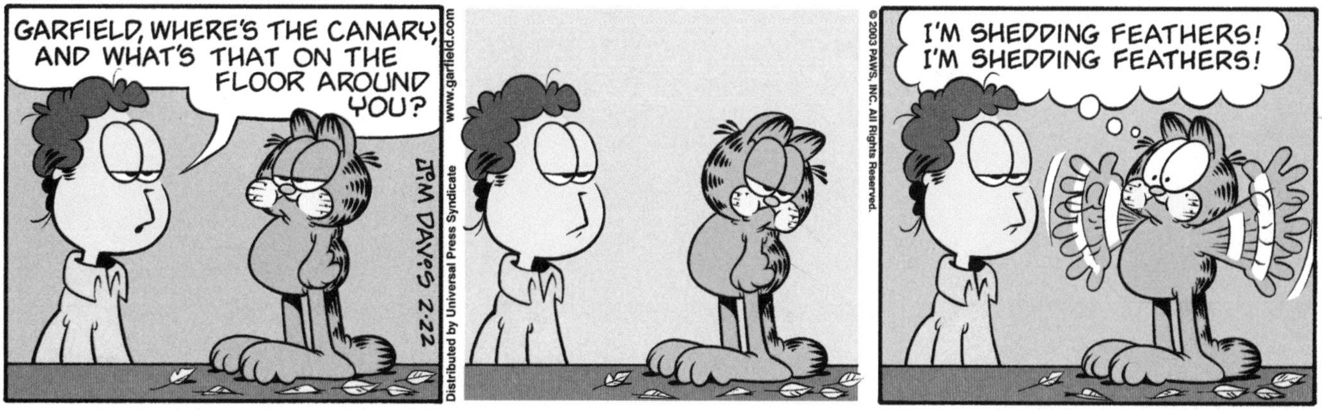
GARFIELD, WHERE'S THE CANARY, AND WHAT'S THAT ON THE FLOOR AROUND YOU?
JIM DAVIS 2-22
www.garfield.com
Distributed by Universal Press Syndicate
© 2003 PAWS, INC. All Rights Reserved.
I'M SHEDDING FEATHERS! I'M SHEDDING FEATHERS!

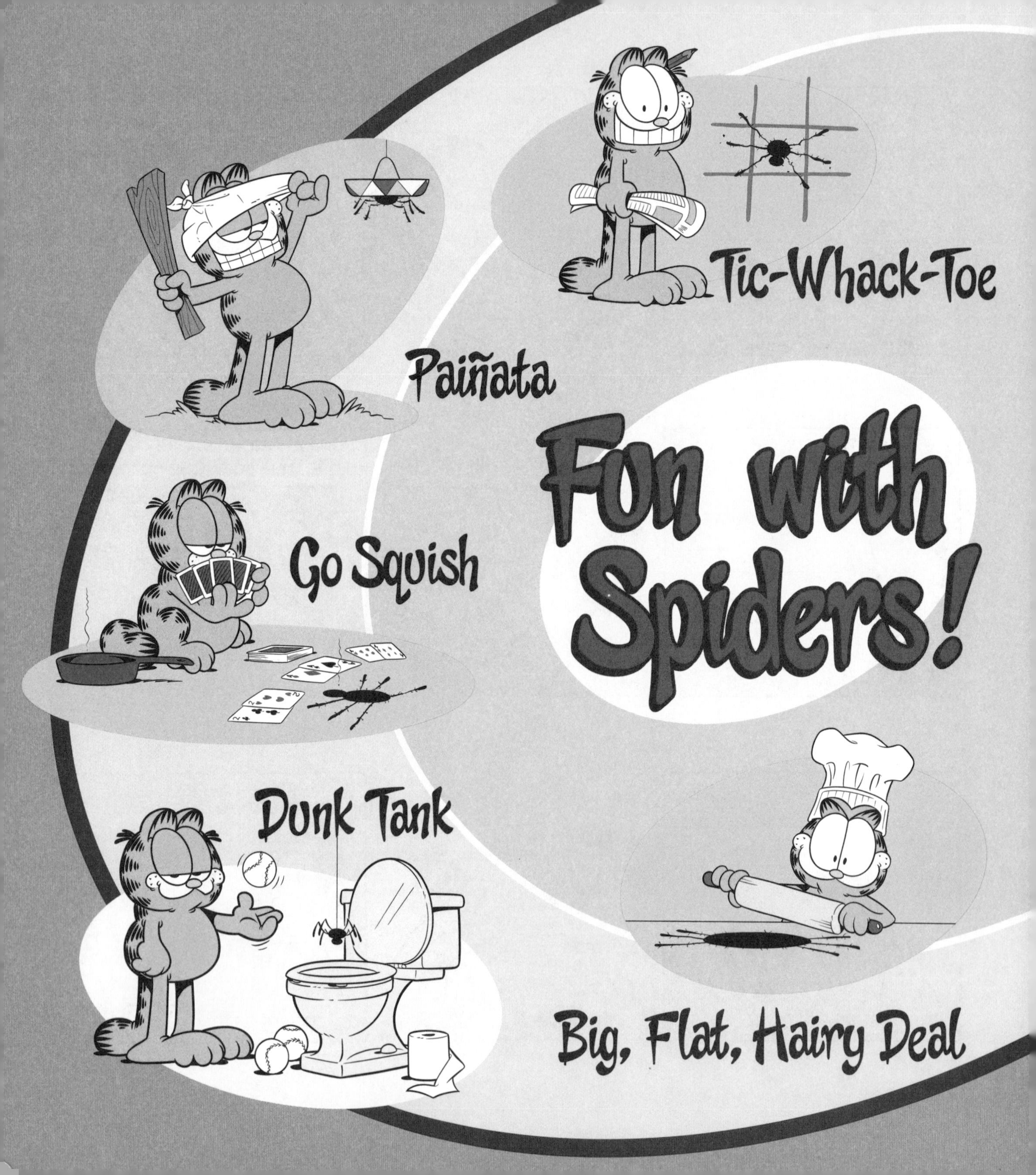
Fun with Spiders!
Tic-Whack-Toe
Paiñata
Go Squish
Dunk Tank
Big, Flat, Hairy Deal

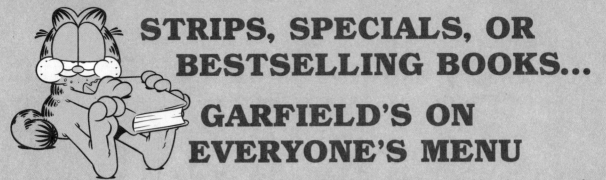

STRIPS, SPECIALS, OR BESTSELLING BOOKS...

GARFIELD'S ON EVERYONE'S MENU

Don't miss even one episode in the Tubby Tabby's hilarious series!

GARFIELD AT LARGE ....(#1) 0-345-44382-9
GARFIELD GAINS WEIGHT.......................(#2) 0-345-44975-4
GARFIELD BIGGER THAN LIFE................(#3) 0-345-45027-2
GARFIELD WEIGHS IN ....(#4) 0-345-45205-4
GARFIELD TAKES THE CAKE...................(#5) 0-345-44978-9
GARFIELD EATS HIS HEART OUT ....(#6) 0-345-46459-1
GARFIELD SITS AROUND THE HOUSE ..(#7) 0-345-46463-X
GARFIELD TIPS THE SCALES..................(#8) 0-345-46909-7
GARFIELD LOSES HIS FEET ....(#9) 0-345-46467-2
GARFIELD MAKES IT BIG ....(#10) 0-345-46468-0
GARFIELD ROLLS ON ....(#11) 0-345-47561-5
GARFIELD OUT TO LUNCH.....................(#12) 0-345-33118-4
GARFIELD FOOD FOR THOUGHT..........(#13) 0-345-34129-5
GARFIELD SWALLOWS HIS PRIDE.........(#14) 0-345-34725-0
GARFIELD WORLDWIDE.........................(#15) 0-345-35158-4
GARFIELD ROUNDS OUT ....(#16) 0-345-35388-9
GARFIELD CHEWS THE FAT ....(#17) 0-345-35956-9
GARFIELD GOES TO WAIST....................(#18) 0-345-36430-9
GARFIELD HANGS OUT ....(#19) 0-345-36835-5
GARFIELD TAKES UP SPACE.................(#20) 0-345-37029-5
GARFIELD SAYS A MOUTHFUL..............(#21) 0-345-37368-5
GARFIELD BY THE POUND ....(#22) 0-345-37579-3
GARFIELD KEEPS HIS CHINS UP..........(#23) 0-345-37959-4
GARFIELD TAKES HIS LICKS.................(#24) 0-345-38170-X
GARFIELD HITS THE BIG TIME..............(#25) 0-345-38332-X
GARFIELD PULLS HIS WEIGHT ....(#26) 0-345-38666-3
GARFIELD DISHES IT OUT ....(#27) 0-345-39287-6
GARFIELD LIFE IN THE FAT LANE ....(#28) 0-345-39776-2
GARFIELD TONS OF FUN.......................(#29) 0-345-40386-X
GARFIELD BIGGER AND BETTER..........(#30) 0-345-40770-9
GARFIELD HAMS IT UP...........................(#31) 0-345-41241-9
GARFIELD THINKS BIG ....(#32) 0-345-41671-6
GARFIELD THROWS HIS
WEIGHT AROUND.................................(#33) 0-345-42749-1
GARFIELD LIFE TO THE FULLEST.........(#34) 0-345-43239-8
GARFIELD FEEDS THE KITTY ....(#35) 0-345-43673-3
GARFIELD HOGS THE SPOTLIGHT ....(#36) 0-345-43922-8
GARFIELD BEEFS UP.............................(#37) 0-345-44109-5
GARFIELD GETS COOKIN'......................(#38) 0-345-44582-1
GARFIELD EATS CROW..........................(#39) 0-345-45201-1
GARFIELD SURVIVAL OF THE FATTEST...(#40) 0-345-46458-3
GARFIELD OLDER AND WIDER ....(#41) 0-345-46462-1
GARFIELD PIGS OUT ....(#42) 0-345-46466-4

DVD TIE-INS

GARFIELD AS HIMSELF...................................0-345-47805-3
GARFIELD HOLIDAY CELEBRATIONS.............0-345-47930-0
GARFIELD TRAVEL ADVENTURES..................0-345-48087-2

AND DON'T MISS...

GARFIELD AT 25: IN DOG YEARS I'D BE DEAD 0-345-45204-6
GARFIELD'S JOKE ZONE/INSULTS..................0-345-46263-7
GARFIELD FAT CAT 3-PACK/ VOL. 1 0-345-46455-9
GARFIELD FAT CAT 3-PACK/ VOL. 2................0-345-46465-6
SEASON'S EATINGS:
A VERY MERRY GARFIELD CHRISTMAS......0-345-47560-7
GARFIELD'S GUIDE TO EVERYTHING............0-345-46461-3
ODIE UNLEASHED! 0-345-46464-8
GARFIELD'S BOOK OF CAT NAMES 0-345-48516-5
THE GARFIELD JOURNAL...............................0-345-46469-9

New larger, full-color format!